lonely planet

Toronto

Sara Benson

LONELY PLANET PUBLICATIONS
Melbourne • Oakland • London • Paris

Toronto
1st edition – June 2001

Published by
Lonely Planet Publications Pty Ltd ABN 36 005 607 983
90 Maribyrnong St, Footscray, Victoria 3011, Australia

Lonely Planet Offices
Australia Locked Bag 1, Footscray, Victoria 3011
USA 150 Linden St, Oakland, CA 94607
UK 10a Spring Place, London NW5 3BH
France 1 rue du Dahomey, 75011 Paris

Photographs
Many of the images in this guide are available for licensing from
Lonely Planet Images.
email: lpi@lonelyplanet.com.au

Photographs of historic footwear courtesy of the Bata Shoe Museum

Front cover photograph
Jazz mural outside Grossman's (Neil Setchfield)

Toronto map section photograph
Inuit art (Jon Davison)

ISBN 1 86450 217 7

text & maps © Lonely Planet 2001
photos © photographers as indicated 2001

Printed by The Bookmaker International Ltd
Printed in China

Contents – Text

PLACES TO EAT   97

ENTERTAINMENT   112

SHOPPING   123

EXCURSIONS   131

INDEX   154

Contents – Maps

TORONTO COLOR MAP SECTION   161

The Author

Sara (Sam) Benson

Sam Benson resides, at least a few months out of the year, in Northern California. A writer by inclination and an itinerant traveler by trade, this is her fourth book with Lonely Planet. But it wasn't until after she covered the hinterlands of Asia that she finally crossed Detroit's Ambassador Bridge and turned her sights on Toronto. For weeks she oriented absolutely everything to the intersection of Bloor St and Spadina Ave, a small corner of which became home. After trekking the city on foot for 16 weeks, she came to know the underground PATH system better than most natives while surviving on late-night pit stops at Mel's deli and Coffee Time.

FROM THE AUTHOR

The foundations of this book were laid by *Canada* Lonely Planet author Mark Lightbody.

Gratitude to LP Oakland for sending me into the Great White North, and thanks all around to the cartographers, editors, staff and even other authors who dispensed professional advice with heaping spoonfuls of patience and goodwill.

I am also indebted to native Torontonians and recent immigrants who shared their top secret 'best of' lists, as well as loopholes in Toronto's horrendous traffic patterns, without which I'd never have gotten out of The Annex. Immense thanks to many UT Campus Co-op folks and all of the gutsy women who got me off to a whirlwind start: Stephanie, Monica, Beth, Sherry, Lisa & Co, Mary J and Tanya K.

Over one seemingly endless summer, Ben Levisohn, Rose Martelli, Sara Zimmerman and my family all became unwitting research accomplices. Special thanks to Masa Kikuchi for going 10,000 miles out of his way to take photos and taste Niagara wines with me. Finally, I owe no thanks at all to the US and Canadian customs officials who stopped me every time I crossed the border.

This Book

This first edition of *Toronto* was produced in Lonely Planet's Oaktown office.

From the Publisher

The Toronto editorial tag-team, overseen by senior editor David Zingarelli, was led by Ben Greensfelder, who handed off to Tullan Spitz, who passed the baton to Christine Lee. Paul Sheridan lent a hand during edit, and proofing was done by Vivek Wagle, Rebecca Northen, Wendy Taylor and Gabi Knight.

Maps were created by Chris Howard, with help from Kat Smith and guidance from senior cartographer Tracey Croom.

Beca Lafore designed the beautiful urban colorwraps while design manager Susan Rimerman laid out the map section and oversaw production. Senior designer Wendy Yanagihara produced the layout with help from Jennifer Steffey. Hugh D'Andrade, Hayden Foell, Beth Grundvig, Justin 'Potted Clown' Marler, Hannah Reineck and Jenn drew the illustrations, which were coordinated by Beca. Wendy designed the cover.

A big thanks to Ken DellaPenta for indexing the book.

Foreword

ABOUT LONELY PLANET GUIDEBOOKS

The story begins with a classic travel adventure: Tony and Maureen Wheeler's 1972 journey across Europe and Asia to Australia. Useful information about the overland trail did not exist at that time, so Tony and Maureen published the first Lonely Planet guidebook to meet a growing need.

From a kitchen table, then from a tiny office in Melbourne (Australia), Lonely Planet has become the largest independent travel publisher in the world, an international company with offices in Melbourne, Oakland (USA), London (UK) and Paris (France).

Today Lonely Planet guidebooks cover the globe. There is an ever-growing list of books, and there's information in a variety of forms and media. Some things haven't changed. The main aim is still to help make it possible for adventurous travelers to get out there – to explore and better understand the world.

At Lonely Planet we believe travelers can make a positive contribution to the countries they visit – if they respect their host communities and spend their money wisely. Since 1986 a percentage of the income from each book has been donated to aid projects and human-rights campaigns.

Updates Lonely Planet thoroughly updates each guidebook as often as possible. This usually means there are around two years between editions, although for more unusual or more stable destinations the gap can be longer. Check the imprint page (following the color map at the beginning of the book) for publication dates.

Between editions, up-to-date information is available in two free newsletters – the paper *Planet Talk* and email *Comet* (to subscribe, contact any Lonely Planet office) – and on our website at www.lonelyplanet.com. The *Upgrades* section of the website covers a number of important and volatile destinations and is regularly updated by Lonely Planet authors. *Scoop* covers news and current affairs relevant to travelers. And, lastly, the *Thorn Tree* bulletin board and *Postcards* section of the site carry unverified, but fascinating, reports from travelers.

Correspondence The process of creating new editions begins with the letters, postcards and emails received from travelers. This correspondence often includes suggestions, criticisms and comments about the current editions. Interesting excerpts are immediately passed on via newsletters and the website, and everything goes to our authors to be verified when they're researching on the road. We're keen to get more feedback from organizations or individuals who represent communities visited by travelers.

Lonely Planet gathers information for everyone who's curious about the planet – and especially for those who explore it firsthand. Through guidebooks, phrasebooks, activity guides, maps, literature, newsletters, image library, TV series and website, we act as an information exchange for a worldwide community of travelers.

Research Authors aim to gather sufficient practical information to enable travelers to make informed choices and to make the mechanics of a journey run smoothly. They also research historical and cultural background to help enrich the travel experience and allow travelers to understand and respond appropriately to cultural and environmental issues.

Authors don't stay in every hotel because that would mean spending a couple of months in each medium-size city and, no, they don't eat at every restaurant because that would mean stretching belts beyond capacity. They do visit hotels and restaurants to check standards and prices, but feedback based on readers' direct experiences can be very helpful.

Many of our authors work undercover; others aren't so secretive. None of them accept freebies in exchange for positive write-ups. And none of our guidebooks contain any advertising.

Production Authors submit their raw manuscripts and maps to offices in Australia, the USA, the UK or France. Editors and cartographers – all experienced travelers themselves – then begin the process of assembling the pieces. When the book finally hits the shops, some things are already out of date, we start getting feedback from readers and the process begins again....

WARNING & REQUEST

Things change – prices go up, schedules change, good places go bad and bad places go bankrupt – nothing stays the same. So, if you find things better or worse, recently opened or long since closed, please tell us and help make the next edition even more accurate and useful. We genuinely value all the feedback we receive. Julie Young coordinates a well-traveled team that reads and acknowledges every letter, postcard and email and ensures that every morsel of information finds its way to the appropriate authors, editors and cartographers for verification.

Everyone who writes to us will find their name in the next edition of the appropriate guidebook. They will also receive the latest issue of *Planet Talk*, our quarterly printed newsletter, or *Comet*, our monthly email newsletter. Subscriptions to both newsletters are free. The very best contributions will be rewarded with a free guidebook.

Excerpts from your correspondence may appear in new editions of Lonely Planet guidebooks, the Lonely Planet website, *Planet Talk* or *Comet*, so please let us know if you *don't* want your letter published or your name acknowledged.

Send all correspondence to the Lonely Planet office closest to you:

Australia: Locked Bag 1, Footscray, Victoria 3011
USA: 150 Linden St, Oakland, CA 94607
UK: 10a Spring Place, London NW5 3BH
France: 1 rue du Dahomey, 75011 Paris

Or email us at: talk2us@lonelyplanet.com.au .

For news, views and updates, see our website: www.lonelyplanet.com

HOW TO USE A LONELY PLANET GUIDEBOOK

The best way to use a Lonely Planet guidebook is any way you choose. At Lonely Planet, we believe the most memorable travel experiences are often those that are unexpected, and the finest discoveries are those you make yourself. Guidebooks are not intended to be used as if they provided a detailed set of infallible instructions!

Contents All Lonely Planet guidebooks follow the same format. The Facts about the Country chapters or sections give background information ranging from history to weather. Facts for the Visitor gives practical information on issues like visas and health. Getting There & Away gives a brief starting point for researching travel to and from the destination. Getting Around gives an overview of the transport options available when you arrive.

The peculiar demands of each destination determine how subsequent chapters are broken up, but some things remain constant. We always start with background, then proceed to sights, places to stay, places to eat, entertainment, getting there and away, and getting around information – in that order.

Heading Hierarchy Lonely Planet headings are used in a strict hierarchical structure that can be visualized as a set of Russian dolls. Each heading (and its following text) is encompassed by any preceding heading that is higher on the hierarchical ladder.

Entry Points We do not assume guidebooks will be read from beginning to end, but that people will dip into them. The traditional entry points are the list of contents and the index. In addition, however, some books have a complete list of maps and an index map illustrating map coverage.

There may also be a color map that shows highlights. These highlights are dealt with in greater detail later in the book, along with planning questions. Each chapter covering a geographical region usually begins with a locator map and another list of highlights. Once you find something of interest in a list of highlights, turn to the index.

Maps Maps play a crucial role in Lonely Planet guidebooks and include a huge amount of information. A legend is printed on the back page. We seek to have complete consistency between maps and text, and to have every important place in the text captured on a map. Map key numbers usually start in the top left corner.

Although inclusion in a guidebook usually implies a recommendation, we cannot list every good place. Exclusion does not necessarily imply criticism. In fact, there are a number of reasons why we might exclude a place – sometimes it is simply inappropriate to encourage an influx of travelers.

Introduction

The English modernist Wyndham Lewis said of Toronto, 'O for a half hour of Europe after this sanctimonious icebox!' Indeed, the long-standing tag of 'Toronto the Good' has been hard to shake. From its beginnings as a safe haven for Loyalists fleeing the American Revolution, the town was ruled by a conservative British colonial society of first families led by politically savvy Anglican clergy. In 1906 the Lord's Day Act was passed, which forbade working and most socializing on Sunday: Eaton's department store drew its curtains to guard against 'sinful' window shopping and city playgrounds were chained up and locked. Shockingly, these anti-vice laws remained on the books until 1950.

Flash forward to the last half of the 20th century: welcome to Toronto's great spring thaw. Following WWII the 'icebox' city has been melted by waves of Portuguese, Greek, Italian, Chilean, Chinese, Southeast Asian, Indian and Caribbean immigrants, their transplanted cultures largely undiminished. Over 40% of today's Torontonians were born overseas and more than 100 languages are spoken on the streets. In fact, diversity is what Toronto often uses to define its character. Here the traveler has the world at the cost of a subway token and the most authentic cuisine dangling from the edge of every fork.

Toronto is a city that has moved incognito into the 21st century. No one has uncovered it yet. 'Is it near Niagara Falls?' people ask. 'Is that where the CN Tower is?' Yes to both, but the city's gold stars are mostly unknown: fine beaches and jungly river ravines, Victorian architecture and cutting-edge music, the Hockey Hall of Fame and the most enormous Carribean festival in North America. Toronto's very own islands lie in the waters of Lake Ontario, facing off against the downtown skyline, and the longest transcontinental rail route in Canada starts here.

Like hypnotized subjects, few travelers can later explain what made Toronto so satisfying. There is no checklist of things to do here because the city is experiential. Its festivals seize you in summer, the spicy corners of its markets call, as do the beachfront boardwalks and the old *and* new world music pouring out of neighborhood eateries. Just beyond the city limits are the rugged zones and wineries of the Niagara peninsula and the quiet life of rural Ontario entwined with Shakespearean plays, Mennonite farmers and First Nations lands.

But the pages of Toronto's history have been also engraved with rebellion, and the wildness of democracy. In 1837 William Lyon Mackenzie led a farmers' militia down Yonge St against the Family Compact government. Almost 150 years later the 'sandbar bohemians' on Toronto Islands stood their ground against the municipal government that was evicting them from their island homes. Although Toronto is still 'the city that works,' an admiring nickname gained for its urban planning successes, there is trouble. The recession of the '90s slashed social spending, which has resulted in increased homelessness and environmental neglect. But for all its challenges, there is every reason for enthusiasm about T.O.'s future. It's an experimental city just finding its feet, and nothing is static. Toronto is a city in evolution.

9

Facts about Toronto

HISTORY
First Inhabitants & the French

When Etienne Brûlé first arrived at what voyageurs came to call 'The Carrying Place' on a mission from Samuel de Champlain in 1615, there were almost a dozen Native tribes residing in southern Ontario, with a total population of approximately 18,000. The site was called Toronto, a Native word meaning 'meeting place,' since it was located at the convergence of several key trading and portage routes. These were used first by Native tribes and later by French fur traders on their way between Lake Ontario and Georgian Bay or the upper inland lakes. Already weakened by European disease, by the mid-1600s, the Huron (who had allied themselves with the French), Petun and Neutral nations living in the area were wiped out by an aggressive war waged by the League of the Iroquois (Seneca, Cayuga, Onondaga, Oneida and Mohawk tribes, later including the Tuscarora and called the Six Nations), who had wanted to expand their trading base from Eastern Ontario.

This left the land around Lake Ontario largely open, so other tribes such as the Algonquin moved down from the north. By the time European exploration and trade arrived in force in the 1700s, the Ojibwa peoples covered a large tract of land north of the Great Lakes and west to the Cree territory of the prairies. It wasn't until around 1720 that the French were able to establish a fur-trading post and mission near the Humber River. By the 1750s, they had built Fort Rouillé (also known as Fort Toronto), one in a series of forts set up to control navigation on the Great Lakes and links with the Mississippi River.

Muddy York

After years of hostility with the French on both sides of the Atlantic, the British took over all of New France, including the area around Toronto, under the Treaty of Paris in 1763. However, it wasn't until after the American Revolution that Loyalists fleeing the States arrived and large-scale settlement began. The British paid £1700 to the Mississauga tribes for the official Toronto Land Purchase of 1787. Four years later the provinces of Upper Canada (now Ontario) and Lower Canada (Québec) were created.

Soon afterward, in 1793, John Graves Simcoe, the new lieutenant-governor of Upper Canada, moved the provincial capital from Niagara-on-the-Lake to a more defensible position at Toronto, which he founded as the town of York. The colonial town was laid out on a 10-block grid with patriotic-sounding street names like King, Queen, George and Duke. Simcoe's men also constructed a trail, which later became Yonge St, leading 48km straight north through the wilderness to the borders of the original Toronto purchase.

The inhospitable muddiness of the new capital gave rise to its notorious nickname 'Muddy York,' but Simcoe had reasoned this made it all the less likely that York would be attacked should the Americans decide to invade. Which, of course, they did during the War of 1812. On April 27, 1813, the American forces reached Fort York and after a short struggle overcame the British and Ojibwa troops. The Americans looted and razed York but held it for only six days before Canadian troops kicked them out and chased them all the way back to the US political headquarters in Washington. Canadian forces raged on until they burned the White House, so named for the white paint that was later used to cover the charred bits.

After the Treaty of Ghent ended the hostilities between the USA and Canada in 1814, the British no longer saw the Iroquois nations as valuable allies and quickly subjected them to increased government control. At the same time, the city of York began to expand and, in 1828, the first stagecoach services began on Yonge St. British and then Irish immigrants began to arrive in Upper Canada in still larger numbers, quadrupling the population to just under 10,000 people.

Rebellion to Unity

By 1824, however, all was not well. Firebrand William Lyon Mackenzie had already started publishing his *Colonial Advocate,* an outcry against the oligarchic Tory government that ruled York. Nicknamed the Family Compact, these staunch Loyalists, comprised of such historic names as Jarvis, Baldwin and Strachan, had come to power as advisers to the now-departed Lieutenant-Governor Simcoe soon after he limited the province's legislative powers in 1791 as means of avoiding an American-style revolution.

In 1834 Mackenzie got himself elected as the first mayor of what was now named Toronto, but the families' continuing political influence proved much too strong for him. Finally out of options, Mackenzie initiated the shortest-lived rebellion in Canadian history on December 5, 1837. He and an assorted band of about 700 disgruntled citizens marched down Yonge St and confronted the Loyalist troops directed by Sheriff Jarvis; shots were volleyed, confusion and panic ensued and both sides broke and ran. Mackenzie went into temporary

Pictohistory

1615 – Etienne Brûlé arrives at 'The Carrying Place'

1649 – League of the Iroquois attacks

1720 – French trading post established at the Humber River

1787 – The British purchase Toronto from the Mississauga tribes

1793 – Founding of the town of York

1803 – St Lawrence farmers' market opens

1813 – Americans invade during the War of 1812

1824 – William Lyon Mackenzie starts to publish the *Colonial Advocate*

1832–34 – Cholera epidemics

1837 – Mackenzie raises the failed Rebellion of Upper Canada

1842 – Gaslights appear on city streets

1849 – First great fire

1853 – The railway arrives

1867 – Confederation of Canada

1869 – Eaton's department store opens

1886 – Women admitted to universities

1883 – The first electric streetcar in North America runs

1893 – The first Stanley Cup game is played

1896 – *Maclean's* magazine begins publishing

1904 – Second great fire

1906 – The Lord's Day Act prohibits work and social activities on Sunday

1907 – Toronto's youngest millionaire builds the Royal Alexandra Theatre

1919 – Citizens vote for prohibition

1920 – Group of Seven exhibitions; Insulin is discovered at UT

1927 – Canadian National Exhibition (CNE) is held on the nation's 60th birthday

1930 – Union Station finally completed

1931 – The first hockey game at Maple Leaf Gardens

1954 – Toronto's first subway line opens

1960s – US exiles arrive fleeing the Vietnam War draft; folk music coffeehouses open in Yorkville

1972 – Pride Week celebrated with Queen's Park march and picnic at Hanlan's Point

1976 – CN Tower opens

1980 – Standoff between city officials and remaining residents on Toronto Islands

1987 – Toronto Stock Exchange relocates from Bay St

1993 – Honest Ed Mirvish builds the Princess of Wales Theatre for *Miss Saigon*

1998 – Protests in Queen's Park over birth of the 'Megacity'

1999 – City council legalizes 'clothing optional' status of Hanlan's Point beach

exile in the USA while unluckier rebels were hanged.

In Mackenzie's absence another news-paperman, George Brown, the publisher of the *Globe* since 1844, became a key political player in Toronto politics. He forged a new liberal party and was a driving force behind the confederation of Canada in 1867, to which most voters agreed more out of fear of another US invasion than any nationalistic ideals. Their fears were not unfounded, considering that Fenian raids (tacitly approved but not acknowledged by the US) were launched across the border as late as 1866. By the time of confederation, the railway had already brought the coalescing nation closer together and it gave Toronto even more prominence as the capital of newly renamed Ontario, even as the city was still economically in the shadow of larger Montréal.

'Toronto the Good'

Throughout the Victorian era of the late 1800s, there was seemingly nothing but progress for Toronto. Eaton's and Simpson's department stores opened on Yonge St, the city was wired for electricity and the first national exhibition was held. By the end of the century specialized farming and industry were growing markedly and more than 200,000 people called Toronto home.

At the turn of the century, masterpieces of Edwardian architecture arose downtown, and the first Italian and Jewish immigrants arrived. Like many big cities, Toronto had already had its great fire, in 1849, but it had another in 1904, when about 5 hectares of the inner city burned, leveling 122 buildings. Amazingly, no one was killed. During this time the city became known as 'Toronto the Good,' a tag that only began to fade in the 1970s. Conservative politicians voted for prohibition (outlawing the production and sale of alcoholic beverages) and strong anti-vice laws (it was illegal to rent a horse on Sunday) that culminated in the Lord's Day Act of 1906 (see Religion later in this chapter).

Meanwhile businessmen like Sir Henry Pellat of Casa Loma fame were amassing their fortunes, and by the 1920s Bay St was booming, in part because nickel, silver and uranium mines had been discovered in northern Ontario. Everything stopped short during the Depression era, pushing anti-immigrant hostilities to an all-time high. This was the period of the anti-Semitic riots at Christie Pits Park and the banning of all Chinese immigration. Racism against blacks was all the more lamentable for Ontario having been a safe haven for Harriet Tubman and other travelers on the Underground Railroad.

The Megacity

It was after WWII that the city began to change. Well over half a million immigrants have arrived since then, mainly Europeans. The influx of new tongues, customs and food has livened up a place once thought to be a hopeless case.

Starting in the 1960s people moved back from the suburbs into the city and restored the old Victorian homes. Bohemian folk-music coffeehouses opened in Yorkville, patronized not least by US citizens who arrived fleeing the Vietnam War draft. But it was the building of the new City Hall in 1965 that really gave Toronto its boost into modernity.

Into the '70s and beyond, Portuguese, Chilean, Greek, Southeast Asian, Chinese and West Indian immigrants rolled over the city in waves. The Harbourfront and new downtown skyscrapers appeared as Toronto finally overtook Montréal in population, becoming one of the fastest-growing cities in North America. The city's optimism and pride expressed themselves in the building of the Canadian National Tower in 1976, continuing right through the 1980s economic boom on Bay St and the city's sesqui-centennial in 1984.

Of course, things had to go bust sometime. They did so during the recession of the early '90s, lean years from which Toronto has largely recovered, thanks in part to continued infusions of immigrants. In 1998, when five surrounding suburbs were incorporated into what was dubbed the 'Mega-city,' Toronto became the largest city in

Canada and the fourth largest in North America. That's certainly a long way from its beginnings as Muddy York, the second-choice prize after Niagara.

GEOGRAPHY & GEOLOGY

The settled part of the province of Ontario, including Toronto, is separated from the prairies of western Canada by the massive Canadian Shield, a stretch of Precambrian rock more than 1600km long and formed by a prehistoric glacier.

All of central Toronto was once under the waters of Lake Iroquois, an ancient sea centered on what is now Michigan in the US. The sea extended as far north as the rise upon which Casa Loma sits today, where the old shore cliffs eroded over millennia are still visible. The modern city sits beside the shores of Lake Ontario, part of the Great Lakes region shared between Canada and the USA. The city's most unique geographic feature is the Toronto Islands, across the harbor from downtown. Originally part of a 9km-long sandbar peninsula, these jewel-like islands were created when a violent storm in 1858 cut through the peninsula and created the Eastern Channel. The sandbar itself was first formed by erosion from the Scarborough Bluffs to the east, massive heights formed by over five different eras of glacial deposits.

Often referred to in southern Ontario, the Niagara Escarpment is a steep rock face that extends for 725km, with a maximum height of 600m, along the ancient shoreline. It begins at the town of Queenston on the Niagara River and passes through Hamilton, Collingwood and Owen Sound on its way north to Tobermory and Manitoulin Island. A major outcropping of the escarpment can clearly be seen from Hwy 401 west of Oakville at the Kelso Conservation Area.

CLIMATE

Just how bad are the winters? That's what most visitors want to know. January is the coldest month, with temperatures averaging between 1°C and 8°C *below* zero. On winter days the windchill factor – a combi-

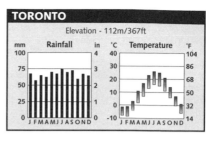

nation of temperature and wind speed – can result in apparent temperatures much lower than the still-air temperature. On such days many folks traverse the city underground via Toronto's PATH system (see the Shopping chapter) to avoid frostbite. (See the Health section of the Facts for the Visitor chapter for more information on frostbite.)

In 1999 Toronto beat its own record for monthly snowfall by surpassing 111cm in the first half of January alone. Gleeful residents stayed home from work (and school) and public transit stopped because of drift snow and iced-over tracks.

Summers can be just as agonizing; the hottest month, July, sees temperatures of 18°C to 27°C. These feel much hotter due to the muggy humidity. During such weather people escape to the Harbourfront area, Toronto Islands and the Beach area, where even if the ambient temperature is only a few degrees cooler, strong lakefront winds make it bearable.

Your chances of seeing some of Toronto's annual precipitation (819mm) are about 50-50 no matter when you visit, because Toronto has an average of 189 'wet' days each year. If you forget yours, the cheapest umbrellas are sold in Chinatown.

ECOLOGY & ENVIRONMENT

Toronto had been tinkering with its environment even before it decided to push around the Don River during the construction of the Don Valley Parkway in the 1950s instead of building more bridges. During the past few decades the Toronto & Region Conservation Authority has wisely based its conservation acts on sounder ecology, evidenced in the astounding success of Tommy Thompson Park (see the Things to See & Do chapter) and the regeneration of natural wetlands at Grenadier Pond and other sites within the city limits.

One of the city's recurring environmental nightmares are the toxic water conditions along the shoreline of Lake Ontario. Because the city's old neighborhood sewage system connects rain downspouts to waste water, any sudden heavy rains cause sewage treatment plants to overflow and all the garbage and bacteria (most notably *E coli*) waiting there to be sent straight out into the lake. Summer beach closures are regularly announced on TV. When water levels are such that the filtration plants work, the lake water becomes *too* clean – shoreline fish die by the hundreds.

Toronto is not LA, but visitors to the CN Tower will notice haze problems. Most city residents are progressive cycling fanatics, but there are still too many motor vehicles on the streets. The city recently enacted a bylaw to prevent motorists from idling their cars more than a few minutes, and in summer, special low-pollutant grades of gasoline are mandatory. Who bears the remaining responsibility for poor air quality? The Ontario environmental commissioner blames the current Tory government for letting environmental priorities slip. The government in turn blames Michigan (notoriously Detroit) and Ohio across the lake. But New York State points the finger back at Canada, noting that their own fossil-fuel emissions standards are much stricter than in Ontario. One thing is clear: the situation isn't improving fast.

Many city residents complain about the Molson Indy car races, which plague central Toronto with noise pollution for days every July. In 2000 a lone band of protesters went over to Mayor Mel Lastman's house and blasted a stereo for hours to see how he liked it. There was no response.

FLORA & FAUNA

The old town of York was plagued in the 1800s by wild moose and loose livestock. The legal courts at Osgoode Hall were even specifically designed with an iron-gated fence to keep out wandering cows. The fence remains today, but the incorrigible bovines and other beasties have been pretty much cleaned out of modern Toronto. Black squirrels, skunks and, particularly, raccoons have learned to adapt quite well and may be seen in city parks and recreation areas, wooded areas around rivers and even along residential streets after dark. Especially on garbage nights! Note that although rabies is not a major problem, it can be caused by any bite, scratch or even lick from an infected animal and medical attention should be sought immediately.

The maligned, adaptable raccoon

When you spot bird life, nine times out of 10 it's the common pigeon or a honking Canada goose. Almost a national symbol, these geese are overfed by humans, leading them to overrun many city parks and crowd out other avian species. Recent conservation efforts have lured other birds back to the lakeshore and the city, most notably Tommy Thompson Park (see the Things to See & Do chapter). One unique way to see species like bald eagles and hawks up close is at the Falconry Centre (see the Excursions chapter).

Though the red maple leaf is Canada's ubiquitous symbol, finding a live maple tree on Toronto's streets can be quite a challenge.

GOVERNMENT & POLITICS

Once the capital of Canada, Toronto is now the provincial capital of Ontario and Ottawa is only a short plane hop away. Relations between the three levels of government – municipal, provincial and federal – are byzantine, with overlapping responsibilities as well as gaps where no one seems to be minding the store.

When Charles Dickens visited the city in the 1840s, he decried its 'rabid Toryism,' and the Union Jack still appears on the provincial flag. But in the late 20th century the Tories were out of power until Premier Mike Harris' 'common sense' revolution of tax cuts and reduced social spending returned them to a majority in 1995. After being elected, they slashed government jobs, shut down hospitals and weakened labor laws. The Tories won again in 1999 by promising to make mandatory the singing of *O Canada!*, the national anthem, in public schools and to arrest and fine 'squeegee kids' (who wipe clean motorists' windows and then demand a few dollars). Toronto politics have been traditionally progressive, but these right-wing provincial politics have shifted the political climate of the city as a whole, not least because it relies on state funding.

In 1997 the provincial government moved to amalgamate Toronto and five surrounding towns into one giant unit, dubbed 'Megacity.' More than 75% of Toronto voters – traditionally liberal-minded – said 'No,' and were promptly ignored. This amalgamation created a strong new suburban voting bloc that swept Mel Lastman, the former mayor of North York and a discount furniture salesman by trade, into the mayor's chair. Although mayors traditionally aren't required to even announce a party affiliation, Mayor Mel is clearly comfortable with the Tories.

Most residents say Mayor Mel hasn't done much for the city, apart from starring in a few startling scandals. Homelessness remains a critical social issue – especially among street youth – and is related to other pressing problems, including reduced social services and new condominium developments that squeeze out affordable housing. Another troubling issue is the $30 million the city government alleges is drained from welfare, health care and social services annually by the immigrants whose sponsors renege support. On a more positive note, the city is fast building its bid for the 2008 Olympics.

For a little political entertainment, check out the oddball former mayoral candidate who sings tuneless late-night karaoke on weekends outside The Bay department store on Bloor St.

ECONOMY

From its roots in the colonial fur trade, Toronto has become pivotal in Canada's economy. The opening of the Toronto Stock Exchange (TSE) in 1937 first pushed the city ahead of Montréal in terms of attracting investors. Now the TSE is one of the top 10 exchanges by volume worldwide, trading just over $100 million each day from its highrise west of Bay St, Toronto's high-powered financial district. Over 200 commercial industries either began or have since established their headquarters in this district, including Canada's five largest banks.

Not only is Toronto a central port for the Great Lakes region, but it straddles two industrial powerhouses: the 'Golden Horseshoe' along Lake Ontario's western shore from Niagara Falls to Hamilton, and the Ontario-Quebec corridor. Together these regions employ over half the nation's workforce in small manufacturing, automobiles, iron and steel.

After the economic boom of the 1980s, the recession of the early '90s brought real-estate prices crashing down – and many corporate fortunes along with them. Manufacturing especially suffered when high Canadian taxes influenced consumers to buy cheaper Japanese or US imports. Toronto has recovered from these lean years, partly because of new growth in communications, tourism and self-employment. Inflation remains steady and low, but the Canadian dollar has fallen as of late.

At the beginning of the 20th century, Britain was Canada's strongest trading partner, but in the 21st the USA snaps up more than three quarters of Canada's exports, especially energy resources and raw materials. Since the passage of the North American Free Trade Agreement (known in Canada as FTA), the border has become ever more porous. Alarmists cry about 'brain drain,' which refers to highly educated Canadian professionals leaving for higher-paying jobs in the US and overseas. However, they overlook how much Toronto gains each year from highly qualified new immigrants.

US tourists are largely responsible for Canada's ranking 10th in international tourism earnings worldwide. In total, about 19.6 million international visitors come to Canada annually, the majority of whom are from the US, UK, Japan, Germany and France, and visit either Niagara Falls or Toronto. Foreign film production alone poured more than $1.2 billion into the city's economy last year, despite crews not having to pay a single cent to film on city streets.

POPULATION & PEOPLE

In 1998, five surrounding towns joined the relatively tiny city of Toronto (around 650,000 people) to form the 'Megacity.' With a population of 2.4 million, this made Toronto the largest city in Canada and the fifth largest in North America after Mexico City, Los Angeles, New York and Chicago. Of course, one out of every eight Torontonians dream of giving it all up and moving to Vancouver, British Columbia. (And did you know that 75% of all Canadians live within 160km of the US border?) The urban sprawl beyond the new Megacity boundaries is known as the Greater Toronto Area (GTA), for a population totaling more than 4.6 million. The GTA continues to swell with new immigrants who arrive steadily from every corner of the globe.

Toronto is in Canada's most culturally diverse province, and has often been called a 'mosaic' of neighborhoods, with more than 70 ethnic groups and 80 languages spoken. About 42% of city residents were born overseas. A full 20% of the current population lived elsewhere before 1980. Most of these newer arrivals are from Southeast Asia or the Caribbean, though a fair number of Anglophones landed here beginning in the '70s after leaving Québec and Francophone politics behind. About 68% of Toronto residents identify as being of other than British or French descent, just the opposite of Montréal.

UNESCO may have named Toronto the world's most diverse city in 1993, but the city has not always welcomed immigrants with open arms. On April 15, 1933, the worst race riots in the city's history broke out against a Jewish team during a baseball game at Christie Pits. During WWII, Canada interned citizens of Japanese ancestry in camps and accepted a mere 5000 Jewish refugees, compared with 200,000 allowed to enter the USA. Immigration troubles continue today with Chinese entering illegally via the west coast and often enduring lengthy stays in detainment camps. This is a minor improvement over the period 1923 to 1947 when they were barred completely after having helped build Canada's transnational railway.

Keep in mind that Toronto's Native population, comprised mostly of First Nations people, is only 1%. A 1997 Supreme Court ruling that Native people, based on their oral histories, have legitimate title to their lands, and government has a 'moral duty' to negotiate with them, hasn't much helped Native groups without a land base, such as those in urban areas like Toronto. The closest established Native community is the Six Nations of the Grand River Territory Reserve (see the Excursions chapter).

EDUCATION

Toronto is arguably the center of English-language education in Canada. Major universities include Ryerson Polytechnic and the prestigious University of Toronto (see the Things to See & Do chapter) with its individual college system. The most famous of the UT colleges is the ultra-starched, traditional Trinity College, where entering collegians are required to wear full academic robes to meals and classes – with nothing underneath, some say.

SCIENCE

Toronto's 'best' claim to scientific fame rests with Dr Charles Herbert Best and Sir Frederick Banting who, along with Collip and Macleod, discovered insulin in 1920. They received a Nobel Prize for their efforts in 1923, and UT hasn't stopped bragging about their discovery for nearly 80 years.

The first working streetcar in North America ran during the 1883 national exhibition, success being relative, however, since the cars short-circuited whenever it rained. The city has had its quirkier inventions, too, like five-pin bowling devised by workers who realized they couldn't fit 10 pins into half-hour lunch breaks.

ARTS
Music

Toronto is still struggling to build an adequate opera house, but Glenn Gould is one famous classical performer the city can claim as its own. Born in the Beach community in 1932, this eccentric piano genius was a distant relation of the composer Edvard Grieg. After recording his famous interpretation of JS Bach's *Goldberg Variations,* he performed in the Soviet Union and Europe and then quietly retired at the age of 32 (he allegedly despised the cult of the virtuoso). He spent the rest of his life composing and, occasionally, making Canadian radio documentaries until his death here in 1982.

In a completely different genre, Toronto has produced plenty of folk and rock & roll bands. Joni Mitchell, Gordon Lightfoot and the Lovin' Spoonful sang (or before that, washed dishes and served) at the bohemian coffeehouses of Yorkville in the 1960s. Neil Young, The Band and Rush all started in Toronto, as did The Tragically Hip, who some say are the definitive Canadian rock band. Cowboy Junkies recorded their *Trinity Sessions* inside the Church of the Holy Trinity (see the Downtown Walking Tour in the Things to See & Do chapter), while countless other rock stars, from Keith Richards to Madonna, had a devil of a time with the Toronto police. Even T.O. natives Barenaked Ladies were once barred from performing in Nathan Phillips Square. They were symbolically handed the keys to the city as a conciliatory gesture when they were invited back to give a concert in September 2000.

Literature

As the de facto English-language capital of Canada, Toronto has been fertile ground for as many homegrown writers as it has wandering authors in exile.

Ernest Hemingway got his start as a cub reporter with the *Toronto Star,* where he penned such smartly titled masterpieces as, 'Before You Go on a Canoe Trip, Learn Canoeing.' William Faulkner came here asking to join the Canadian Air Force during WWII because his sweetheart back home had rejected him. Cyberpunk writer William Gibson spent long stretches of time in the city and loved Kensington Market, which shows excellent taste (literally).

In its earlier days, the city hosted Dickens, Yeats, Arthur Conan Doyle and Walt Whitman, who loved the omnibuses and thought Toronto 'a wild dashing place' (he was perhaps the only person ever to say so). More critical guests included Oscar Wilde, who lambasted the city's architecture during his 'The House Beautiful' North American tour, but was welcomed anyway because he was Irish. The English modernist Wyndham Lewis got stranded here during WWII and had nary a good word to say about the city he considered 'a sanctimonious icebox.'

Local writers have written with an equally critical and socially conscious eye. After joining Hemingway and other expatriates in Paris, Torontonian Morley Callaghan returned home to write several acclaimed novels about the problems of modern urban life, for which he won the Governor General's award in 1951. Working around the same time, Mazo de la Roche is a fixture in the Canadian literary canon for her *Jalna* novels set in the Toronto suburbs, some of which have been translated from the French-language originals. Hugh Garner is well known for *Cabbagetown,* a classic reminiscence of growing up in an Irish working-class neighborhood during the Depression era.

Many modern Canadian literary giants have studied at the University of Toronto, including Margaret Atwood and Sri Lankan-born Michael Ondaatje. Ondaatje became famous for his novel *The English Patient*, but his earlier work *In the Skin of a Lion* is an equally moving examination of working-class life during the construction of the 'Palace of Purification.' Great critics hailing from Toronto include Northrop Frye and pop culture maven Marshall McLuhan. And don't miss the visual ('concrete') poem by bpNichol drilled into bpNichol Lane, running north off Sussex Ave between Huron and St George Sts. It's inscribed beside the historic Coach Press, which was also associated with the avant-garde Open Letter movement of the 1970s.

On the pop fiction front, straitlaced Toronto is the original publishing home to none other than the Harlequin Romance series. Modern potboilers by hometown boy Timothy Findley are also set mostly in Toronto and beloved children's writer Dennis Lee penned the rhyming poems of *Alligator Pie* and the lyrics to Fraggle Rock here.

Architecture

Although its exact age is unknown, the oldest building in the city is certainly the Scadding log cabin, which was moved from the banks of the Don River to its present site in Exhibition Place; it remains open as a museum. In 1793 when the town of York was founded, colonials built their churches and mansions in the Georgian style. During the Victorian era, wealthier citizens built Gothic manor houses, Italianate and Romanesque villas and Queen Anne row houses. Toronto's distinctive 'Bay & Gable' house also appeared at this time, usually

Doors Open Toronto

Have you ever seen a building so stunning or so unusual that you wanted to open up the door and walk right in? That's what the annual Doors Open Toronto festival is all about. Begun in May 2000, Doors Open is based on a wildly successful festival that started in Glasgow over a decade ago, an idea that has now spread to more than 40 countries in Europe, with 19 million participants last year alone.

The festival's debut took place over one sunny weekend, during which Toronto's architectural treasures, both famous and forgotten, were flung open to the public. The air truly buzzed with enthusiasm as amicable Torontonians lined up to peek inside the three-sided Flatiron (Gooderham) Building, or to hear tales of the Italian consulate's hidden mosaics, '100 hounds room' and secret passageway to the house of the former ambassador's mistress. The longest queues were at the Victorian-era Don Jail, which was ironic considering that most of its guests over the last century or so spent much of their time trying to get out.

Who knew that Torontonians had an appetite for architecture? Mostly the city has shown a lack of respect for its past: Many of its finest historic buildings have been successively torn down since the 1950s, when the Guild Inn (see the Places to Stay chapter) started collecting pieces of them on its front lawn. Those venerable buildings still left standing often have private citizens like Honest Ed Mirvish or nongovernmental organizations to thank, all of whom saw their valiant (and expensive) efforts rewarded again during the hugely popular festival. The restored Elgin & Winter Garden Theatre Centre got a boost in attendance that weekend, as did historic community jewels like Kensington Market's Anshei Minsk Synagogue and St Anne's Anglican Church.

Doors Open Toronto's two open-house days seem all too short considering it only happens once a year. But next year's selection of buildings will be different, with equally intriguing doors to knock on. If you're lucky, maybe the city will even open the ghostly subway station rumored to still exist underneath Bay St.

Web site: www.doorsopen.org

consisting of two semidetached dwellings, each with a bay window and pointy Victorian gable, and a patch of garden in front. Warehouses and factories were being built on Front St, one of which processed pigs, giving rise to one of Toronto's nicknames, 'Hogtown.'

Around the beginning of the 20th century, the great civic buildings of a burgeoning Edwardian metropolis were constructed: Old City Hall, the Royal Ontario Museum (ROM) and Union Station. Many were worked on by EJ Lennox, often called the 'Architect of Toronto,' who also designed the provincial legislature and Casa Loma. These new Edwardian masterpieces were all part of a 'City Beautiful' scheme that envisioned parkways radiating from downtown, but the city only managed to build University Ave before the Depression hit.

Starting in 1834 Toronto mandated that buildings be made of brick, and so the great fires of 1849 and 1904 didn't destroy as much of the city as they might have otherwise done. After strict zoning limitations were lifted in 1905, at last taller buildings began to rise on the city's horizon, though most of its skyscrapers were done in the dull 'form follows function' International Style during the 1950s. Even today Toronto remains relatively low-lying and flat. Still the enclosed quiet residential blocks found throughout the central area boast shady trees, quiet one-way streets (called 'Traffic Calming Zones') and mix & match row houses dating from the 1920s that make Toronto a particularly pleasant place to live, architecturally speaking.

The most refreshing architecture in contemporary Toronto is being done by the firm of Moriyama & Teshima, who believe in 'healthy' architecture that is harmonious and ecologically sound, and involves community cooperation at the design stage. Much of the firm's work shows an elegance and clarity of Japanese influences reminiscent of Frank Lloyd Wright's Prairie School of architecture; however, Moriyama & Teshima's designs are more dynamic, less predictable and meant for ordinary people. Just visit the quirky Bata Shoe Museum, the Ontario Science Centre or the Metro Toronto Reference Library, which has interior water fountains and great glass windows overlooking the Don River Valley. Web site: www.mtarch.com.

The Ontario Heritage Foundation (see the Downtown Walking Tour in the Things to See & Do chapter) has been instrumental in protecting and restoring many of the city's architectural treasures, such as the Elgin & Winter Garden Theatre Centre and the George Brown house, as well as the Niagara Apothecary museum in Niagara-on-the-Lake (see the Excursions chapter).

Painting & the Visual Arts

The landscape painters known as the Group of Seven first came together in the 1920s. Fired by an almost adolescent enthusiasm, this all-male gung-ho group of painterly talent spent a lot of time traipsing the wilds of northern Ontario, capturing the rugged Canadian wilderness through the seasons and under all weather conditions. The energy they felt then can be seen today in some stunning paintings – vibrant, light-filled canvases of Canada's mountains, lakes, forests and townships. The original seven members (the group later expanded to become the Canadian Group of Painters) were Franklin Carmichael, Lawren Harris, AY Jackson, Frank Johnston (later replaced by AJ Casson), Arthur Lismer, JEH MacDonald and FH Varley.

Although he died before the group was officially formed, the painter Tom Thompson was considered by other members as the group's leading light. An experienced outdoorsman, Thompson drowned in 1917 just as he was producing some of his most powerful work. His deep connection to the land can be clearly seen in his vivid paintings. When the group took studios in Toronto (they sketched outside but produced finished work indoors), Thompson preferred working and living in his small rustic shack out back.

Today works by the Group of Seven hang in the Art Gallery of Ontario, the Thompson Gallery (see the Downtown Walking Tour in the Things to See & Do chapter)

Outdoor Moose-eum

Moose hadn't been seen on the streets of Toronto since they were herded out the Yonge St toll gate during colonial times. But Mayor Mel Lastman launched a grand 'Outdoor Moose-eum' campaign in summer 2000 to bring them back.

Like public art projects in Chicago (using cows) and Buffalo (using buffalo, what else?), more than 300 life-sized fiberglass moose were set up around Toronto. Each moose was painted with its own whimsical design, often reflecting its corporate sponsor, for example, the Pizza Hut moose, the Go-Go GO Transit Moose or even Microsoft's Hotmail moose. But others were free of their capitalist shackles, like the moose in the Moose Stop waiting for the bus on Bloor St or the quizzical one poised on the diving board above the fountain in Nathan Phillips Square.

This public art campaign had three purposes: to employ artists, lure tourists and raise money for charity. But moose vandalism raged that summer in Toronto, as frustrated citizens targeted the hapless mascots which they said had wasted $1.5 million in municipal funds that should have been spent on affordable housing or better social services. Shortly after making their appearance, the moose population was repeatedly spray-painted (and this in a city where graffiti is rarer than hen's teeth). A certain pinstriped banking moose on Bay St was symbolically emasculated each weekend by the theft of his spring-loaded antlers.

In emergency response the city set up a moose vandalism hotline and the moose enthoosiasts at www.AntlerWatch.com used digital cameras to safeguard Toronto's forlorn herd. AntlerWatch stands for 'Alliance of Nervous Torontonians Leery of Evil Ruffians Who Abscond Taking Cervidae Headgear'; it was formerly known as CCRAP (Citizens Concerned about Removal of Antler Parts).

By the end of the summer, the anarchy had passed and the remaining moose were left untouched until they were auctioned off, leaving Toronto bare and moose-less once again.

and the McMichael Collection in Kleinburg (see the Excursions chapter). Three original members also worked on the interior murals of St Anne's, a Byzantine-style Anglican church dating from 1907 at 270 Gladstone Ave, northeast of Dundas St W and Dufferin Ave.

Contemporary Toronto doesn't seem to quite grasp the importance of public art. In the 1960s when the new City Hall was being built, the English sculptor Henry Moore offered to practically donate his work to the city, and the city council turned him down. Outdoor murals are few, except for the Flatiron Building (see the Downtown Walking Tour in the Things to See & Do chapter). Halfhearted attempts at city-funded art are limited to such things as the Moose-eum (see boxed text 'Outdoor Moose-eum') and the odd metalworks along the Spadina streetcar line.

For traditional Native work you'll be hard-pressed to find anything apart from museum and gallery collections, most of which are imported from British Columbia and the Arctic Inuit nations.

Cinema & TV

Toronto is unquestionably the Hollywood of the North (see the boxed text in the Facts for the Visitor chapter), except there's less glitz and schlock and instead more fine, independent cinema produced here. The Toronto International Film Festival has a sterling international reputation and more films stars and directors come from the region than you might think. (For a full-on Canadian history of Hollywood, check out www.northernstars.net.)

Like their Vancouver cousins, Torontonians are used to tripping over film sets and trailers as they go about their business (or where they actually do business). Entire city blocks are often roped off and traffic rerouted, all for the sake of the contributions that film crews, drawn by generous federal tax concessions, make to the city's economy. The Elgin & Winter Garden Theatre Centre stars in *Blues Brothers 2000;* Maple Leaf Gardens and the Silver Dollar Room blues club in *Adventures in Babysitting;* the old Don Jail and Lee's Palace in *Cocktail;* and Union Station, Allan Gardens and Casa Loma in *Johnny Mnemonic,* to name just a few locations.

David Cronenberg, the director of out-there films like *Videodrome, The Fly, Naked Lunch,* and most recently *eXistenZ,* was born right here in Toronto. Atom Egoyan, another renowned Canadian director, started making movies while a student at UT. His works, including *Exotica* and *The Sweet Hereafter,* are often big doses of bitter reality.

Another UT alumnus, Norman Jewison worked as a director and producer at the CBC during television's 'Golden Age' before moving to the US to launch *Your Hit Parade* and make feature films. He got his big break when he was called in to finish Sam Peckinpah's *The Cincinnati Kid,* but his crowning achievement was directing the 1967 Academy Award-winning *In the Heat of the Night,* a film about racial tensions in the US. It was in part his success that revived the Canadian film industry during the 1960s. Jewison's more recent movie titles include *The Thomas Crown Affair* and *Hurricane.*

When it comes to actors, Toronto has produced some funny women and men. Many got their start at the Second City comedy club (see the Things to See & Do and Entertainment chapters), like Gilda Radner, Dan Aykroyd and Mike Myers, all of whom eventually moved on to New York's Saturday Night Live (SNL). Myers grew up just next door to Toronto in Scarborough and remains to this day a die-hard Toronto Maple Leafs fan. If you ever wondered why the donut shop was such a big deal in *Wayne's World,* blame it on Mike being a true Canuck. His 1993 *So I Married an Axe Murderer* mostly flopped, but local teens made it into a cult classic, yelling 'Head! Move!' in Scottish accents for quite some time afterward.

Another successful Scarborough boy, but one who took a different career path, is Jim Carrey. After working as a factory janitor during his teens, he began doing open-mike performances at Yuk Yuk's comedy club (see the Entertainment chapter). His physical routines and wild impersonations went over so well that he took off with his newfound fame to LA, where Rodney Dangerfield and Buddy Hackett finally 'discovered' him.

Toronto's dirty little secret is that Keanu Reeves, who was born in Beirut, Lebanon, actually grew up in Toronto. Take that, Canada!

Theater

Toronto is the third largest theater city in the world, after London and New York. But its theatrical past has been stormy, as reflected in the topsy-turvy fortunes of the historic double-decker Elgin & Winter Garden Theatre Centre (see the Things to See & Do chapter). In the heyday of vaudeville, the likes of George Burns and Gracie Allen, Milton Berle and Sophie Tucker all performed on its stages. Patrons paid only 15¢ to stay all day if they liked. The advent of 'talkies' in the 1920s closed the fantastical Winter Garden theater and converted the Elgin into a movie house. When TV was invented, even the historic Elgin theater went into a slow decline. It wasn't until the 1960s when Honest Ed Mirvish restored the Royal Alexandra theater and brought on productions of big musicals with international casts like *Godspell* and *Hair* that live theater in Toronto began to revive (See the Theatre Block entry in the Downtown Walking Tour section in the Things to See & Do chapter). Experimental and new dramatic works by contemporary Canadian playwrights exploded onto the scene starting as far back as the '70s, and by the time the Ontario Heritage Foundation started restoring the Elgin & Winter Garden in the early '90s, it was able to mount an all-Canadian production of *Cats* that was a sellout for months. Toronto's theater scene was definitely back to stay (for information on theaters, see the Entertainment chapter).

SOCIETY & CONDUCT

Describing 'Toronto the Good' circa 1984, Jan Morris wrote that the people here were 'incoherently polite' and that 'even the imminent explosion of a nuclear bomb would not induce its citizens to ignore a red light at a pedestrian crossing.' In general, Torontonians are still very mannerly, if a bit standoffish.

In the latter part of the 20th century the city cultivated an exemplary culture of tolerance in any category you want to name (race, religion, sexual orientation, etc). Except, of course, for those fine citizens who, thinking there are no Americans to hear them, critique the USA using the grossest, most arbitrary stereotypes imaginable. It's almost a civic duty to do so.

RELIGION

The nickname 'Toronto the Good' dates back to the 1906 Lord's Day Act banning all paid employment and virtually all cultural and social activities on Sunday. Eaton's department store drew its curtains to prevent 'sinful' window shopping and playground sets were chained and locked. This morally Christian legislation had its socially conscious aspect, since it ensured the working classes got at least one day off per week. The laws persisted, however, until 1950.

Today Canadians are even more lax about religious practice than their US counterparts and don't mix religion with politics, although abortion is still hotly debated. The largest Christian denomination is surprisingly not Anglican, but Roman Catholic, after which comes the Protestant United Church of Canada. Meanwhile progressive Christianity is in full force at the high number of 'affirming' congregations in the Annex neighborhood that ordain and welcome the lesbigay community, and downtown at the Church of the Holy Trinity, where most members come for the social activism and not the Sunday service.

Historically, Jews have been a strong presence in Toronto. The first Jewish immigrants in the early 20th century settled around Kensington Market and founded the Anshei Minsk Synagogue (see Places of Worship in the Facts for the Visitor chapter).

Since the 1970s Toronto's immigrant groups have brought along their own religious traditions. Buddhism predominates among Asian communities, and appeals to a significant number of non-Asian Canadians as well. Toronto has also been a haven for a small but notable Tibetan Buddhist community.

LANGUAGE

We dare you to tell us a language that isn't spoken in Toronto. The official notices of the Toronto municipal government are not just bilingual but *sexti*-lingual, printed in Chinese, English, French, Greek, Italian and Portuguese, while driver's license tests are given in 12 languages.

Admittedly, Toronto is still in practice predominantly Anglophone (English-speaking). Residents may not speak the Queen's English, but many British terms and spellings (eg, 'centre' instead of center) are still in common use. Active support for French bilingualism is on the decline and most of Toronto's bilingual signs are written in English and Chinese, not French. The few bilingual French signs are most visible near the US border, as if Ontario wanted to hit new US arrivals over the head with the message, 'We are Canadian! We are bilingual! Voilà!'

So you definitely won't need to bring along a French phrase book, though an English-Canuck (Canadian) one might be useful. As a quick glossary, 'ski-doo' means snowmobile, a 'toque' (rhymes with duke) is a hat, 'peameal bacon' is what US citizens aptly call Canadian bacon, and afternoon 'high tea' is more like a meal.

The proper pronunciation of the city's name (and many of its streets) troubles visitors. You can pick them out the newbies by how they say 'Toh-RAWN-toh,' enunciating each syllable, while natives slur it into almost a grunt, 'Tuhranna.'

Facts for the Visitor

WHEN TO GO
In Toronto the peak summer season runs from Victoria Day (late May) until Labour Day (early September), and the squeeze on accommodations and lines at major attractions become unreal. The weather is hot, everything stays open late and there are street festivals and outdoor performances every weekend.

From November to March, the wind whipping down Bay St chills the bones. Many shops, restaurants and attractions reduce their hours or even close during winter. Still, the coldest December day can be made bearable by a fireside pint, and don't forget – it's hockey season.

WHAT TO BRING
Casual Torontonians don't compete with their *haute couture* cousins in Montreal. You'll only need to 'dress up' for an evening theater performance or top-end restaurant. If you've forgotten to pack your club gear, Toronto has plenty of original designers and vintage clothing shops to outfit you.

Many residents won't wear heavy down jackets, even when it's 30 degrees below zero outside (just so they look hip) – go figure. For others, cheap ski jackets, gloves, scarves and hats (called '*toques*,' pronounced tukes) are sold at thrift stores and discount stores. Even in winter, pack a bathing suit, which weighs next to nothing, for heated indoor pools and saunas.

In any season, bring a good, sturdy pair of walking shoes since the city can put a lot of mileage on your tootsies.

ORIENTATION
The land around Toronto is flat and the city tends to sprawl. Its grid-style layout, with nearly all the streets running north-south and east-west, means it's easy to get oriented. The subway, though not too extensive, is quick, safe and simple to navigate, as are the old-fashioned streetcars that run along all major thoroughfares in the city center.

Yonge St (pronounced Young), the main north-south artery, begins at Lake Ontario and runs north to the city boundary, Steeles Ave, and beyond. The central area is bounded by Front St to the south, Bloor St to the north, Spadina Ave to the west and Church St to the east. Street names change from 'East' to 'West' at Yonge St, and the street numbers begin there.

At the foot of Yonge St is Lake Ontario and the semi-redeveloped waterfront area called Harbourfront. Several blocks north is Queen St, which runs east across the Don River to The Beach neighborhood and west beyond Bathurst St, filling up with shops and cafés that just get artier the further you go.

Spadina Ave, once a strictly Jewish area, is now the heart of Chinatown. Kensington Market borders its west side and both extend as far north as College St (called Carlton St, east of Yonge St). West of Euclid Ave is Little Italy.

University Ave, lined with offices and trees, is Toronto's widest street. It leads north, just skirting to the west of City Hall, to Queen's Park and the provincial legislature. North of the park is the museum district, while to the west lies the University of Toronto (UT) campus and The Annex, a student neighborhood. East of the park several of the city's museums are on Bloor St, which borders the chi-chi enclave of Yorkville, once at the vanguard of the 1960s bohemian scene.

Farther east towards the river is Cabbagetown, an increasingly gentrified neighborhood that retains some Irish immigrant character. On the east side of the river, Bloor St becomes Danforth Ave, the restaurant-blessed Greek area of town, often called the Danforth, with Chinatown East and Little India areas just south along Gerrard St E.

MAPS
This guidebook's detailed neighborhood maps will be enough for all but the most in-depth explorations of Toronto.

Toronto Transport Commission (TTC) maps are available free at subway stations and are printed in the Yellow Pages. While these are excellent for subway navigation, detailed bus and streetcar routes are only found on the virtually theft-proof plasticized maps hanging inside shelters at passenger stops.

Widely available at newsstands and bookstores, MapArt's 'Toronto' ($2.95) has full city coverage, a street index and an enlargement of the downtown area. For excursions, the Canada Map Store (Map 4; ☎ 416-862-0881), 61 Front St E, has excellent hiking and canoeing contour maps, and Ontario Tourism offices offer free maps covering the whole province.

TOURIST OFFICES
Local Tourist Offices

At the Ontario Tourism office (Map 5; ☎ 416-314-0944, 1-800-668-2746, French speakers ☎ 416-314-0956 or 1-800-268-3736) inside Eaton Centre, the well-informed staff speak eight languages. Walk-in visitors will find racks of brochures on accommodations, entertainment and outdoors activities across the city and province – pick up the *Toronto 2001 Visitor Guide*. It's open 10 am to 9 pm weekdays, 9:30 am to 7 pm Saturday and noon to 5 pm Sunday. On the Web (www .ontariotravel.net) you can access seasonal events information and request Ontario travel planners (available in English or French).

Ontario Tourism Travel Centres at land border crossings provide information and currency exchange services. These offices are open 8:30 am until at least 6 pm daily in summer, closing earlier in winter.

Niagara Falls (☎ 905-358-3221) 5355 Stanley Ave

Sarnia (Blue Water Bridge; ☎ 519-344-7403) 1415 Venetian Blvd

Windsor (Ambassador Bridge; ☎ 519-973-1310) 1235 Huron Church Rd

You can make accommodations requests and purchase discount tickets for major attractions through the privatized TraveLinx Ontario (☎ 1-800-603-3837) between 9 am and 5 pm daily or via their Web site (www .travelinx.com).

Tourism Toronto (☎ 416-203-2500, 1-800-499-2514) staffs a limited summer kiosk at City Hall that stays open until Labour Day. Telephone agents are available year-round from 8 am to 5 pm daily; after hours, you can use the touch-tone information menu.

Apart from stocking a few brochures, the 'Info TO' (Map 4; ☎ 416-599-1548) desk at the Metro Convention Centre, open 8 am to 5pm daily, only sells tickets for the CN Tower, SkyDome tours, etc.

Tourist Offices Abroad

For basic help in planning a visit, call the closest Canadian embassy, consulate or high commission, or visit their Web site for entry requirements, customs regulations, working holidays, and where to get more in-depth travel information (see Embassies & Consulates, later in this chapter).

Although its main purpose is marketing Canada to the global tourist industry, the Canadian Tourism Commission (CTC; www .travelcanada.ca) maintains a helpful introductory Web site with destination overviews and practical information. US residents can request visitors' guides and travel planners by calling ☎ 1-877-822-6232; in the UK, dial ☎ 0906-871-5000.

The toll-free Ontario Tourism number (☎ 1-800-668-2746) works in the continental US and Hawaii.

TRAVEL AGENCIES

For budget, youth or student travelers, Travel CUTS (Canadian University Travel Service; ☎ 1-800-667-2887, www.travelcuts .com) offers a wealth of information and services. There are six offices in Toronto, including one at 187 College St (Map 6; ☎ 416-979-2406); 74 Gerrard St E (Map 5; ☎ 416-977-0441); 49 Front St E (Map 4; ☎ 416-365-0545); and 313 Queen St W (Map 5; ☎ 416-977-6272).

For discount and last-minute fares, check the newspaper classifieds, especially the free weekly *Now*, and with Last Minute Ticket Centre (Map 10; ☎ 416-469-1161), 405 Danforth Ave. A chain called Flight Centre

(Map 8; ☎ 416-934-0670), 382 Bloor St W, claims unbeatable prices, but don't be fooled – independent travel agents, especially in Toronto's immigrant neighborhoods, often advertise better bargains. Many agencies are found in The Annex, including African Wings Travels & Tours (Map 8; ☎ 416-588-7626), 835 Bloor St W, and Andes Travel (Map 8; ☎ 416-537-3447), 616 Bloor St W.

DOCUMENTS
Passport
Visitors from almost all countries need a passport. The few exceptions include people from Greenland (Denmark) and Saint Pierre & Miquelon (France) who do not need passports if they are entering from their areas of residence. They do need to have valid identification, however.

For US and Canadian citizens, a driver's license is often sufficient in practice to prove residency when entering via land border crossings. However, a birth certificate or certificate of citizenship or naturalization may be required before admission is granted. Permanent residents of the US who aren't citizens should carry their green card.

Visas
For Canada Visas aren't required for visitors from nearly all western countries. Visa requirements change frequently, so it's a good idea to check with the Canadian Immigration Centre (in Toronto ☎ 416-973-4444, www.cic.gc.ca) or your consulate to see if you're exempt. Visas are necessary for residents of developing countries, Hong Kong, Korea, Taiwan, South Africa and parts of Eastern Europe. A separate visa is required for visitors intending to work or attend school in Canada. A multiple-entry visa costs $150 and can be used over a two-year period, provided that no single stay exceeds six months.

A passport and/or visa does not guarantee entry. Proof of sufficient funds or possibly a return ticket out of the country may be required, though legitimate travelers often aren't asked. Minors under 18 years old should carry a permission letter from a guardian. HIV-positive visitors may only be refused entry if they admit to needing treatment during their stay in Canada. If you are refused entry but have a visa, you have the right of appeal at the port of entry. If you're arriving by land, the best course is simply to try again later (after a shift change) or at a different border crossing.

For the USA Visitors to Canada who plan to spend time in the USA should be aware that admission requirements to the USA when you're arriving by land can be quite different than by air or sea. These regulations are also subject to rapid change, and the duration of the visit – whether an afternoon at Niagara Falls or a cross-continental journey of three months – doesn't matter.

Visitors to the USA from nearly all western countries don't need visas, but there are exceptions, one being South Africa. For details, contact the US embassy or consulate in your home country or Toronto (see Embassies & Consulates later in this chapter). Visitors can apply for US visas in Canada but it's generally easier and quicker to apply at home; this also reduces your chances of being refused. Visas cannot be obtained upon arrival in the USA.

Those who do not need a visa are subject to a US$6 entry fee (visa waiver) at US land border crossings. Check that your entry permit to Canada includes multiple entries, otherwise you may find your afternoon trip into the USA involuntarily extended when border officials won't let you back into Canada.

Travel Insurance
You should seriously consider taking out travel insurance to cover any eventual medical expenses and luggage theft or loss, as well as cancellation or delays in your travel arrangements. International student policies handled by STA Travel, Council Travel, Travel CUTS (Voyages Campus in Québec) and other student travel agencies are usually reasonably priced.

Some policies offer lower and higher medical expenses options; when signing, bear in mind that Canada's excellent medical, hospital and dental care is very expensive. Most policies require that you pay on the spot and submit a claim later to your insurer.

The largest seller of medical insurance to visitors to Canada is John Ingle Insurance. It offers hospital medical care policies that cover you for periods lasting from seven days up to one year. The 30-day basic coverage costs $90 for an adult under the age of 55 and includes hospital and doctors' fees, extended health care and other benefits. Policies can be bought before or after arrival in Canada from the Toronto head office (☎ 416-340-8115, 1-800-216-3588), 438 University Ave, Suite 1200, Toronto, ON M5G 2K8).
Web site: www.ingle-health.com

Driver's License & Permits
A valid driver's license from any home country is normally valid for six months in Canada. An International Driving Permit (IDP), available in your home country, is cheap and good for one year almost anywhere in the world.

Short-term US visitors can bring in their own vehicles without special permits, provided they have insurance. If you've rented a car, trailer or any other vehicle in the USA and you are driving it into Canada, bring a copy of the rental agreement to save any possible hassle by border officials. US citizens traveling extensively in Canada should get a Nonresident Interprovince Motor Vehicle Liability Insurance Card, handy if you're involved in an accident. It's only available in the USA; contact your insurance agent.

Discount Cards
A Hostelling International (HI) will insure a discount (and is often required) at affiliated youth hostels, but it may get you small discounts at other backpacker hostels, museums, restaurants, attractions and shops. If you don't pick one up before leaving home, one/two-year memberships cost $25/35 at any HI hostel or Travel CUTS office. Call

Canada HI at ☎ 1-800-663-5777 for further details.
Web site: www.hostellingintl.ca

An International Student Identity Card (ISIC) can pay for itself through half-price admissions and discounted air and ferry tickets. If you're under 26 but not a student, you can apply for a GO25 card. Teachers are eligible for the International Teacher Identity Card (ITIC). In Toronto, these discount cards are issued by Travel CUTS (see Travel Agencies earlier in this chapter) for $16. Bring proper documentation – this isn't Bangkok or Athens.
Web site: www.istc.org

Photocopies
Before you leave home, you should photocopy all important documents (passport, credit cards, travel insurance policy, air/bus/train tickets, driver's license, etc.). Leave one copy with someone at home and keep another with you, separate from the originals.

It's also a good idea to store details of your vital travel documents in Lonely Planet's free online Travel Vault in case you lose the photocopies or can't be bothered with them. Your password-protected Travel Vault is accessible online anywhere in the world – create it at www.ekno.lonelyplanet.com.

EMBASSIES & CONSULATES
Your Own Embassy
It's important to realize what your own embassy can and can't do to help you if you get into trouble. Generally speaking, it won't be much help in emergencies if the trouble you're in is remotely your own fault. Remember that you are bound by the laws of the country you are in. Your embassy will not be sympathetic if you end up in jail after committing a crime locally, even if such actions are legal in your own country.

In genuine emergencies, you might get some assistance, but only if other channels have been exhausted. If all your money and documents are stolen, it might assist you with getting a new passport, but a loan for onward travel is out of the question – the embassy would expect you to have insurance.

Canadian Embassies Abroad

For a list of other Canadian diplomatic representation abroad, consult the Canadian government Web site (www.dfait-maeci.gc
.ca/english/missions/menu.htm).

Australia
High Commission: (☎ 02-6273-3844), Commonwealth Ave, Canberra ACT 2600, www.canada
.org.au
Consulate: (☎ 02-9364-3000, Visa Immigration Office ☎ 02-9364-3050), 111 Harrington St, Level 5, Quay West, Sydney, NSW 2000
Consulate: (☎ 03-9811-9999), 123 Camberwell Rd, Hawthorn East, Melbourne, Vic 3123
Consulate: (☎ 08-9322-7930), 267 St George's Terrace, Perth, WA 6000

Denmark
Embassy: (☎ 33-48-32-00), Kr Bernikows Gade 1, 1105 Copenhagen K, www.canada.dk

France
Embassy: (☎ 01-44 43-29-00), 35 Avenue Montaigne, 75008 Paris, www.amb-canada.fr
Consulate: (☎ 04-72-77-64-07), 21 rue Bourgelat, 69002 Lyon

Germany
Embassy: (☎ 30-20-31-20) Friedrichstrasse 95, 23rd Floor, 10117 Berlin, www.dfait-macci.gc.ca/
~bonn/

Ireland
Embassy: (☎ 01-478-1988; after hours 01-478-1476), Canada House, 65/68 St Stephen's Green, Dublin 2

Italy
Embassy: (☎ 06-44-59-84-46), Via Zara 30, 00198 Rome, www.canada.it

Japan
Embassy: (☎ 03-5412-6200), 3-38 Akasaka 7-chome, Minato-ku, Tokyo 107-5803, www.dfait-maeci.gc.ca/ni-ka/contacts/tokyo/menu-e.asp

Netherlands
Embassy: (☎ 070-311-1600), Sophialaan 7, 2500 GV The Hague, www.ocanada.nl

New Zealand
High Commission: (☎ 04-473-9577, toll-free from Auckland ☎ 09-309-8516), 61 Molesworth St, 3rd Floor, Thorndon, Wellington, www.dfait-maeci
.gc.ca/newzealand/welcome-e.asp

Spain
Embassy: (☎ 91-423-32-50), Edificio Goya, Calle Nuñez de Balboa 35, 28001 Madrid, www
.canada-es.org

Sweden
Embassy: (☎ 08-453-3000), Tegelbacken 4, 7th Floor, S-103 23 Stockholm, www.canadaemb.se

Switzerland
Embassy: (☎ 031-357-3200) Kirchenfeldstrasse 88, 3005 Berne, www.canada-ambassade.ch
Permanent Mission to the Office of the UN, Consular Section: (☎ 22-919-9200), 1 PrÈ-de-la-Bichette Street, 1202 Geneva

UK
High Commission: (☎ 020-258-6600), Canada House, Trafalgar Square, Pall Mall East, London SW1Y 5BJ, www.canada.org.uk
Visa Information: (☎ 09068-616644), 38 Grosvenor Street, London W1X 0AA
Consulate: (☎ 0131-220-4333), Standard Life House, 30 Lothian Road, Edinburgh, EH1 2DH Scotland
Consulate: (☎ 01232-660-212), 378 Strandmillis Road, Belfast, BT9 5BL Northern Ireland

USA
Embassy: (☎ 202-682-1740), 501 Pennsylvania Avenue NW, Washington, DC 20001, www
.canadianembassy.org
Consulate General: (☎ 716-858-9500), 1 Marine Midland Center, Suite 3000, Buffalo, NY 14203-2884
Consulate General: (☎ 312-616-1860), Two Prudential Plaza, 180 N Stetson Avenue, Suite 2400, Chicago, IL 60601
Consulate General: (☎ 313-567-2340), 600 Renaissance Center, Suite 1100, Detroit, MI 48243-1798
Consulate General: (☎ 212-596-1600), 1251 Avenue of the Americas, Concourse Level, New York City, NY 10020-1175

There are many other cities with Canadian Consulate Generals in the USA, including Atlanta, Boston, Dallas, Honolulu, Los Angeles, Minneapolis and Seattle. For a full list of Canadian diplomatic representation abroad, consult the Canadian government Web site: www.dfait-maeci.gc.ca/english/missions/menu.htm.

Consulates in Toronto

The following consulates are generally open 9 am to 1 pm weekdays, although some open again from 2 to 4:30 pm.

Australia (Map 6; ☎ 416-323-1155) 175 Bloor St E, North Tower Suite 314

Cuba (☎ 416-234-8181) 5353 Dundas St W, Suite 401, Kipling Square

Denmark (Map 6; ☎ 416-962-5669) 151 Bloor St W, Suite 310, www.ambassade-info.dk/dkcanadtorcg.htm

France (Map 6; ☎ 416-925-8041) 130 Bloor St W, Suite 400, toronto.consulfrance.org

Germany (☎ 416-925-2813) 77 Admiral Rd

Ireland *Honorary Consul:* (☎ 416-366-9300) *Embassy:* (☎ 613-233-6281) 130 Albert St, Ottawa, ON K1P 5G4.

Israel (Map 6; ☎ 416-640-8500) 180 Bloor St W, Suite 700, www.israelca.org

Italy (Map 5; ☎ 416-977-1566) 136 Beverley St, www.toronto.italconsulate.org

Japan (☎ 416-363-7038) 77 King St W, Royal Trust Tower 33rd Floor, www.japancg-toronto.org

Netherlands (Map 5; ☎ 416-598-2520) 1 Dundas St W, Eaton Centre Suite 2106, www.netherlands-consulate.org/Toronto.htm

New Zealand *Honorary Consul:* (☎ 416-947-0000) *High Commission:* (☎ 613-238-5991) 99 Bank St, Suite 727, Ottawa, ON K1P 6G3, www.nzhcottawa.org

Spain (Map 4; ☎ 416-977-1661) 200 Front St W, Suite 2401

Sweden (Map 6; ☎ 416-963-8768) 2 Bloor St W, 15th Floor

Switzerland (Map 4; ☎ 416-593-5371) 154 University Ave

UK (Map 6; ☎ 416-593-1290) 777 Bay St, Suite 2800

USA (Map 5; ☎ 416-595-1700, 1-800-529-4410) 360 University Ave, www.usembassycanada.gov/toronto.htm

The noteworthy Consulate General of Indonesia (☎ 416-360-4020), 129 Jarvis St, is inside a tiny gated compound protected by stone Garuda birds, Indonesia's national symbol. You can't see that at the Royal Ontario Museum.

CUSTOMS

How thorough Canadian customs is upon arrival depends on your nationality, age, point of departure and/or appearance. Drivers are more likely to be searched if their vehicle looks suspiciously full – stow your belongings in the trunk. Some border personnel are polite, others rude; arguing is of little use. If an agent wants to frisk or

strip search you, you are entitled to be given a reason for his or her suspicion. You are also entitled to legal counsel if you wish to refuse.

Adults age 19 and older can bring in 1.14L of liquor (or a case of beer), 200 cigarettes, 50 cigars and 400g of tobacco. You can also bring in gifts valued up to $60 plus a 'reasonable amount' of personal effects, including cars, computers, cameras and sports equipment. Boats powered by motors under 10hp can be brought in without any special licenses. Duty-free shops are found at every major arrival and departure point, but you must have spent at least 48 hours in the country to be entitled to use them. To avoid delays, don't bring any perishable items since fruits, vegetables and plants may all be confiscated.

Don't get caught bringing drugs into Canada, as sentences can be harsh. This warning includes marijuana and hashish. Mace, pepper spray, pistols, fully automatic weapons and smaller firearms (except for hunting purposes) are also prohibited. For the latest customs information, contact the Canadian embassy or consulate in your home country or phone ☎ 1-800-461-9999.

MONEY

Since the 1990s the US$ has held strong against the Canadian dollar ($, for purposes of this book), giving American visitors favorable exchange value for their money. However, once Canadian federal and provincial taxes are factored in, that buying power loses its strength. All prices quoted in this book are in Canadian dollars, unless otherwise noted.

Currency

Canadian coins come in one-cent (penny), five-cent (nickel), 10-cent (dime), 25-cent (quarter), $1 (loonie) and $2 (toonie) pieces. The 11-sided, gold-colored 'loonie' features the common loon. When the two-toned 'toonie' was introduced in 1996, Canadians

Unless otherwise noted, all prices in this book are in Canadian dollars.

went on a rampage trying to separate the aluminum-bronze core from the nickel outer ring; the most successful method is to put one in the freezer for a while and then hit it with a hammer.

With the demise of the $2 bill, paper currency is found in $5 (blue), $10 (purple), $20 (green) and $50 (red) denominations. The $100 (brown) and larger bills are less common and could prove difficult to cash. Some denominations have two styles as older versions in fair condition continue to circulate.

Exchanging Money

It's best to change your money at a recognized bank or other financial institution. American Express (Map 4; ☎ 416-363-3883), 100 Front St W, inside the Royal York Hotel, is open 8:30 am to 5 pm Monday to Thursday (until 7 pm Friday) and 9 am to 4 pm Saturday. Its Holt Renfrew Centre branch (Map 6; ☎ 416-967-3411) stays open later. Thomas Cook (Map 4; ☎ 416-366-1961), 10 King St E, is open 9 am to 5 pm weekdays and has a booth at Pearson International Airport. Its counter inside the Sheraton Centre (Map 4; ☎ 416-363-4867), 123 Queen St W, keeps extended summer hours of 8 am to 8 pm weekdays, 9 am to 7 pm Saturday and 9 am to 4 pm Sunday.

If it's late or the weekend, your choices are limited. Try the currency exchange booths on Front (especially Union Station), Yonge or Bloor Sts. The Money Mart (Map 6; ☎ 416-920-4146), 617 Yonge St, is open 24 hours. Calforex Currencies International (Map 6; ☎ 416-410-6918) 170 Bloor St W, is open 8:30 am to 7 pm weekdays, 9 am to 6 pm Saturday and 10 am to 5 pm Sunday.

Some hotels and souvenir shops exchange money, but rates aren't likely to be good. Ontario Tourism Travel Centres (see Local Tourist Offices earlier) and drive-through services at the border itself also handle currency exchange. Also most tourist enterprises near the border and even McDonald's will calculate on-the-spot exchange rates for cash transactions, though rates are unfavorable and change is given only in Canadian money.

You can withdraw money using an ATM debit card (see ATMs, later). The exchange rate on such transactions is usually good.

country	unit		Canadian dollar
Australia	A$1	=	C$0.83
EU	€1	=	C$1.41
France	FF1	=	C$0.22
Germany	DM1	=	C$0.72
Hong Kong	HK$1	=	C$0.19
Japan	¥100	=	C$1.29
New Zealand	NZ$1	=	C$0.67
UK	UK£1	=	C$2.22
USA	US$1	=	C$1.50

Cash & Personal Checks Most Canadians do not carry large amounts of cash for everyday use, relying instead on credit cards, ATMs and direct debit cards. Personal checks are rarely accepted, unlike in the USA.

Traveler's Checks American Express, Thomas Cook and Visa traveler's checks in Canadian dollars are the best; they are accepted as cash at many hotels, restaurants and stores. The savings you might make on exchange rates by carrying traveler's checks in a foreign currency (even US$) don't make up for the hassle of having to exchange them at banks or other financial institutions.

American Express and Thomas Cook offices cash their own traveler's checks fee-free. Banks usually offer better rates than currency exchange booths, but keep in mind that all will charge transaction fees of up to 3% of the total amount, with $2 minimum. Bank of Montréal and Scotiabank usually charge the lowest fees. If it's a flat fee and not a percentage, be sure to cash several checks at once.

For stolen or lost traveler's checks, call American Express (☎ 1-800-221-7282), Thomas Cook (☎ 1-888-823-4732) or VISA (☎ 1-800-227-6811). If you keep records and can supply a list of which checks are gone, a refund should be forthcoming with minimal inconvenience.

ATMs ATMs often offer superior exchange rates, and most give cash advances using Visa, American Express or MasterCard (see Credit Cards below). There are plenty of ATMs in Canada linked to the international Cirrus, Plus and Maestro networks. ATMs are found in convenience stores, gas stations, shopping centers, bus and train stations, airports etc. Royal Bank and Bank of Montréal ATMs most readily accept foreign-issued cards. Beware: many Canadian ATMs charge a $1.50 fee per use, and your home bank may charge you another fee on top of that.

Credit Cards Carrying a credit card is a good idea in Canada. They are more or less essential for deposits when booking accommodation, purchasing tickets, renting cars or even a bicycle. Credit cards also get you cash advances at banks, generally for a 3% or minimum $5 transaction fee.

Visa, MasterCard, American Express and JCB cards are widely accepted in Canada. American Express (☎ 1-800-668-8680), Citibank (☎ 1-800-387-1616), MasterCard (☎ 1-800-307-7309) and VISA (☎ 1-800-847-2911) all offer toll-free ATM locator services. Call immediately if your card gets lost or stolen.

Beware that many US-based credit cards now convert foreign billing charges using highly unfavorable exchange rates and extra fees.

International Transfers Telegraphic transfers are not very expensive, but can take up to a week to reach their destination. It's quicker and easier to have money wired via American Express (☎ 1-800-668-8680), which charges a fee of US$50 for US$1000. Western Union's Money Transfer system (☎ 1-800-325-000) and Thomas Cook's MoneyGram service (☎ 1-800-926-9400) are also popular. Completing a transfer should take no more than 15 minutes.

Costs

Arguably the most expensive city in Canada, Toronto is not exactly a bargain travel destination. Most prices that you see posted do not include taxes, which can add significantly to your costs. Bargaining is generally only done at markets, though haggling on big-ticket items like cars or outdoors equipment could knock 10% or more off the price.

If you are on a strict budget (ie, staying in hostels, self-catering and limiting your entertainment), you could scrape by on $40 a day. Staying in a cheap B&B, eating in budget restaurants and allowing yourself more freedom with your entertainment dollar runs $60 to $70. Anything more (say, an unlimited expense account) and it's the Royal York, sky boxes at the SkyDome and dinner at top-end Canoe for you.

Tipping & Bargaining

The minimum tip in restaurants is 15% of the pre-tax amount; exceptional service merits 20%. Either hand the tip directly to your server or discreetly leave it behind on the table. A few restaurants may include a service charge for large parties; no tip should be added in these cases. Tipping is also expected in bars, and it especially helps if a fat tip is given on the first order – after that, you won't go thirsty all night.

Smaller tips of at least 10% are also given to taxi drivers, hairdressers and barbers. Hotel bellhops and redcaps (porters) are tipped a dollar or two per item.

Taxes & Visitor Refunds

The federal goods and services tax (GST), variously known as the 'Gouge and Screw' or 'Grab and Steal' tax, adds 7% to just about every product, service or transaction, on top of which is an 8% provincial sales tax.

Visitors are eligible for refunds on GST paid for accommodation and non-consumable goods, provided they spend at least $200 and that each eligible receipt totals over $50. All original receipts (credit-card slips are not sufficient) must be stamped by customs before leaving the country. Drivers can obtain instant cash refunds for claims less than $500 at participating land border duty-free shops.

If you're leaving Canada by any other method, you'll need to mail your stamped

receipts within one year of the purchase date, along with boarding passes and a completed GST rebate booklet to: Visitor Rebate Program (☎ 902-432-5608, 1-800-668-4748), Summerside Tax Centre, Canada Customs & Revenue Agency, 275 Pope Rd, Suite 104, Summerside PE, C1N 6C6. Allow four to six weeks for processing.
Web site: www.ccra-adrc.gc.ca

Don't be misled by private companies that distribute 'official tax refund' booklets at tourist offices and duty-free stores. They offer to obtain your refund for you and then take up to 20% (minimum $7.50) for their 'services,' usually no faster or easier than if you do it yourself. National Tax Refund (www.nationaltaxrefund.com) charges extortionate fees, but many visitors find their instant cash tax refund office on the lower level of Eaton Centre convenient.

Visitors may also be eligible to reclaim the provincial 8% retail sales tax paid on goods, but not accommodation. Contact the Ministry of Finance (☎ 905-432-3332, 1-800-263-7965), Retail Sales Tax Branch, Refund Unit, 4th Floor, 1600 Champlain Ave, Whitby, ON L1N 9B2.

POST & COMMUNICATIONS
Post
The national mail service, Canada Post/Postes Canada (☎ 1-800-267-1177) is neither quick nor cheap, but it's reliable. Standard 1st-class air-mail letters or postcards to destinations within Canada cost 46¢ for up to 30g, 55¢ to the US or 95¢ to all other destinations (limit 20g). There are many post offices and drugstore postal outlets around the city. Hotel concessions, newsstands and tourist shops also sell stamps. Deposit mail into red mailboxes, usually found on street corners.

For posting heavier parcels, depending on the sender's time and money limitations, air, surface or a combination of methods can be used. Packing supplies and pamphlets explaining the various options, rates and requirements are available at post offices.
Web site: www.canadapost.ca

Poste-restante mail can be sent c/o General Delivery, Toronto, ON Canada M5W 1A1, and will be held for 15 days before being returned. Mail can be picked up at the Main Post Office at 25 The Esplanade (Map 4; ☎ 416-365-0656), from 8 am to 5:45 pm weekdays. Any packages will be ruthlessly inspected by customs officials, who will then assess duties that must be paid (no arguing) before you claim your goodies.

The American Express and Thomas Cook offices (see Money earlier in this chapter) will also hold mail for customers.

Telephone
Local calls cost 25¢ from public pay phones. There is no charge for dialing ☎ 0 (the operator), ☎ 411 for information, or ☎ 911 for emergencies. Toll-free numbers beginning with 1-800, 888, 877 or 777 can also be called at no cost. Some are good anywhere in North America, others within Canada only and still others may cover just one province. You don't know until you try the number. Note that most hotels, motels and guest houses charge a service fee of 50¢ per call, even for local or toll-free numbers.

Phone numbers within Canada consist of a three-digit area code followed by a seven-digit local number. You must dial all 10 digits, even to make a local call within the same area code (this is new; see the boxed text 'Additional Area Codes' for more information). Downtown Toronto phone numbers have a 416 or 647 area code, and some telephone numbers within the Greater Toronto Area (GTA) have 905 or 289 as the three-digit code. Calls from the 416/647 downtown area to 905 or 289 numbers are local calls. For inquiries on long-distance calls, dial ☎ 1 (area code) 555-1212.

Long-distance international calls can be made from any phone, but the rate varies depending on when and how. A direct call made without the assistance of an operator is not only cheapest but quickest (see Phonecards below). With operator assistance, collect (reverse charge) and person-to-person calls are much pricier.

If you're calling from overseas, the international country code for Canada is 1, the same as for the US (though international rates apply).

Additional Area Codes

Toronto has outgrown its one-area-code status; beginning March 5th, 2001, new phone numbers will be assigned a 647 area code.

Although this won't affect existing phone numbers with a 416 area code, Toronto will implement 10-digit dialing. This means you'll have to dial the area code for any phone number, even if you're calling from within that area code.

The area surrounding Toronto will follow suit in June 2001, when new numbers in the 905 area will be assigned a 289 area code and 10-digit dialing will be necessary.

Phonecards Private, prepaid phone cards give rates far superior to the country's Bell networks and are sold at smaller convenience stores, especially in Koreatown. These cards have catchy names like Millenium, Chit-Chat, Ola and WOW and come in denominations of $5, $10, $20, $30 and $50. At the time of writing, Nuvo charged a flat 5.6¢ per minute for calls anytime between Toronto, Montréal, Ottawa and Vancouver; 7.5¢ for calls to the US and UK; and 9.3¢ for calls to Australia and New Zealand. There's no connection charge, and the first 10 seconds are free.

eKno Communication Service Lonely Planet's eKno global communication service provides low-cost international calls – for local calls you're usually better off with a local phonecard. eKno also offers free messaging services, email, travel information and an online travel vault, where you can securely store all your important documents. You can join online at www.ekno .lonelyplanet.com, where you will find the local-access numbers for the 24-hour customer-service centre. Once you have joined, always check the eKno Web site for the latest access numbers for each country and updates on new features. To use eKno from Canada, dial the access number ☎ 1-877-635-3575.

Fax & Photocopies

For making photocopies or sending and receiving faxes, Kinko's Copies at 459 Bloor St W (Map 8; ☎ 416-928-0110) and 505 University Ave (Map 5; ☎ 416-979-8447) are open 24 hours. Cheaper copy shops in the UT area charge comparable fax service rates ($1 to $2 per page). Other fax machines are found at major hotels and shipping outlets like Mail Boxes, Etc (Map 6; ☎ 416-921-6282), 599 Yonge St.

Email & Internet Access

If you plan to carry your notebook or palmtop computer with you, remember that the power supply voltage in Canada may be different. Invest in a universal AC and plug adapter, which will enable you to plug in these devices anywhere without frying their innards. If you usually access your email through your office or school network, you'll find it easiest to open a free Web-based email account before you leave home. You can then use cybercafés and other public access points to receive and send email.

Most hostels and some B&Bs offer relatively expensive Internet access, usually for about $6 per hour. Toronto's cheapest cybercafés are in Koreatown, including Webst@tion Internet Cyber Café (Map 8; ☎ 416-533-6795), 594 Bloor St W, which never closes and charges $3 per hour (minimum $2). Chapters bookstore (Map 6; ☎ 416-920-9299), 110 Bloor St W, has self-serve Internet terminals (10¢ per minute), open 9 am to midnight daily. Gray Region Comics (Map 6; ☎ 416-975-1718), 550 Yonge St, has streetside computers for net surfing ($2 per hour).

Free Internet access can be found at public libraries. The Metro Toronto Reference Library (Map 6; ☎ 416-393-7000), 789 Yonge St, has the largest number of terminals, but you must reserve a time slot in advance.

INTERNET RESOURCES

The World Wide Web is a rich resource for travelers. You can research your trip, hunt down bargain airfares, book hotels, check on weather conditions and chat with locals

19th-century French chestnut-crushers, Bata Shoe Museum

You can find just about anything in Chinatown – in bulk!

SARA BENSON

Moose-eum 2000 project, Yonge St

P RICHARDSON

Art Gallery of Ontario

BATA SHOE MUSEUM

Inuit sealskin kamiks

KEN EAKIN

Skatin' around at Nathan Phillips Square

and other travelers about the best places to visit (or avoid!).

There's no better place to start your Web explorations than the Lonely Planet Web site (www.lonelyplanet.com). Here you'll find succinct summaries on traveling to Canada, postcards from other travelers, the Thorn Tree bulletin board and subWWWay section links to the most useful travel resources elsewhere on the Web. Here are the smartest, kookiest and most practical of them all:

www.attractionscanada.com
This site offers stirring descriptions of Canada's main tourist draws and contains oodles of hard information.

www.icomm.ca/emily
Self-titled 'An American's Guide to Canada,' this sassy, well-linked site gets nitty-gritty about the critical differences between the US and its northern neighbor (ie, which one has more donut shops per capita). It also contains extensive media links and a helpful glossary for non-Canucks.

www.cio-bic.gc.ca/facts/index_e.html
Here you'll find all the facts about Canada, including what Royal Mounties actually do out there on the prairies, straight from the federal government's mouthpiece.

www.toronto.com
This upbeat Web site reviews and highlights upcoming special events, restaurants, entertainment venues, accommodations and anything else visitors or residents might need to know.

www.city.toronto.on.ca
There's more to the official municipal government site than meets the eye, especially for outdoors enthusiasts.

www.toronto.hm, www.anewtoronto.com
Filling in the gaps, these Web sites are all links for the specialist of special needs.

Other specific Web sites for Toronto news, transport, sights, accommodations etc, are listed throughout this book.

BOOKS
Most books are published in different editions by different publishers in different countries. As a result, a book might be a hardcover rarity in one country but readily available in paperback in another. Your local bookstore or library is best placed to advise you on availability.

For a list of novels by Canadian authors, see Literature under Arts in the Facts about Toronto chapter.

Lonely Planet
If you just can't bear to leave the land o' maple leaves, Lonely Planet's *Canada, Montréal* and *Great Lakes* titles will sustain you long after the pages of this guidebook have become dog-eared. And for those venturing out west, Lonely Planet also has comprehensive guides to Vancouver and British Columbia.

Guidebooks
Scott Mitchell's *Secret Toronto: the Unique Guidebook to Toronto's Hidden Sites, Sounds, & Tastes* promises to 'lead you astray' on artsy and ethnic-inspired jaunts.

A Magical Place: Toronto Island and Its People by Bill Freeman takes readers effortlessly through the islands' turbulent history, historic sites and even lighthouse ghosts.

Travel
The Diary of Mrs John Graves Simcoe by early pioneer Elizabeth Simcoe is a newsy, human account of mid-19th-century life in Upper Canada. During roughly the same time period, Susanna Moodie wrote *Roughing it in the Bush; or Life in Canada* and the sequel *Life in the Clearings vs the Bush*, the latter based on her trip to Niagara Falls.

More aptly described by its Canadian title *City to City*, Jan Morris' sharp essays in *O Canada: Travels in an Unknown Country* vividly capture the 1980s era of change in Toronto, Montréal and Ottawa, among other places. *Wild is Always There: Canada Through the Eyes of Foreign Writers* is another collection of well-edited pieces, as is *Streets of Toronto,* with its tales of the city by Canadian authors.

History & Politics
Chris Raible's *Muddy York Mud: Scandal and Scurrility in Upper Canada* dishes the dirt on major players in the old town of

York – the Baldwins, the Mackenzies et al – through a retelling of the famous 1826 Types trial. For a history of Toronto's jump into modernity, read Robert Fulford's *Accidental City*.

Sensational and long-winded, Peter C Newman narrates Toronto's 1980s economic boom that went bust in *The Canadian Revolution: from Deference to Defiance*. He has also produced an intriguing history of the Hudson's Bay Company, *Caesar's of the Wilderness*. For all the tales of tightrope walkers and daredevils in barrels, read Pierre Berton's entertaining *Niagara: A History of the Falls*.

Brian Miracle's account of returning to live on the Six Nations Grand River Reserve after 40 years away in *Back on the Rez: Finding the Way Home* is a primer for present-day Native community issues.

Cookboooks

Anita Stewart is best know for her classic *Flavours of Canada*. Her *Great Canadian Cuisine* features recipes collected from Canadian Pacific luxury hotels across the nation. With Julia Aitken she co-wrote the *Ontario Harvest Cookbook*, full of down-on-the-farm recipes collected from growers, vineyards and country kitchens. For more provincial cooking, try Brenda Matthews' *Niagara Flavours*.

The Chef's Table by Lucy Waverman, James Chatto and Tony Aspler records the creations of top Toronto chefs with superb background color on the city's culinary scene. *The Bamboo Cooks!* by Patti Habib and Richard O'Brien has original recipes and Caribbean classics, but it's only available at the Queen St Bamboo Club (see the Places to Eat chapter) itself or specialty bookstores.

General

A one-stop guide to all things Canadiana is *Mondo Canuck!* by Geoff Pevere and Grieg Dymond, who highlight pop culture you didn't even know *was* Canadian (which is the whole point). The book even describes why Canadian sitcoms just aren't funny.

Will Ferguson's provocatively titled *Why I Hate Canadians* decimates the myth of making love in a canoe and denies that Canadians are all that 'nice' – and yes, the author is himself a true-blooded Canuck.

FILMS

Innumerable films have been shot in Toronto, but very few movie storylines are set here, two wacky exceptions being *Strange Brew* with Rick Moranis and *Last Night*. Francis Ford Coppola filmed *The Black Stallion* here at Woodbine Racetrack, St Lawrence Market and Exhibition Place. *Good Will Hunting* and the *X-Men* were also made in part in Toronto, to name just a few out of hundreds of titles that Torontonians pick out with glee.

NEWSPAPERS & MAGAZINES
Major Daily Newspapers

The elder statesman is the conservative *Globe & Mail*, (www.globeandmail.ca) similar to the *New York Times*, except that the heavy weekend edition comes out on Saturday. The conservative *National Post* (www.nationalpost.com) has dramatic headlines and front-page color photos that are sure to catch your eye. The *Financial Post* is similar to the USA's *Wall St Journal*.

Ernest Hemingway once worked as a cub reporter for the liberal-minded *Toronto Star* (www.thestar.ca), but it seems the writing has gone downhill since the good ol' days. The *Toronto Sun* is a sensational tabloid-style daily with pin-up girls (and boys) that's good only for gossip and sports coverage.

Weeklies

Toronto's free weeklies are found in news-boxes on the street and piled up at restaurants, bookstores, etc. They'll give you the complete low-down on entertainment, special events and off-beat news. The biggest one is *Now,* though *eye* and the major gay weekly *Xtra* keep a better watch on clubs.

L'Express de Toronto is a French-language weekly newspaper published every Tuesday, available at Librarie Champlain (see the Shopping Chapter).

Magazines

Maclean's is a weekly Canadian news-magazine, albeit a little on the light side. The high-brow *Saturday Night* bills itself as 'Canada's magazine,' but the current events, sports, politics and arts features do lean to the right. The antidote is *This Magazine*, winner of the Utne Reader Alternative Press Award, which takes on Canadian and world politics, arts and culture from all fronts.

Indispensable *Toronto Life* markets itself to yuppies, but its entertainment and shopping pages are up-to-date, and the gossip columnists don't hesitate to blast anything from City Hall foibles to the latest superstar chef's bistro flop. Web site: www.torontolife.com

Toronto's position at the center of English-language arts and literature in Canada means numerous small press offerings like *Ink Magazine*. For reviews and reprints from Canada's underground 'zine scene, check out *Broken Pencil*. Canadian feminism and art are still hot on the pages of *Fireweed*.

Toronto's many tight-knit immigrant communities put out smaller publications that are worth a read. *Zdorov!*, the 'Magazine of Ukrainian Things,' recently questioned the wisdom of having emigrated in the first place with a cover article on the '9 Pros & Cons of Moving Back to Ukraine.'

RADIO & TV

The Canadian Broadcasting System (CBC) has one television station and two radio frequencies in Toronto. CBC1 (94.1FM) has mostly classical music, including Saturday Afternoon at the Opera from 1:30 to 6 pm. In the same time slot, CBC2 (99.1FM) airs 'Definitely Not the Opera,' a Canadian pop culture show that's aimed at the young and overeducated.

Toronto's premier new-rock station is Edge 102.1FM. Tune in weeknights from 6 to 8 pm for 'Live in Toronto,' a newsy insiders' show. Mix 99.9FM, Chum 104.5FM and Kiss 92.5FM spin mainstream dance and Top 40 while the shock-rock DJs at Q-Rock 107.1FM play classic rock. Chin 100.7FM and CIRV 88.9FM serve Toronto's multi-lingual communities; tuning in is sure to turn up something weird and wonderful for your ears. At the bottom of the FM dial are the eclectic university stations, 89.5 CIUT and 88.1 FM Ryerson.

The Chum CityTV complex on Queen St is home to Toronto's upstart CityTV, the Bravo arts channel and MuchMusic (a sort of Canadian MTV). Ever-popular QueerTV programming broadcasts Sunday at midnight and Monday at 11:35 p.m.

Global, a cable station, imports all of the gems as well as the dross from south of the border (ie, the USA). More Canadians watch it than are willing to admit to it.

PHOTOGRAPHY

Pharmacies, department stores and convenience shops generally carry only basic Kodak and Fuji print film. For a roll of 24-exposure Kodak Gold, expect to pay about $5 for 100 ASA (ISO) and $7 for 400 ASA. Camera shops do on-site developing as fast as one hour, costing $12 for 24 color prints, depending on the size. A second set of prints often costs just $3 more. Cheaper rates apply for 1-day or 3-day processing.

Transparency film, digital and video camera equipment and supplies are generally available only at specialty camera shops, including West Camera (Map 9; ☎ 416-504-9432), 514 Queen St W, and Japan Camera (Map 5; ☎ 416-598-1474) on Level 1 at Eaton Centre. ALT Camera (Map 5; ☎ 416-362-6400), 69 Queen St E, handles repairs and used camera equipment exchange and sales. For professional transparency (slide) developing, Absolute Color Slides (Map 10; ☎ 416-868-0413), 197 Dundas St E, does fantastic work.

The X-ray scanning machines at Canadian airports should pose no problems to most films, except specialized film with an ASA speed of 400 or higher. When in doubt, pack your film in a transparent plastic bag (a Ziploc is good) to show separately to airport security officials. Don't leave your camera in the car on a hot day; film can be damaged by excessive heat.

For photographers, the number one skyline view of Toronto is from the Gardiner

Expressway exit ramp onto Lake Shore Blvd – so breathtaking, you'd better take along a designated driver.

VIDEO SYSTEMS

Four types of videotape are in common use across Canada: VHS, VHS C, Beta and 8mm. These tapes are readily available at Shoppers Drug Mart and electronics retailers such as Future Shop. VHS tapes are dirt cheap: A regular Sony 120-minute tape should cost less than $3. VHS C tapes (common for handheld video cameras) cost about $6 for 120 minutes.

Note that the PAL system predominant in most of Europe and Australia isn't compatible with the American and Japanese NTSC or French SECAM standards. V/Tape (Map 4; ☎ 416-351-1317), 401 Richmond St W, restores and dubs videotape into different formats, but not cheaply (see www.vtape.org/home.htm).

TIME

Toronto is in the Eastern time zone (EST/EDT), the same as New York City. This may seem odd to travelers coming from the USA, as the zone immediately south of the Ontario border is Central, which is one hour behind Eastern. When it's noon in Toronto, it's 9 am in Vancouver and Los Angeles, 1 pm in Halifax, 5 pm in London, 6 pm in Paris and 3 am (the following day) in Sydney. Clocks are set ahead one hour during daylight saving time, from the last Sunday in April to the last Sunday in October, making summer days seem endless. Official times (train schedules, film screenings etc) are often indicated using the 24-hour clock, eg 6:30 pm is '18:30.'

ELECTRICITY

Canada, like the USA, operates on 110V, 60-cycle electric power. Non-North American visitors should bring a plug adapter if they wish to use their own small appliances such as razors or hairdryers. Note that gadgets built for higher voltage and cycles (such as 220/240V, 50-cycle appliances from Europe) will function poorly. Canadian electrical goods have a plug with two flat, vertical prongs (the same as the US and Mexico) or sometimes a three-pronger with the added ground.

WEIGHTS & MEASURES

Canada officially changed from imperial measurement to the metric system in the 1970s. Most citizens accepted this change only begrudgingly, so the two systems coexist. All speed-limit signs are in kilometers per hour, and gasoline is sold in liters. However, supermarket items are often sold by the pound. All measurements in this book are given in metric; for help in converting between the two systems, see the chart on the inside back cover.

LAUNDRY

Every neighborhood has self-serve coin-operated laundromats that stay open until 11 pm daily. A wash and dry costs a couple of dollars, usually in $1 or 25¢ coins. Some convenient laundromats include Coin-o-Rama (Map 8), 172 Harbord St, across from Harbord Fish & Chips; The Laundry Lounge (Map 6), 531 Yonge St, behind Captain's Fish & Chips (see the pattern?); and Inglis Laundry (Map 9) on Queen St W, opposite McDonald's (Filet-o-Fish and french fries).

Many campgrounds, hostels and some B&Bs have a washer and dryer that guests may use for a fee. Major hotels and dry cleaners shops will clean and press your clothes for you at significantly higher prices.

HAIRCUTS

UK import House of Lords (Map 6; ☎ 416-962-1111), 639 Yonge St, has treated the tresses of David Bowie and Alice Cooper. Although less than punk these days, they still do dreadlocks, and basic cuts for men/women cost just $15/21 (walk-ins accepted).

More cutting-edge Coupe Bizzarre (Map 9; ☎ 416-504-0783), 704 Queen St W, is the DJs' choice.

TOILETS

That dirty word, 'toilet,' is rarely used in Canada. Canadians refer to it as the bathroom, the men's or women's room, the rest room (!) or the washroom. Almost all bathroom facilities are sex-segregated, although abstract signs don't always make it clear who should go where. Public washrooms are virtually nonexistent, except in some city parks. Instead, stride right into a posh hotel or restaurant as if you were a legitimate paying customer. As a last resort, there's always the corner gas station.

LUGGAGE STORAGE

Inside Union Station there are small and medium-sized coin lockers costing $2 per 24 hours, but none are big enough for rucksacks. For information on Pearson airport luggage storage, see the Getting There & Away chapter.

Some hostels and hotels offer lockers or day check services. They may also be amenable to long-term luggage storage (for an additional fee, of course).

HEALTH

Canada is a typical First World destination when it comes to health. Toronto's tap water is generally safe to drink. At campgrounds, ask about local water quality; if in doubt, boil it vigorously for five minutes or treat it chemically.

No vaccinations are required from visitors, except if you are coming from an area with a history of certain diseases – immunization against yellow fever or cholera are the most likely requirements. However, some routine vaccinations or booster shots are recommended nonetheless for all travelers. They include hepatitis B, polio, tetanus and diphtheria, and sometimes measles, mumps and rubella.

It's a good idea to pack a basic medical kit (antiseptic solution, aspirin or paracetamol, band aids etc) even when your destination is a place like Canada where first-aid supplies are readily available. To avoid problems at customs, keep prescription medication in its original packaging and bring a copy of your prescription for any medication or syringes.

Medical Treatment

There are no reciprocal healthcare arrangements between Canada and other countries. Non-Canadians must pay cash up front for treatment, so taking out travel insurance is strongly advised (see Travel Insurance earlier). Before seeking medical attention you can (and sometimes must) contact your insurer for referrals. Your own consulate in Toronto keeps lists of recommended physicians and dentists, too.

Medical treatment in Canada is expensive; the standard rate for a bed is around $500 and up to $2500 a day for nonresidents. Emergency room services have improved, through you may still have to wait some time if your case isn't diagnosed as 'urgent'. However, the quality of treatment (when it comes) is generally excellent.

Many of Toronto's major hospitals are clustered on or near University Ave:

Hospital for Sick Children (Map 5; ☎ 416-597-1500), 555 University Ave

Mount Sinai Hospital (Map 5; ☎ 416-596-4200), 600 University Ave

Toronto General Hospital (Map 5; ☎ 416-340-4611), 200 Elizabeth St

The Hassle-Free Clinic (for men ☎ 416-922-0603; for women ☎ 416-922-0566), 556 Church St (Map 6), has drop-in and appointment-only hours for STD/HIV testing and reproductive health. If you're under 25 and without travel insurance, try Shout Clinic (Map 10; ☎ 416-927-8553), 467 Jarvis St, which provides dental, chiropractic and sexual health services to Toronto's street youth.

Environmental Hazards

Doctors are warning that the ozone layer over Canada is thinning. This means that, even on cloudy days, people will be subject to more UV radiation and should always take precaution to avoid skin damage and possibly skin cancer. In any case, sunburn and windburn should be primary concerns for anyone planning to spend time cycling, lazing on the beach or just walking around the city. Using sunscreen lotions with an SPF rating of 30 or higher and a moisturizer on exposed skin is advised.

On winter days when frostbite is a possibility (usually when low temperature and high wind combine to make what's called the windchill factor dangerously low) you will know about it. Everyone discusses the freezing cold, and radio stations broadcast warnings and state how many minutes it's safe to expose your skin. On such days, take the opportunity to scuttle underground into Toronto's PATH system (see the Shopping chapter).

Travelers should think twice before jumping into the waters of Lake Ontario. Every summer the city periodically closes its public beaches due to toxic levels of pollution. Since these closures aren't signposted well, travelers who miss the TV news announcements may not know whether the water is safe or not. When in doubt, keep your tootsies out.

Infectious Diseases

Infection with the human immunodeficiency virus (HIV) may lead to acquired immune deficiency syndrome (AIDS), which is a fatal disease. Any exposure to blood, blood products or body fluids may put the individual at risk. The disease is often transmitted through sexual contact or dirty needles – vaccinations, acupuncture, tattooing and body piercing can be potentially as dangerous as intravenous drug use. The government estimates the number of AIDs cases in Canada at around 20,000, and nearly 46,000 people are registered as HIV-positive.

Catie (1-800-263-1638) runs a nationwide HIV/AIDs helpline, open 10 am to 6 pm weekdays. Staff provide information and advice on relevant topics such as transmission risks, the side effects of a particular drug or alternative therapy.

WOMEN TRAVELERS

Toronto sets high standards for women's safety, especially when compared to major US cities. The usual advice applies: Avoid walking alone late at night, especially along the Harbourfront or in high-crime areas (see Dangers & Annoyances, later in this chapter). On main streets busy foot traffic continues past midnight. Moreover the TTC system makes excellent provisions for

women riding public transport after dark (see the Getting Around chapter).

It is illegal in Canada to carry pepper spray or mace; some women recommend carrying a whistle instead. If you are violently assaulted, call the Toronto Rape Crisis Centre (☎ 416-597-8808) or SOS Femmes (French Crisis Line; ☎ 416-759-0138). These organizations are underfunded and often understaffed: If you get a busy signal, keep trying. They can refer you to hospitals that have sexual assault care centers.

The YWCA has several locations in Toronto and operates a 24-hour women's hostel and emergency shelter (see the Places to Stay chapter). Many other social service organizations for women operate out of the 519 Community Centre (see Lesbigay Travelers section, next).

The Toronto Women's Bookstore (see the Shopping chapter) has bulletin boards and free publications on women-oriented activities, rallies, classes and other happenings. If you don't see the event you're looking for advertised, ask the knowledgeable staff.

LESBIGAY TRAVELERS

The legal age at which a person in Canada may consent to all sexual activity is 18. Tolerance of homosexuality is generally high in Toronto. Public displays of affection (PDA) will generally attract no more notice than would similar activity by straight couples, though you may encounter some unwanted hassle in more conservative ethnic neighborhoods. In general, Torontonians are overly careful *not* to stare.

In the city's gay district, sometimes called the gay village, on Church St, men's bars and clubs outnumber lesbian venues about 10 to one (as they do everywhere in the world). But queer women should take heart because Toronto is home to the Drag Kings (women who cross-dress and perform as men), women-only bathhouse nights and Clit Lit reading series (see the Entertainment chapter). On-line directories for other social opportunities (gay hockey, anyone?) can be found at www.gaytoronto.com and www.lesbiantoronto.com.

The 519 Community Centre (Map 6; ☎ 416-392-6874, 519 Church St) houses activist and community groups, including the Lesbian and Gay Immigration Task Force (LEGIT; ☎ 416-925-9872 x2211) which helps members of same-sex relationships who are applying for permanent Canadian resident status. Brochures (in English or French) are available upon request by mailing LEGIT-Toronto, PO Box 111, Station F, Toronto ON M4Y 2L4.

The Canadian Lesbian and Gay Archives (☎ 416-777-2755, 56 Temperance St, Suite 201) has one of the world's largest collection of periodicals, photographs, films, recordings, art, even protest buttons. Begun in 1973, it's entirely run by volunteers, so hours vary.
Web site: www.clga.ca/archives/

The gay free weekly, *Xtra* (☎ 416-925-6555), maintains a large archive on its Web site (www.xtra.ca). For lesbians, there's the free weekly *Siren*. Both publications are available at This Ain't the Rosedale Library, Glad Day (see the Shopping chapter) and many other bookstores and restaurants around town.

There are gay-operated and gay-friendly B&Bs off Church St and in Cabbagetown (see the Places to Stay chapter). Anyone is welcome, but the clientele is often exclusively gay and male.

DISABLED TRAVELERS

Across Canada, seeing-eye dogs may legally be brought into restaurants, hotels and other businesses. Many public service phone numbers and some public payphones are adapted for the hearing-impaired. In Toronto 90% of curbs are dropped and most public buildings are wheelchair accessible. It's even easier to get around using Toronto's underground PATH system, which is 100% wheelchair accessible (see the Shopping chapter). Although only some public city buses are wheelchair-equipped, the TTC runs separate Community Routes and WheelTrans (☎ 416-393-4111) services with lifts at the cost of a regular bus ticket. See the Getting Around chapter for recommended taxi companies.

All parking lots have designated parking spots for the physically disabled. These spots, located closest to the door or access point, cannot be used by others under threat of a serious fine. Permits must be applied for in advance through the Ministry of Transportation at ☎ 416-235-2999.

Airlines provide early boarding and disembarking as standard practice and VIA Rail can accommodate wheelchairs given 48 hours advance notice. All long-distance buses take wheelchairs providing they collapse into luggage compartments. Car-rental agencies can provide special accessories such as handcontrols but again, advance notice is required.

For specific advice on the accessibility of over 850 hotels, attractions, restaurants and services around Toronto, call the 24-hour courtesy line of Beyond Ability International (☎ 416-410-3748, fax 416-604-2340). Access Toronto (☎ 416-338-0338) can provide printed access guides and for any other referrals, call Community Information Toronto (see Useful Organizations later).

Mobility International USA (☎ 541-343-1284, info@miusa.org), PO Box 10767, Eugene, OR 97440 specializes in international exchange opportunities for the disabled.
Web site: www.miusa.org

SENIOR TRAVELERS

Visitors over the age of 65 (sometimes 60) can qualify for big discounts on transportation and entry to many attractions, parks, museums, historic sites, and even cinemas. You may be asked to show proof of age, so carry photo ID with you. Some hotels and motels may also offer reductions – it's always worth asking.

The Elderhostel office in Kingston, Ontario has changed its name to Routes to Learning Canada (☎ 613-530-2222, 1-877-426-8056, fax 613-530-2096, 4 Catarqui St, Kingston, Ontario, K7K 1Z7). It still coordinates Elderhostel programs in Canada with the US Elderhostel office (☎ 877-426-8056, 75 Federal St, Boston, MA 02110-1941, USA). Elderhostel specializes in inexpensive, educational packages for people 55

years or older. In Ontario, opportunities have included studying the history of Toronto theater, wine country experiences, even snowshoe-making and skiing. Accommodation is in university dorms and the programs are so popular that a lottery is often conducted to decide which applicants can participate.
Web site: www.elderhostel.org.

For those over 50 years of age, the Canadian Association of Retired Persons (CARP; ☎ 1-800-363-9736) offers information on senior travel and substantial savings on auto and medical travel insurance. An annual membership costs $16, but its comprehensive Web site (www.fifty-plus.net) resources are free. The Toronto CARP office (Map 5; ☎ 416-363-8748) is at 27 Queen St E, Suite 1304, Toronto, ON M5C 2M6. Members of the US-based American Association of Retired Persons (AARP; ☎ 1-800-424-3410) can take advantage of similar savings on travel services while in Canada, including discount car rental and roadside assistance.

TORONTO FOR CHILDREN

Traveling successfully with children at any age requires preparation and effort – that's why you should let them take part as much as possible. When sketching out an itinerary, try to balance educational activities with fun and relaxation, and don't overdo it. Lonely Planet's *Travel with Children* by Maureen Wheeler can give you some more tips.

In Toronto kids are welcome just about anywhere. They are entitled to discounted admission at many attractions; family passes (two adults and two children) are an even better deal. In more traditional ethnic neighborhoods like Little Italy or Greektown, they will be fussed over and even smilingly taken off your hands for a few minutes. Few restaurants have children's menus, but high-chairs are widely used.

Finding affordable accommodation with children is tricky. Some B&Bs do not accept children, while others brazenly charge full price. Hotels and motels usually allow children under 18 to stay with their parents for free and can recommend baby-sitting serv-

ices if none are available in house. The top hotel for families is the Delta Chelsea (see the Places to Stay chapter), providing a supervised play center, kids' swim club and low-cost childcare services.

Special events for children take place throughout the year (see Special Events later in this chapter). Two are the Milk Festival and the Canadian National Exhibition. At any time of year, interactive museums such as the Children's Own Museum or Ontario Science Centre and sports events at the Air Canada Centre or the SkyDome are winning ideas. In summer it's easy (if expensive) to keep them entertained at Paramount Canada's Wonderland or Ontario Place amusement parks. Your little city slickers can get a taste of country life at popular historical sites like Riverdale Farm and Black Creek Pioneer Village. For outdoors relaxation, try the Harbourfront and Beach areas and the Toronto Islands.

Specialty bookstores include cozy Parentbooks (Map 8; ☎ 416-537-8334) at 201 Harbord St.

USEFUL ORGANIZATIONS

The Canadian Automobile Association (CAA) of Central Ontario (Map 6; ☎ 416-221-4300, 1-800-268-3750), 461 Yonge St, is an 'auto club' that provides free maps, trip planning services, travel discounts and emergency roadside assistance to members. See the Web site www.caa.ca for details. New members pay a $15 joining fee plus annual dues of $57. Members of affiliated clubs like the American Automobile Association (AAA) are eligible for CAA services. Convenient offices near land-border crossings to the USA include Sarnia (☎ 519-344-8686), 1095 London Rd, and Windsor (☎ 519-255-1212), 1255 Ouellette Ave.

The Sierra Club (☎ 1-888-810-4204) is an international organization dedicated to environmental advocacy and protection. Its Eastern Canada Chapter (Map 8; ☎ 416-960-9606, eastern.canada.chapter@sierra-club.org), 517 College St, sponsors half- and full-day Ontario wilderness outings in all seasons, including special kids' programs.
Web site: www.sierraclub.ca/eastern/

Hostelling International (HI) Canada (☎ 613-237-7884, 1-800-663-5777) has its head office at 205 Catherine St, Ottawa, ON K2P 1C3. The local HI Great Lakes Region office operating out of the HI Toronto hostel (see the Places to Stay chapter) sells memberships, dispenses travel information and handles bookings.

The charitable Travellers' Aid Society has been helping lost, ill, disabled and stranded travelers since the days when war widows, orphans and farmers first arrived penniless at Union Station. There are information counters at Union Station (Map 4; ☎ 416 366 7788), Pearson International Airport (☎ 905-676-2868) and the Metro Toronto Coach Terminal (Map 5; ☎ 416-596-8647), all open 9 am to 9 pm daily.

For inquiries about city services, parks and recreation, Access Toronto (☎ 416-338-0338) can connect you between 8 am and 5 pm weekdays. The knowledgeable, helpful operators at Community Information Toronto (☎ 416-397-4636) dispense detailed, up-to-date information on community organizations and social services from 8 am to 10 pm every day.

LIBRARIES & CULTURAL CENTERS
The Metro Toronto Reference Library (Map 6; ☎ 416-393-7000), 789 Yonge St, is open 10 am to 8 pm Monday to Thursday, 10 am to 5 pm Friday and Saturday, and 1:30 to 5 pm Sundays (except during summer). Though visitors can browse, they do not have check-out privileges. Remember that major bookstore chains like Chapters and Indigo have couches and cafés where you can read and research using their books without buying a single thing (don't spill).

Toronto's many cultural centers, of which the following are only a sample, usually have small libraries or resource centers, art exhibitions and social events. For example, the Native Canadian Centre offers language classes, teaching circles and Thursday evening drumming socials.

Alliance Française (Map 8; ☎ 416-922-2014), 24 Spadina Rd, www.alliance-francaise.com

The Black Secretariat (Map 6; ☎ 416-924-1104), 590 Jarvis St

Centre Francophone de Toronto (Map 4; ☎ 416-203-1220), 20 Lower Spadina Ave at Lake Shore Blvd

First Portuguese Canadian Club (Map 8; ☎ 416-531-9971), 722 College St

Goethe-Institut (Map 4; ☎ 416-593-5257), 163 King St W, www.goethe.de/uk/tor/enindex.htm

Hellenic Culture Centre (Map 3; ☎ 416-425-2485), 30 Thorncliffe Park Dr

Italian Cultural Institute (Map 6; ☎ 416-921 3802), 496 Huron St, www.iicto-ca.org/istituto1.htm

The Japan Foundation (Map 6, ☎ 416-966-1600), 131 Bloor St W, www.japanfoundationcanada.org

Native Canadian Centre of Toronto (Map 8; ☎ 416-964-9087), 16 Spadina Rd

Russian Canadian Cultural Aid Society (Map 3; ☎ 416-653-1361), 91 Kersdale Ave

Spanish Centre (Map 6; ☎ 416-925-4652), 40 Hayden St, www.spanishcentre.com

Toronto Australia New Zealand Club (TRANZAC; Map 8; ☎ 416-923-8137), 192 Brunswick Ave

PLACES OF WORSHIP
If you're looking for a spiritual home away from home, Toronto has a few unusual choices. Anshei Minsk Synagogue (Map 9; ☎ 416-595-5723), 10 St Andrew St. Services have been held here since the 1920s and the musical Friday night *shabbat* dinners are popular with travelers and UT students. It's also home to Ronnie Wiseman, the local 'King of Jewish Reggae,' and his band Kedusha.

Tengye Ling Tibetan Buddhist Temple (Map 6; ☎ 416-966-4656), 11 Madison Ave, holds dharma talks open to all on Tuesday evenings. The fascinating director and abbess, Lama Tenzin Kalsang, was ordained by the Dalai Lama in India, quite a long way from her hometown of Kenora, Ontario.

Although it seems that nobody builds churches on the grand scale anymore, the Slovak Byzantine Catholic Cathedral (☎ 905-887-5706), 10350 Woodbine Ave near Hwy 404 in Markham, is one heck of an exception. Its copper-topped spire measures 62.7m high and its main bell rings in at 16,650kg, second in size only to the one in Sacré Coeur in Paris. It's also the first cathedral in the western hemisphere to be blessed by a pope – John Paul II did the honors.

Other houses of worship, including numerous affirming congregations open to lesbigay visitors, are listed in the yellow pages of the telephone book.

DANGERS & ANNOYANCES

Some areas of Toronto are more vulnerable to crime than others, namely downtown and the area east of Yonge St, anywhere from the Gardiner Expressway north to Carlton Street, where women walking alone at night are likely to be mistaken for prostitutes by curb-crawling johns. The southern section of Jarvis St, between Carlton and Queen Sts, especially around the Allan Gardens, should be avoided by everyone late at night. Although violent crime rates are steadily falling, property theft, especially of automobiles, is increasing.

Because many social service agencies have recently closed, there are an increasing number of homeless people and street youths begging on the streets. Be compassionate: keep in mind that homeless people are more likely to be assaulted or harassed than to do so to you, and many street youths have run away from genuinely dangerous home situations but are too young to qualify for governmental programs, so they have nowhere else to go.

Police estimate a total of 80 gangs operating in Toronto, but only a small percentage of their activities are hard core. Biker wars that have recently racked Québec are just starting to make their way into Ontario via the Hells Angels, Para-Dice Bikers and other groups. If you see them out on the highway, it's best to give them a wide berth.

The average traveler, however, isn't likely to encounter anything much more annoying than inhospitable winter weather, congested city streets, a dearth of parking spaces and unbelievable traffic snarls on Toronto's major expressways.

EMERGENCIES

Dial ☎ 911 for police, fire, accident and medical emergencies. For non-emergency matters, contact the closest police station.

Medical services and crisis lines are listed in the Health, Women Travelers and Lesbigay Travelers sections earlier. When in doubt, call ☎ 0 and ask the operator for assistance.

Should your passport get lost or stolen, contact your own consulate. It will be able to issue a temporary replacement and inform you when and how to go about getting another. You may not need another depending on your travel plans.

For lost or stolen traveler's checks or credit cards, contact the issuer or its representative (see Money earlier in this chapter). For other types of theft, if you plan to make an insurance claim contact the police as soon as possible for an incident report.

LEGAL MATTERS

In Ontario the legal drinking age is 19. It is an offense to consume alcohol anywhere other than a residence or licensed premises, which puts parks, beaches and the rest of the great outdoors technically off limits.

Visitors are unlikely to meet Canadian police officers except when random spot checks for drunk driving are held at bar closing time and on holidays. Driving any motorized vehicle while impaired (meaning blood alcohol levels of greater than 0.08%) is considered a very serious offense. You could find yourself in jail overnight, followed by a court appearance, heavy fine, a suspended license and/or further incarceration.

If you are arrested, you have the right to remain silent. However, never walk away from law enforcement personnel without permission. If arrested, you must be informed of the charges and have the right to an interpreter and one phone call. For low-cost legal advice, contact Legal Aid Ontario (☎ 416-598-0200), 375 University Ave.

Despite the wild popularity of Toronto's rave scene, recreational drugs are *not* legal. Smuggling drugs, including pot, across the border is a serious crime. The Canadian federal government is working on legislation permitting the use of marijuana for medicinal purposes. If no laws are passed before the court's set deadline, marijuana will become legal nationwide. Don't hold your breath, dude.

BUSINESS HOURS
The issue of Sunday shopping has been hotly debated for years, but no consensus has been reached (see the Shopping chapter). The vast majority of convenience shops remain open 24 hours, as do some gas stations, supermarkets and drug stores (chemists). Canada Post offices are generally open 9 am to 5 pm on weekdays, while postal outlets in stores stay open later and on weekends. Banking hours are usually shorter, from 10 am to 4:30 pm Monday to Thursday, and later on Friday; only certain branch locations open Saturday morning.

PUBLIC HOLIDAYS
On national public holidays, all banks, schools and government offices (including post offices) are closed and transportation, museums and other services are on a Sunday schedule. Holidays falling on a weekend are usually observed the following Monday.

Summer begins with Victoria Day in late May, often called '2-4 Weekend' even when it doesn't fall on 24 May because traditionally many Canadians spend it drinking a case (24 cans) of beer. It ends with Labour Day, when many businesses, attractions and services change hours of operation or shut down for the winter.

Although not a statutory holiday, National Aboriginal Day falls on 21 June, the first day of the summer solstice, when Canada's heritage of First Nations, Inuit and Métis cultures is celebrated at public and private institutions. Halloween, October 31, is based on a Celtic pagan tradition, and Toronto lesbigay nightclubs are often the scene of wild masquerades.

Major 2001 public holidays in Ontario are:

New Year's Day January 1
Good Friday April 13
Easter Monday April 16
Victoria Day May 21
Canada Day July 1
Simcoe Day (Civic Holiday) August 6
Labour Day September 3
Canadian Thanksgiving October 8
Remembrance Day November 11
Christmas Day December 25
Boxing Day December 26

SPECIAL EVENTS
In addition to festivals listed in the Entertainment and Excursions chapters, some of Toronto's major events are:

May
Toronto International Powwow The two-day event celebrates Native Indian culture with dancers, costumes and crafts. It's held at the SkyDome in the middle of May.

Milk International Children's Festival On Victoria Day weekend, Harbourfront stages come alive with international puppetry, theater, dance and musical performances especially for kids, as well as storytelling events and films.

June
Caravan A nine-day cultural exchange of ethnic groups offers music, dance and food native to their homelands. A passport ($18) entitles you to visit the 25 different pavilions set up around the city towards the end of June. Ask at the tourist office for a complete list of events and things to see.

Pride Week Larger and more flamboyant every year, towards the end of June, Gay Pride Week culminates in outrageous downtown out-of-the-closet parades on Church St. Recent crowds have been estimated as high as 100,000.

International Dragon Boat Festival In a 2000-year-old Chinese tradition, these large, brightly decorated 'dragon' canoes are raced in waters around the Toronto Islands in late June.

Aboriginal Voices Festival A five-day celebration of Native arts and culture takes place around National Aboriginal Day (21 June) at city parks, the Toronto Islands, movie theaters and clubs.

Du Maurier Downtown Jazz Festival For more than 10 days (and nights) in late June and early July, excellent jazz shows ranging from freebies on the streets to nightclub performances and concert hall recitals fill the city. Workshops, films and even jazz cruises are part of the event. The jazz is varied, featuring local, US and European players, and more gospel, blues and world beat influences have been creeping into the mix.

Benson & Hedges Symphony of Fire True to its name, this is a downtown fireworks extravaganza set to music by international pyrotechnic teams who compete at Ontario Place during late June and early July.

July

Great Canadian Blues & BBQ Festival The longest-running blues festival in the country takes place in early July at Harbourfront. It's usually held on the same weekend as the Toronto Street Festival (various locations).

The Molson Indy Toronto's only major car race is held in mid-July. Well-known drivers from the international circuit compete in front of large crowds during the two days of practice and qualifying trials, with the big race on the third day at Exhibition Place.

Fringe Theatre Festival With over 400 performances in six venues over 10 days, generally in July, this budget festival (☎ 416-534-5919) has become a major hit. The participants are chosen by lottery, so expect the unexpected of drama, comedy, musicals and cabaret-style shows.

August

Caribana This major Caribbean festival is held along Lake Shore Blvd W and on the Toronto Islands at the beginning of August. It's primarily a weekend of reggae, steel drum, and calypso music and dance with a huge finale parade featuring outrageous costumes á la carnival in Rio. The parade has thousands of participants (and spectators) and can take five hours or more in passing.

Canadian National Exhibition (CNE) The CNE claims to be the oldest and largest annual exhibition in the world with agricultural and technical exhibits, lumberjack competitions, an air show, concerts, a horse show, Midway carnival games and rides, and fireworks. The exhibition is held at Exhibition Place during the two weeks prior to, and including, the Labour Day holiday. Grounds admission costs $8/5 adults/ children. Parking, however, is exorbitant – take the streetcar.

December

Christmas Celebrations In the weeks leading up to Christmas, traditional seasonal celebrations are

Hollywood o' the North

It started off as an idea tossed around 25 years ago over lunch by two unlikely candidates, a lawyer and a mayoral assistant. Except that the lawyer was already a fixture at the famous Cannes film festival and the assistant was a film producer. The 1973 Women and International Film Festival had already started people thinking about a potential media cocktail made of Toronto and movies, but it wasn't until 1976 when the so-called Festival of Festivals opened with *Cousine, Cousine* at Ontario Place's Cinesphere that an embryonic Toronto International Film Festival got rolling. At first it was run on a hope and a prayer – films were delivered by bicycle, creditors were put off and there were wild rumors of stars that never showed. Back then, it cost $150 for the VIP treatment. Nowadays, gold packages that include invites to all the galas with stars like Ben Kingsley (and just about anyone else you could name) cost $3000 – and they sell out.

Critics and the film industry acknowledge that Toronto's festival has grown into one of the most prestigious and influential in the world, perhaps second only to Cannes. Last year over half of the 328 films from 56 countries screened over 10 days were premieres. Films from the quarter-century-old festival have won a total of 291 Academy Awards. Along the way the Toronto International Film Festival has been instrumental in launching directors like Atom Egoyan and reviving the entire Canadian film industry. Toronto has been called Hollywood North and you may well come across one of a number of ongoing movie shoots around town at any time of year.

Tickets to the Toronto International Film Festival (☎ 416-968-3456) go on sale in early July by phone, fax or over the Internet (www.bell.ca/filmfest). The early bird pass costs $278 and coupon books for 10 ($90) or 30 ($225) movies can be bought separately. In any case, festivalgoers need to show up a week before opening night in late August to pick up a program, submit ticket request orders and cross their fingers to get the shows they want to see. Single tickets for what's left are sold for $12.50, and same-day rush tickets are available from the theaters one hour before showtime. Check the free weeklies and major newspapers for special guides and reviews.

held at Casa Loma, Black Creek Pioneer Village and other venues. The Church of the Holy Trinity puts on a musical Christmas pageant that's not to be missed. On New Year's Eve, 'First Night' is a family-oriented festival of the visual and performing arts.

DOING BUSINESS

As the most popular Canadian city for conventions and trade shows, Toronto hosts almost 100 of these annually at the Metro Convention Centre on Front St and Exhibition Place. Despite cries of 'Buy Canadian!' foreign companies seem to do quite well here, as evidenced by US ownership of many Golden Horseshoe industries and, more recently, the invasion of Starbucks.

Although it doesn't much help tourists, Tourism Toronto (see Local Tourist Offices at the beginning of this chapter) is extremely well set up for assisting business travelers and offers corporate incentives. Their on-line business directory has extensive business services listings, including office and meeting-space rental and document translation.
Web site: www.toronto.com/Toronto/Tourism _Toronto/Directory/

WORK

It is difficult to get a work permit, as employment opportunities go first to Canadians; you will need to take a validated job offer from a specific employer to a Canadian consulate or embassy outside Canada.

Visitors to Canada are technically not able to work. However, employers hiring casual, temporary, service workers (hotel, bar, restaurant) and construction, farm or forestry workers often don't ask for permits. Visitors working here legally have Social Insurance numbers. If you don't have this, and get caught, you will be told to leave the country.

Each year, a limited number of one-year working holiday visas are made available to Australians and New Zealanders between the ages of 18 and 30. Competition is stiff, so apply as early as possible and allow 12 weeks for processing. Application forms are available through the Canadian Consulate General in Sydney (see Embassies & Consulates earlier in this chapter).

The Student Work Abroad Program (SWAP) facilitates an additional 3500 working holidays every year for students and youths between 18 and 25 years old. Participants come from nearly 20 countries, including Australia, Britain, France, Japan, South Africa, the USA and New Zealand. After paying a registration fee, you will be issued with a one-year, non-extendable visa allowing you to work anywhere in Canada. Most 'Swappers' find service jobs – at restaurants, bars, hotels or on farms. SWAP Canada (swapinfo@travelcuts.com) or any Travel CUTS office (see Travel Agencies earlier in this chapter) can tell you which student travel agency to contact in your own country for further details.

Getting There & Away

AIR

Toronto is served by two airports, Pearson International Airport and the Toronto City Centre Airport. See the Getting Around chapter for details on options for getting from the airports to central Toronto.

Pearson International Airport

By far the busiest airport in the country, Pearson International Airport (Map 1; ☎ 416-247-7678), is 27km northwest of downtown Toronto near Etobicoke. The major Canadian airlines fly in and out of Pearson, as do many international carriers. The complex shuffling of airport operations following Air Canada's merger with Canadian Airlines is over. All Air Canada and Canadian Air international flights use Terminal 1; their domestic and US flights depart from Terminal 2 (reverse this for Air Ontario flights). Star Alliance partners share space with Air Canada in Terminal 1;

all other international airlines are assigned to Terminal 3. Almost all tickets for flights departing Canada, whether purchased in Canada or abroad, include departure tax.

Air Canada representatives say they are already looking ahead to moving yet again into the new $3.3 billion terminal, now under construction. For now, transit passengers can use the pedestrian tunnel between terminals 1 and 2 or inter-terminal courtesy shuttle buses that run every eight to 15 minutes. All three terminals have food courts, duty-free stores, ATMs, medical emergency clinics, currency exchange booths and information desks. If you get stranded at the airport, airport representatives can grant you access to 'quiet areas' set aside for fatigued travelers. Baggage storage is provided by Canadian Locker (Terminal 3) and the Travel Store (Terminals 1 and 2) for $3 to $6 per day, or $8 per bike.

Toronto City Centre Airport

This small airport (Map 1; ☎ 416-203-6942) on Toronto Islands is used by regional and charter airlines. Air Ontario commuter flights between Montréal and Ottawa are a lot quicker than the major flights because you're already downtown – and you get a better look at the city, too.

Airlines

The following are the major airlines that have offices in Toronto or at its airports.

Air Canada (Map 4; ☎ 416-925-2311) 100 Front St W, Royal York Hotel

Air China (☎ 416-581-8833) 700 Bay St, Suite 1900

Air France (☎ 1-800-667-2747) 151 Bloor St W

Air India (☎ 416-865-1030) 390 Bay St

Air New Zealand (☎ 1-800-663-5495)

Air Transat (☎ 1-877-872-6729)

Alitalia (☎ 1-800-361-8336)

American Airlines (Map 5; ☎ 416-612-3752, 1-800-433-7300) 44 Gerrard St W

GETTING THERE & AWAY

The XYZs of Canadian Airports

Unlike in the US where airport codes often reveal a quirky story, Pearson International Airport is quizzically labeled 'YYZ.' It often makes travelers to Toronto feel like they've gone to the ends of the earth and exhausted the entire alphabet. In fact, many major Canadian airport codes begin with YY, which makes you wonder how much missing luggage might end up at YYB (North Bay), YYC (Calgary), YYJ (Victoria) or even more disastrously, YYG (Charlottetown, Prince Edward Island) or YYH (Taloyoak, Nunavut)!

Back in the day when Canada swiped almost all of the airport codes beginning with X, Y or Z, they weren't fast enough to catch funny YUM (Yuma, Arizona) or YAK (Yakatut, Alaska). Still, if Toronto (and all of its thousands of young ravers) ever wanted to redesignate Pearson International Airport, the code XTC has never been taken.

British Airways (☎ 416-250-0880, 1-888-334-3448) 4120 Yonge St

Canada 3000 (☎ 416-674-0257)

CanJet Airlines (☎ 1-800-809-7777)

Cathay Pacific (☎ 1-800-268-6868) 928-70 York St

Continental Airlines (☎ 1-800-231-0856)

Delta Air Lines (Map 4; ☎ 1-800-221-1212) 100 Front St W, Royal York Hotel

El Al Israel Airlines (☎ 416-967-4222) 151 Bloor St W

Iberia Airlines (☎ 1-800-772-4642)

Japan Airlines (Map 4; ☎ 416-364-7229, 1-800-525-3663) 130 Adelaide St W

Korean Air (☎ 1-800-438-5000)

Lufthansa (Map 4; ☎ 416-360-3600) 100 Front St W, Royal York Hotel

Mexicana Airlines (Map 6; ☎ 1-800-531-7921) 2 Bloor St W

Northwest Airlines/KLM (☎ 1-800-225-2525) 777 Bay St

Olympic Airways (Map 6; ☎ 416-920-2452) 80 Bloor St W, 10th Floor

Qantas (☎ 1-800-227-4500)

Royal Airlines (☎ 1-888-828-9797)

Royal Air Maroc (☎ 1-800-361-7508)

Scandanavian Airlines (☎ 1-800-221-2350)

Singapore Airlines (Map 4; ☎ 416-860-0197, 1-800-387-0038) 70 York St, Suite 1660

Swissair (☎ 1-800-267-9477)

Thai Airways (☎ 416-971-5181, 1-800-668-8103) 20 Dundas St W

TWA (☎ 1-800-221-2000)

United Airlines (Map 4; ☎ 1-800-241-6522) 100 Front St W, Royal York Hotel

US Airways (Map 4; ☎ 1-800-428-4322) 100 Front St W, Royal York Hotel

Varig Brazilian Airlines (Map 6; ☎ 416-926-7500, 1-800-468-2744) 77 Bloor St W, Suite 1108

Round-the-World Tickets

If you are covering a lot of distance, a Round-the-World (RTW) ticket that includes travel in Canada could be worthwhile. Depending on which countries and therefore airlines you select, the price of the fare will change, with an absolute minimum of £500, A$2000 or US$1200. The maximum ticket validity is usually 12 months. Most tickets will not allow you to fly in and out of the same airport twice, effectively putting half the world out of reach.

Within Canada

The domestic air market is dominated by Air Canada and its affiliates, particularly Canadian Airlines. Good deals are occasionally offered, but usually with plenty of restrictions.

Some competitors offering cut-rate flights to Toronto include Royal Airlines (www.royalairlines.com), AirTransat (www.airtransat.com) and Canada 3000 (www.canada3000.com). Regional carriers such as CanJet Airlines (www.canjet.com) and WestJet Airlines (www.westjet.com) are also well worth a look. Check ads in free entertainment weeklies like *Now* for special deals. Along the heavily-traveled Toronto-Montréal route, return fares start at just

$122, including tax – cheaper than the train or bus. CanJet also offers good one-way tickets, including Ottawa ($82), Montréal ($82) and Halifax ($140). Royal Airlines offers return fares to Vancouver from Toronto for as little as $232; prices balloon to $400 or more in summer.

The USA
Direct flights between major US and Canadian cities are abundant and frequent on Air Canada and major US airlines.

The cheapest flights to Toronto are from the Midwest. For example, roundtrip flights from Chicago start at US$195 to US$275. A short hop from Detroit costs from US$125 with Continental or Air Canada.

Air Canada flies between New York City and Toronto for $255 roundtrip, and this fare is often matched by United, Continental, US Air and others. Pakistani Air flights from New York City's La Guardia Airport to Toronto cost even less.

Fares from the west coast vary, with Los Angeles usually being the cheapest gateway. Canada 3000 has nonstop flights from LAX for US$210 to US$270 roundtrip; discount fares on other airlines start at US$400. Standard fares from San Francisco or Seattle easily cost at least 50% more.

Travel agencies specializing in student and discount airfares like Council Travel (☎ 1-800-226-8624) and STA Travel (☎ 1-800-781-4040) have offices in major cities across the USA. You can check out their Web sites at www.counciltravel.com and www.statravel.com, respectively. Under-26, student and teacher fares shave up to 50% off the cost of many routes, with excellent deals on one-way flights possible. In Canada, Travel CUTS (see Travel Agencies in the Facts for the Visitor chapter) offers competitive roundtrip fares of $297 to New York City, $299 to Miami or $389 to Los Angeles.

The weekly travel sections of the *New York Times, Chicago Tribune, San Francisco Chronicle* and *LA Times* contain ads for travel agencies that specialize in cut-rate airfares. Many US airlines and Air Canada advertise their own last-minute and Internet-only fares on their Web sites.

Cuba
Many US tourists fly first to Canada because direct flights to Cuba are illegal south of the border. Typical Havana-Toronto roundtrip fares start at $600 to $800. Air Canada has connecting flights to Havana, while Mexicana, Lacsa and Cubana all offer direct service. Beware that Cubana has the third worst safety record of any airline in the world!

Australia & New Zealand
From Australia, Canada 3000, Japan Airlines, Korean Air, Qantas and Canadian Airlines offer some of the best deals to Toronto. Most flights from Australia include a free stopover on the way, usually in Hawaii or the USA. In the high season, expect to pay from A$1699 to A$2100 for a roundtrip flight. In the low season, the best deals are with Canada 3000, starting at A$1385.

From New Zealand, Canada 3000, Japan Airlines and American Airlines have some of the best deals. During the high season, fares from Auckland to Toronto start from NZ$1949 to NZ$2344 while low season fares start from NZ$1699 to NZ$2101. Flights from New Zealand often include a free stopover either in the Pacific – Fiji, Rarotonga and Hawaii – or the USA.

These fares are only the airlines' official fares. You will find the best prices by shopping around – travel agencies, classified ads and the Internet are good sources. In Melbourne and Sydney, Flight Centre and STA travel agencies have competitively priced tickets. STA also operates an office in Auckland, New Zealand.

The UK & Continental Europe
Air Canada offers the most flights to Toronto, but there are plenty of competitors including Air France, British Airways, Continental, KLM, SAS, United Airlines and US Airways. Prices vary seasonally, with the highest fares during summer and around Christmas/New Year's. Keep an eye open for youth and standby fares, as well as special offers posted by airlines on the Web.

From London, roundtrip fares for under-25s start as low as £260/500 in low/high

Air Travel Glossary

Cancellation Penalties If you have to cancel or change a discounted ticket, there are often heavy penalties involved; insurance can sometimes be taken out against these penalties. Some airlines impose penalties on regular tickets as well, particularly against 'no-show' passengers.

Courier Fares Businesses often need to send their urgent documents or freight securely and quickly. Courier companies hire people to accompany the package through customs and, in return, offer a discount ticket that is sometimes a phenomenal bargain. However, you may have to surrender all your baggage allowance and take only carry-on luggage.

Full Fares Airlines traditionally offer 1st class (coded F), business class (coded J) and economy class (coded Y) tickets. These days, so many promotional and discounted fares are available that few passengers pay full economy fare.

Lost Tickets If you lose your airline ticket, an airline will usually treat it like a traveler's check and, after inquiries, issue you with another one. Legally, however, an airline is entitled to treat it like cash: If you lose it, it's gone forever. Take good care of your tickets.

Onward Tickets An entry requirement for many countries is a ticket out of the country. If you're unsure of your next move, the easiest solution is to buy the cheapest onward ticket to a neighboring country or a ticket from a reliable airline that can later be refunded if you do not use it.

Open-Jaw Tickets These are return tickets that permit you to fly into one place but return from another. If available, these tickets can save you backtracking to your arrival point.

Overbooking Because almost every flight has some passengers that fail to show up, airlines often book more passengers than they have seats. Usually excess passengers make up for the no-shows, but occasionally somebody gets 'bumped' onto the next available flight. Guess who it is most likely to be? The passengers who check in late.

Promotional Fares These are officially discounted fares, available from travel agencies or direct from the airline.

Reconfirmation If you don't reconfirm your flight at least 72 hours prior to departure, the airline may delete your name from the passenger list. Call to find out if your airline requires reconfirmation.

Restrictions Discounted tickets often have various restrictions – for example, they may need to be paid for in advance, or altering them may incur a penalty. Other restrictions include minimum and maximum periods you must be away.

Round-the-World Tickets RTW tickets give you a limited period (usually a year) in which to circumnavigate the globe. You can go anywhere the carrying airlines go as long as you don't backtrack. The number of stopovers or total number of separate flights is decided before you set off, and these tickets usually cost a bit more than a basic roundtrip flight.

Transferred Tickets Airline tickets cannot be transferred from one person to another. Travelers sometimes try to sell the return half of a ticket, but officials can ask you to prove that you are the person named on the ticket. On an international flight, tickets are compared with passports.

Travel Periods Ticket prices vary with the time of year. There is a low (off-peak) season and a high (peak) season, and often a low-shoulder season and a high-shoulder season as well. Usually the fare depends on your outward flight – if you depart in the high season and return in the low season, you pay the high-season fare.

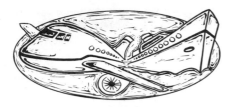

season, taxes included – US Airways and British Airways offer the best deals. The over-26 prices average £288/603, significantly less if you fly Canada 3000 or Royal Aviation. Stopover privileges in Canada for tickets such as London-Montreal-Toronto-Vancouver-London are sometimes offered.

Advertisements for travel agents appear in the travel pages of weekend newspapers as well as in *Time Out*, the *Evening Standard* and *TNT*. Also try discount 'student' travel agencies, including STA Travel (☎ 020 7361 6161) and Usit Campus (☎ 020 7730 3402), or check their Web sites, www.statravel.com, www.statravel.co.uk and www.usitcampus.co.uk, respectively.

From Frankfurt, continental Europe's busiest airport, a roundtrip ticket to Toronto can cost as little as DM595 in low season (DM1100 in high season). Roundtrip flights from Paris cost FF2400 to FF4000; tickets from Amsterdam, f670 to f1000.

You could fly to the Northeastern US and make your way by bus or train to Toronto (a 10- to 12-hour journey). Roundtrips from London to New York City, for instance, can be picked up for as low as £150 to £175, FF1800 from Paris. If your schedule is flexible, Airhitch (☎ 310-574-0090, 1-800-326-2009 in North America, 01 47 00 16 30 in Paris) has standby flights that can get you to/from Europe for US$169.
Web site: www.airhitch.org

Asia

Many flights from Asia travel over the Pacific, usually connecting in Vancouver or US gateway cities, such as Detroit, Chicago or New York. Other flights are routed via Europe, stopping in London, Frankfurt or Paris. The only direct services from Asia are offered by Air Canada from Japan and Cathay Pacific from Hong Kong, but these are expensive. During the Asian holiday periods, including Chinese Lunar New Year and *ōbon* in Japan, fares skyrocket and seats can be well-nigh impossible to get.

Air Canada, Japan Airlines, Northwest and American offer the lowest fares from Japan, starting at ¥91,000 roundtrip, not including taxes. Asiana and Korean Air fly roundtrip from Bangkok for as low as B41,600. Fares jump quite a bit if you're flying from Hong Kong (HK$13,250) or Singapore (S$3270).

Many discount travel agencies in Bangkok, Hong Kong and Singapore sell cut-rate tickets for far less than the major airlines. One-way fares to Toronto from Bangkok, sometimes including a stopover in the USA, cost from B15,000. A few such discount agencies are of the cut-and-run variety, however, so ask around before you buy.

From Asia, it's often cheaper to fly first to the USA rather than directly to Canada. After arriving in Chicago, Detroit, Buffalo or New York City, a train or bus will take you (after many hours) to Toronto. Northwest often advertises special $450 roundtrip fares between Tokyo and Detroit on its Web site (www.nwa.com).

BUS

Buses are fairly clean and safe. They are also cheaper than trains, though not nearly so quick and comfortable. Always ask for the direct or express bus – the price is generally the same, and you may save hours. Most advance tickets do not guarantee a seat, so you will need to show up at least an hour before departure to line up. On evenings prior to holidays or long weekends, expect crowds.

The Metro Toronto Coach Terminal (Map 5; ☎ 416-393-7911) is at 610 Bay St at the corner of Dundas St. Numerous bus lines covering Ontario originate here, as do Greyhound buses traveling within Canada and to US destinations. Lockers are found on the lower level, and there's a restaurant upstairs. Some buses also depart from an adjacent terminal on the western side, including GO Transit (☎ 416-869-3200) commuter services. For information on

GETTING THERE & AWAY

other bus lines serving destinations in Ontario and beyond, call the Metro Coach terminal information line at ☎ 416-393-7911. Fares with Coach Canada (☎ 1-800-461-7661), formerly Trentway-Wagar, match Greyhound fares (see the following section) to Montréal, Niagara Falls and Buffalo, NY.

Alternative hop-on, hop-off adventure bus trips around Ontario and Quebec are described under Organized Tours, later in this chapter.

Greyhound (☎ 416-367-8747, 1-800-231-2222) covers much of southwestern Ontario, including the Niagara region, Kitchener and Stratford. Long-distance routes stretch west as far as Vancouver ($313, 65 to 70 hours, three departures daily) and east to Ottawa ($56.60, six hours, eight daily) or Montréal ($74.70, 7½ hours, seven daily). Additional overnight buses to Ottawa and Montréal leave around midnight.
Web site: www.greyhound.ca

Cross-border Greyhound services to the USA include: Detroit ($61.60, six hours, five daily); Chicago ($103.50, 11½ to 13½ hours, four daily); Buffalo ($25.40, 2½ hours, nine daily); and New York City ($104.25, 10 to 12 hours, eight daily). Most departures are in the morning and then again after 6 pm. Note that Greyhound Ameripass holders travel free between Toronto and Detroit or New York.

Discount Fares & Passes

All of the prices quoted above are regular one-way adult fares. Significant discounts are given for roundtrip and advance purchase fares. ISIC cardholders (25% off) and seniors and youth (10%) must buy their tickets seven days in advance. With the purchase of any full-fare adult ticket, the second adult goes half-price or one child under age 16 rides free. Greyhound USA offers slightly different discounts, including on weekday travel.

Greyhound's Canada Coach Pass, which costs the same whether purchased overseas or after arrival, comes in seven- ($249), 15- ($379), 30- ($449) and 60-day ($599) variations, plus tax. Passes cover five provinces – from Ontario west to British Columbia – as

well as the Yukon and Northwest Territories. All passes must be bought at least one week prior to making your first trip.

The International Canada Coach Pass Plus, which can only be purchased abroad, extends to Quebec City and includes New Brunswick, Nova Scotia and Prince Edward Island. It comes in 15- ($409), 30- ($529) and 60-day ($679) variations, plus tax.

TRAIN

Canadians feel a special attachment to the 'ribbons of steel' from coast to coast, although they don't take the train very often. Generally, long-distance train travel is more expensive than taking the bus and not as streamlined as Europe or Japan, but trains arguably remain Canada's most enjoyable (and romantic) way to travel.

Grand old Union Station (Map 4) downtown is served by VIA Rail and GO Transit commuter trains. The Yonge-University-Spadina subway line goes right into the station, which has several fast-food outlets, currency exchange booths, a Travellers' Aid desk and, most critically, a bar.

Within Canada

VIA Rail Passenger services on VIA Rail (☎ 416-366-8411, 1-800-561-8630) are best along the so-called Québec-Windsor corridor, an area of heavy traffic between Québec City, Québec and Windsor, Ontario (near Detroit, USA), including Montréal, Ottawa, Toronto and Niagara Falls. Overnight trains between Montréal and Toronto depart either city at 11:30 pm every night except Saturday, arriving at 8 am (with a complimentary breakfast) the next morning. One-way fares in a sleeper cabin start at $90, tax included.

One-way peak fares to other cities are: Ottawa ($75, four hours); Montreal ($104, five hours); and Niagara Falls ($21.50, two hours), with transfers to Windsor ($77, 3¾ hours). There are usually no discounted return or excursion fares. Train schedules and routes are listed in the free *National Timetable* or on the Web at www.viarail.ca.

Reservations for all VIA Rail trips are important, especially on weekends and holidays. VIA fares vary with the phone call, even within the hour, so it's worth trying several times over a day or two to check. On long trips, you can save literally hundreds of dollars! Remember that one week's notice drops the fares as much as 40%, except for Friday or Sunday travel. Students, seniors and children also get discounts.

For those who intend to travel a lot, the Corridor Pass is good for 10 days and costs $255 in economy class, or $234 for students with ISIC card and seniors. VIA Rail also offers the Canrailpass, which is good for 12 days of coach-class travel within a 30-consecutive-day period. It costs $399/639 in low/high season, or $359/575 for students, seniors and under-25s. The longest continuous route in the country starts in Toronto and goes through the Rocky Mountains to Vancouver. Named the *Canadian,* the train looks like a 1950s stainless steel classic with two-story windowed 'dome' car, perfect for sightseeing.

GO Commuter Network This train network (☎ 416-869-3200) serves the suburbs of Toronto east to Whitby and west to Hamilton. Ticket inspection is random, and service is fast and steady throughout the day; unfortunately, it doesn't serve any destinations travelers are likely to visit.

The USA
Amtrak The US equivalent of VIA Rail is Amtrak (☎ 215-824-1600, 1-800-872-7245). Information on Amtrak routes and services is available from the information desk in Union station.

Amtrak has several routes between the USA and Canada, including: Toronto to New York City (US$65 to US$99 one-way, 12 hours via Niagara Falls); New York City to Montréal (US$52 to US$65, 10 hours); and Chicago to Toronto (US$86 to US$98, 11½ hours). International passengers are responsible for securing the necessary documentation (ie, visas) prior to on-board customs and immigration procedures.

Reservations are necessary for all trains, and roundtrip tickets are often heavily discounted. For fares and schedules call Amtrak or visit its Web site (www.amtrak.com).

CAR & MOTORCYCLE
In 1862 Anthony Trollope remarked, 'But if the streets of Toronto are better than those of other towns, the roads around it are worse.' It's still true. Expressways on all four sides of the city experience continual congestion and, except during winter, construction never ends.

At the southern edge of the city along the lake, the Gardiner Expressway (parallel to Lake Shore Blvd) runs west into Queen Elizabeth Way (QEW) to Niagara Falls. At the city's western border is Hwy 427, which runs north past Hwy 401 up to the airport. Hwy 401 parallels the lake north of downtown, heading east to Montreal and west to Stratford and Windsor. The often bumper to bumper segment of the 401 between Hwy 427 and Yonge St can be nightmarish. On the eastern side of the city, Don Valley Parkway is an alternate, slower connection between the Gardiner and Hwy 401.

Hwy 407, running east-west from Markham to Mississauga for about 40km just north of the city, is an electronic toll road. If you don't have a prepaid electronic gizmo on your car, a bill is mailed to you (maximum $5). Bills are sent out of province and to some US states but payment is not enforced.

On weekends and holidays, especially during summer, major land border crossings with the USA become jammed with

Road Sign Wrangling

Since 1997, Ontario has been deregulating its highways. As these roads are returned to their county or local authorities for maintenance, the shapes of the highway shields and occasionally even the numbers are changing officially, but resignposting has not always kept pace. During this transitional period, travelers should be aware that there may be some inconsistencies between highway signs and published maps. Contact the Ontario Ministry of Transportation at ☎ 416-325-4686 for more information on this situation.

shoppers, vacationers and visitors. Delays in the Windsor-Detroit tunnel of over an hour are not uncommon (the Ambassador Bridge is quicker). Smaller, secondary border points like Sarnia, on Lake Huron bordering Michigan, are usually quiet, sometimes so quiet that the officers have nothing better to do than tear your luggage apart.

Driving costs in Canada are reasonable, with gasoline prices considerably lower than in Europe. Major highway service stations offer no bargains and often jack up gas prices on long weekends and at holiday time in order to fleece captive victims. Those arriving from the USA should always have a full tank before crossing the border, since in Ontario gas averages 72¢ per liter, which works out to more than US$2 per gallon. Drivers from Québec should wait until they're over the border to refuel.

For driving rules and regulations, see the Getting Around chapter.

Ride-Sharing

EcoRide is based on a great idea – getting drivers and cars together with passengers. Its Web site (www.ecoride.com) mainly lists rides offered by drivers headed to Montreal and Ottawa ($20 to $35 one-way), but sometimes destinations like New York City or Vancouver pop up, too. Drivers set their own fees and pick-up and drop-off points. Start checking the site about a week before your planned departure.

Recent government crackdowns have eliminated most ride-sharing services, as a favor to Greyhound and other major bus lines. At the time of writing, however, ecoRide was still active.

Drive-Aways

One of the best driving deals is the uniquely North American drive-away system. The agency matches you and your desired destination with a car that needs to be delivered to that place. You put down a hefty deposit and are given a certain number of days to make the journey. If you don't show up on time, the police are notified. Gasoline is generally at your own expense and be sure

to get in writing what happens if the car breaks down (ie, who is responsible).

Toronto Drive-Away Service (☎ 416-225-7754, 1-800-561-2658) has cars for Canadian and US destinations, including Florida and California.

Web site: www.torontodriveaway.com

HITCHHIKING

Hitchhiking is never entirely safe in any country in the world, and Lonely Planet does not recommend it. Travelers who decide to hitchhike should understand that they are taking a small but potentially serious risk. You will be safer if traveling in pairs and if you let someone know where you are planning to go.

Within Toronto city limits, hitchhiking is illegal on the expressways. If you're heading east for Montreal, take public transit to the corner of Port Union Rd and Hwy 401 in Scarborough. For destinations west, try the corner of Carlingview Dr and International Blvd almost at Hwy 401. If you're northbound, you're stuck. The best bet is to take the bus to Barrie and then hitch the rest of the way on Hwy 400 or Hwy 11, depending on your destination. If you feel you've waited a long time to be picked up, remember that the ride you get may take you over 1500km.

BOAT

Hydrofoil Lake Jet Lines (Map 10; ☎ 416-214-4923, 1-800-313-3237), 225 Queen's Quay E at Sherbourne St, operates speedy, one-hour boat trips to Queenston along the Niagara Parkway. The $25 one-way fare includes a shuttle bus to either Niagara Falls or Niagara-on-the-Lake. Call for reservations and to check schedules.

Web site: www.seaflight2000.com/rates.htm

There's talk of a high-speed international ferry service between Toronto and Buffalo starting in 2003. For now the only option to/from the USA is the Lake Erie ferry crossing between Sandusky, Ohio, and Pelee Island, Ontario. Vehicles cost $30 and adults/children $13.75/6.75 each, one-way. It operates from approximately May to September, depending on the weather – call

☎ 1-800-661-2220 for seasonal schedules and reservations (required).

ORGANIZED TOURS

Organized group tours are best arranged through travel agencies or the tour companies themselves. Two companies with established names are Suntrek (☎ 707-523-1800, 1-800-786-8735) and TrekAmerica (☎ 973-983-1144, 1-800-221-0596, in the UK 01295-256777). TrekAmerica offers three-week Canada Frontier tours that start in New York or Seattle and visit Toronto, Montréal and Vancouver along the way (US$1119).
Web sites: www.suntrek.com and www.trekamerica.com

Adventure & Alternative Buses

Many small, innovative alternative transportation companies gear services to budget travelers and hostelers. Some of these low-cost, high-convenience, good-fun trips are just a few hours in duration, others go for weeks, making the trip as meaningful as the destination.

From mid-May to mid-October, Moose Travel (☎ 905-853-4762, 1-888-816-6673, info@moosenetwork.com) operates three different jump-on, jump-off adventure-hostel trips around Toronto, Ottawa, Algonquin Park, Montréal and Quebec City, costing $279 to $379 (the price is for transport only).
Web site: www.moosetravelco.com

The founders of CanaBUS Tours (☎ 416-977-8311, 1-877-226-2287) claim to have 'built themselves some buses out of beer bottles, hockey pucks, lacrosse sticks and snowboards.' Like Moose Travel, the tours stop in cities, at historic sites and for white-water rafting or canoeing in provincial parks; passengers pay extra for the activities they choose (some are free). Note that CanaBUS tours are not hop-on, hop-off trips. Base prices range from $200 for the Georgian Bay Loop to $320 for the eight-day Grand Experience covering Ottawa and the Bruce Trail.
Web site: www.canabus.com

Further Still (☎ 905-371-8747, 1-877-371-8747) offers low-budget trips around Ontario to concerts, festivals and even ski resorts in recycled school buses decorated à la the hippie aesthetic. Their main specialty, however, is two-week trips around eastern Canada ($589, plus $116 for food) or three-week adventures to the west coast ($899 plus $305) leaving monthly between May and October. HI members receive a 10% discount. Accommodation en route is mainly camping (equipment provided) or in hostels.
Web site: www.magicbuscompany.com

From May to October, Free Spirit Tours (☎ 416-219-7562) has hiking and rock-climbing on the Bruce Peninsula with overnights at Collingwood hostel. The small-group, three-day, two-night all-inclusive package is $175. Other outdoor trips run in winter.

Getting Around

TO/FROM THE AIRPORTS
Pearson International Airport
The cheapest way to Pearson is on the No 58A Malton bus from the Lawrence West subway station on the north-south Yonge-University line for a grand total of $2. Allow at least an hour from downtown. At the airport catch this bus outside Terminal 2.

You can also take either branch of the Yonge-University subway line north to York Mills or Yorkdale station (20 minutes). From there GO Transit Brampton-bound buses leave for the airport every half hour between 5:45 am and 1:15 am ($2.95, 30 minutes), as do Airport Express (☎ 905-564-6333, 1-800-387-6787) buses for $8/13 one-way/roundtrip, but they don't make the journey any faster.

Airport Express buses also leave from Islington subway station, one stop before the western terminus of the Bloor-Danforth line; trips are every 40 minutes from 5:30 am until 12:15 am ($7.10/11.50 one-way/round-trip, 30 minutes).

Airport Express operates a 24-hour downtown service that connects the Metro Toronto Coach Terminal (Map 5), Union Station (Map 4) and major hotels every half hour or better, taking about 80 minutes, depending on traffic. One-way/roundtrip tickets cost $13.75/23.65, though some hotel connector services cost a few dollars more. Students and seniors receive 10% off one-way fares.

A metered taxi from Yonge and Bloor Sts to the airport will cost around $40 and take about 45 minutes, depending on traffic. However, many taxi companies will charge a comparable flat fee for airport fares.

If you're driving, avoid using Hwy 401 during morning and evening rush hours; instead, take the Gardiner Expressway west and go north on Hwy 427. Parking at the airport garage costs $5 for the first hour, $3 for each additional half hour. Long-term off-site parking at the reduced-rate lot costs $59 per week, with free terminal shuttles.

Toronto City Centre Airport
Ferries to TCCA leave from the foot of Bathurst St on the lakefront. A shuttle bus (free for Air Ontario ticket-holders) runs to the TCAA ferry slip from the Royal York Hotel (Map 4), across from Union Station. Shuttle service starts at 6:15 am on week-days, 8 am on weekends, with the last run sometime after 7 pm. You could also take the No 511 Bathurst streetcar south to Lake Shore Blvd and walk down. Ferries leave every 15 minutes from 6:15 am until around 11 pm, taking just minutes for the short sail.

PUBLIC TRANSPORTATION
Toronto Transit Commission (TTC) has a good subway, bus and streetcar system throughout the city. Call ☎ 416-393-4636 for recorded route and fare information, 24 hours a day. Ride Guides are available at subway ticket booths and inside some subway cars. Parking is available free at most TTC lots on weekends and holidays.

The regular adult fare on all TTC transportation is $2. Exact change is required except at subway ticket booths. You can transfer to any other bus, subway or streetcar within one hour at no extra charge, provided you get a transfer from the driver or from the machine inside the subway turnstiles. If you are relying on public transit, buy 10 tokens or tickets for $17. Day passes cost $7 per person and are valid for unlimited rides on weekdays after 9:30 am, weekends from the start of service, until 5:30 am the following morning. On weekends and holidays, a family pass costs the same and is good for up to two adults and four children.

For farther-flung travel, the TTC system connects with bus routes in surrounding suburban cities such as Mississauga, Markham and Brampton. For information on these routes, call GO Transit at ☎ 416-869-3200.

Streetcar
Toronto is one of the few North American cities still using streetcars. Although not as

55

fast as the subway, many people prefer them because they're simple to use and stop every block or two. Routes are numbered in the 500s and they roll on St Clair Ave and College, Dundas, Queen and King Sts (all of which run east-west) and on Bathurst St and Spadina Ave (north-south). The Spadina streetcar turns east at the southern end of that street and runs along Queen's Quay W to Union Station. The No 509 Harbourfront streetcar partially covers the same route from Union station past the Harbourfront and out to the CNE grounds near Ontario Place.

Subway

The subway system is clean, quick and air-conditioned, but it's skeletal. There is one east-west line, which goes along Bloor St/Danforth Ave and a north-south line shaped like a horseshoe with two branches extending from Union Station up Yonge St and University Ave and out to Toronto's north suburbs. The subway starts running at 6 am (9 am on Sunday) and runs until around 1:30 am. All subway stations have clearly marked Designated Waiting Areas (DWAs) monitored by security cameras and equipped with a bench, pay phone and an intercom link to the station manager. They are located where the subway guard's car stops along the platform.

Bus

Visitors won't find much use for the public buses, which are slow and get held up in traffic. Bus hours vary; some run late but are infrequent. Women traveling between 9 pm and 6 am can request special stops anywhere along regular bus routes. Bus stops with blue-banded poles are part of the limited Blue Night Network operating on basic routes around the city between 1:30 and 5 am, every 30 minutes or better. Detailed bus route maps are posted at every bus (and sometimes streetcar) stop, but it's confusing. Before you get off one bus, ask the driver for information on making connections.

CAR & MOTORCYCLE

Once Toronto was called 'Muddy York' after the wearying conditions of its roads. Today driving in the city is still nothing but a headache, so park your car and ride the TTC 'Rocket' (a slight exaggeration) instead.

If you insist on driving, know that congestion is a real problem. Morning and evening rush hours are impossible, especially on city

Do-It-Yourself (Mostly) TTC Tour

Along with a few cities such as New Orleans and San Francisco, Toronto has some of the only running streetcars in North America. Granted, 'running' is a relative term here when streetcars sit in traffic and even the pedestrians are moving faster. Still, most tourists hop a streetcar the first chance they get, and riding one is unbeatable for watching the city roll by.

Start at Union Station and take the No 510 Spadina streetcar along the Harbourfront and north through Chinatown to College St. Transfer to the No 506 streetcar westbound through Little Italy and either stay on until the terminus or get off at Caledonia Rd and walk a few blocks south. Either way, you want to catch the No 505 Dundas streetcar heading back east through Little Portugal. Back near Chinatown at Bathurst St, transfer to the No 511 south to Queen St. From there, the No 501 heading east gives you a long, straight shot past City Hall, over the Don River and out to The Beach.

To get back downtown using an alternative route, catch any bus going north up Woodbine Ave to Gerrard St E, then hop the No 506 Carlton streetcar taking you west through Little India and Chinatown East back over the river. No one really knows how many times one person could get away with re-using the same TTC transfer, but if you don't want to push the limits of the law, a day pass costs $7.

streets leading to Lake Shore Blvd and the Gardiner Expressway. Very few streets have left-turn lanes or signals, and traffic can become backed up for blocks, especially downtown. During the day, avoid Kensington Market and Spadina Ave in Chinatown; at night, don't even think about driving near the entertainment or theater districts.

If you'll be leaving city streets behind to drive on Ontario's highways, see 'Road Sign Wrangling' in the Getting There & Away chapter for a note on their potentially confusing deregulation.

Road Rules

The use of seat belts is compulsory throughout Canada. You can turn right on a red light after first having made a full stop; flashing green lights mean protected left turns. All vehicles must stop for streetcars, behind the rear doors, while the streetcar is loading or unloading passengers. Drivers must also stop for pedestrians at crosswalks whenever the overhead signals (look carefully) are flashing.

Motorcyclists are required to drive with their lights on and driver and passengers both must wear helmets.

Parking

In Toronto, parking is expensive – usually about $2.50 to $3.50 for the first half hour, with an average daily maximum of $8. Most places have a flat rate after 6 pm. Cheapest are the city of Toronto municipal lots, which are scattered around the downtown area and marked by green signs. They cost the same as metered street parking, which (if you can find any) is usually $2 per hour. Incidentally, some meters do accept US coins, albeit at Canadian rates. Many metered spaces have a central payment kiosk for an entire row. Purchase the appropriate amount of time using cash or a credit card and be sure to display the receipt on your dashboard. It's not free to park next to a broken meter – it's illegal.

Parking on main city streets is prohibited during rush hours (7 to 9 am and 4 to 6 pm). Tow trucks show no mercy and getting your vehicle back will cost a bundle in cash and aggravation. Unless, of course, you happen

Terrible Torontonian traffic!

to be local lawyer John Wiengust, who regularly beats almost 60 parking tickets every year with his astute knowledge of hundreds of gaps in the parking bylaws.

Rental

Renting a car is only recommended for excursions outside Toronto where public transit options just don't exist. Most car rental agencies have a daily rate of about $30 to $50 plus a kilometer fee of 12¢ after the first 100km. Many require that you be at least 21 years old; extra fees apply for those under age 26. If you own a car, check to see if your car insurance covers rentals or offers a rental clause before purchasing insurance at inflated rates from the rental agency. By the time you finish with insurance, gasoline, the number of kilometers, provincial sales tax, GST and any other bits and pieces, you can be handed a pretty surprising bill.

Rates vary from location to location, even within the same company, with downtown usually being cheaper than the airport. Heavily discounted weekend rates of under $100 may include 'extra days,' say noon Friday until 9 am Monday morning. Special discounts may be available for long-term rentals, senior citizens, CAA/AAA members or members of frequent flyer programs. Count on needing a credit card since cash is not usually considered good enough.

There are countless rental agencies in Toronto, but advance reservations are almost always necessary. Major agencies with reservation desks at Pearson International Airport, as well as numerous city offices, include:

Budget (☎ 416-622-1000 local, 905-673-3322 all locations, 1-800-268-9000). Over 50 Toronto locations.

Discount Car (Map 5; ☎ 416-593-7146) at Atrium on Bay; (Map 4; ☎ 416-593-9777) 101 Spadina Ave; (☎ 1-800-263-2355 outside Toronto); Web site: www.discountcar.com

National Car Rental (Map 4; ☎ 416-364-4191, 1-800-227-7368), 65 Front St W, outside Union Station

Thrifty Car Rental (Map 4; ☎ 416-947-1385), 100 Front St W, Royal York Hotel

Smaller independent agencies offer lower rates and less fuss, but may have fewer cars available. Wheels 4 Rent (Map 9; ☎ 416-585-7782, wheels@istar.ca), 77 Nassau St, rents used cars if you have a credit card and are over 25. Rates are excellent at $29 a day, including insurance, plus 9¢ per kilometer over the first 100km (200km in winter).

Also worth a call is No Frills E (Map 5; ☎ 416-599-1230) at 102 Gerrard St. Used compact cars cost from $27 a day (plus 12¢ per kilometer after the first 200km). There are cheaper weekly and monthly rates, too.

A-Plus Car and Truck Rental (Map 6; ☎ 416-413-1222), 548A Church St, is open seven days a week and has quality Hondas, Nissans, Mazdas etc, starting at $99 for the weekend with 600km free.

TAXI

Taxi drivers in Toronto are generally reliable and will take you where you want to go without taking you for a ride. Just hail one on the street and watch them brake, U-turn or otherwise do whatever it takes to pick you up. Taxis also wait outside hotels, museums, theaters and shopping districts, making them easy to find. Metered fares start at $2.50 plus approximately $1 for each additional kilometer, depending on traffic. Dependable companies include Crown Taxi (☎ 416-750-7878, from local payphones ☎ 1-877-750-7878) and Diamond Taxicab Association (☎ 416-366-6868), as well as Royal Taxi (☎ 416-777-9222), which has a fleet of wheelchair-accessible taxis.

FERRY

In summer Toronto Islands ferries (☎ 416-392-8193) run every 15 to 30 minutes from 8 am to 11 pm, earlier (but not later) on weekends. Make sure to check the time of the last return trip from your planned departure terminal; if you miss it, you'll have to sprint a few kilometers to the next closest terminal or be stuck taking a pricey water taxi. One-way tickets cost $5/2 per adult/child, and the return trip is free. Bicycles are allowed on some, but not all ferries. During spring and fall, hours are reduced, running every 45 minutes. The ferries run through winter (though less frequently) and service only Ward's Island. From there, the other islands can be reached on foot, but note that pretty much everything else is shut tight.

Queues can be long on weekends and holidays, so show up early. Alternatively, there's a private ferry service to the Toronto Islands Marina leaving from the York St slip next to Queen's Quay Terminal. If you can persuade the captain to take you, it'll cost $2.50 and deposits you within walking distance of central Centre Island.

BICYCLE & IN-LINE SKATES

Maybe it's due to the insane parking situation, but Torontonians treat their bicycles with all the respect accorded a second (or even first) vehicle. Bicycles are permitted on all TTC buses, streetcars and subways except during the 6:30 to 9:30 am and 3:30 to 6:30 pm rush hours.

When cycling or in-line skating, be careful on the streetcar rails; cross at right angles or you'll land on your ear. Helmets are not mandatory. Lights must be used from dusk until dawn.

Toronto has 40km of specially marked routes for bicycles only, often meaning a separate lane on the street if you're lucky. The Toronto Cycling Commission (☎ 416-392-7592) publishes a free *Toronto Cycling Map*, available at city hall and tourist offices. In-line skaters mostly stick to sidewalks, but that's illegal for cyclists.

You'll need ID and usually a credit card for making a deposit in order to rent bicycles or in-line skates. The most convenient place for well-maintained racers and mountain bike hybrids is McBride Cycle (Map 4; ☎ 416-203-5651), 180 Queen's Quay W. Rates start at $12 for two hours and from

$24/75 for daily/weekly rentals. Nearby Wheel Excitement (☎ 416-506-1001), 5 Rees St, charges slightly higher day rates, but two-day rentals of either in-line skates or bicycles cost $36. On Toronto Islands, Centre Island Bicycle Rental (Map 12; ☎ 416-203-0009) is on the south shore more or less straight back from the ferry landing. Bicycles/tandems/quadricycles costs $5/12/15 per hour, requiring only a two-hour equivalent cash deposit.

All of the following bicycle and in-line skate shops are excellent sources of information, maps, accessories, tune-ups (starting at $25) and quick repairs. Curbside Cycle (Map 8; ☎ 416-920-4933), 412 Bloor St W, carries MapArt's 'Toronto with Bicycle Routes' ($3.95) and the *Official Lake Ontario Waterfront Trail Mapbook* ($9.95). In line skates rent for $22 per 24 hours. The shop is closed Monday. Bike rental is done at their other location, Bikes on Wheels (Map 9; ☎ 416-966-2453), 309 Augusta Ave (closed Sunday). Closer to downtown, Duke's Cycle (Map 9; ☎ 416-504-6138), 625 Queen St W, does lickety-split repairs and skate sharpening. If they're busy, try Cycle Shoppe (☎ 416-703-9990) at No 630-A across the street.

Farther east, in the Beach community, Quiet Storm (Map 11; ☎ 416-693-7368), 2229 Queen St E, and Planet Skate (Map 11; ☎ 416-690-7588), 2144 Queen St E, rent in-line skates while Recycle (Map 11; ☎ 416-698-3756), 2230 Queen St E, handles bike rental and repair.

PEDICAB

Pedicabs are deluxe bicycle rickshaws pedaled by sweating, fit young men and women who can be hired during summertime in the downtown, Harbourfront and Yorkville neighborhoods. The price is $3 per person per block.

ORGANIZED TOURS
Walking Tours

The quirky, well-qualified guides at A Taste of the World (☎ 416-923-6813) lead over a dozen different off-beat walking and cycling tours of Toronto's nooks and crannies; one visits the hidden ice-cream parlors of the city, another tries to unveil the ghosts of Yorkville. Prices vary from $15 to $45 for adults, depending on whether bike rental and snacks are included.
Web site: www.torontowalksbikes.com

Civitas (☎ 416-966-1550, civitas@compuserve.com) offers three summer City-Walks focusing on colonial, Victorian or modern architecture with historical tales of scandal and disaster thrown in. Tours run on weekends only, take about 1½ hours and cost $12 for adults. Call between 8 am and 10 pm to reserve a spot and check meeting times and places.

Heritage Toronto (☎ 416-392-6827 x230, info@torontohistory.on.ca) organizes over 50 free historical walks on weekends between late April and mid-October. Each of the unique tours, led by Heritage foundation members, museum staff or neighborhood historical society members, is given only once each summer.

Volunteers from the Royal Ontario Museum (ROM) lead free historical walking tours, rain or shine, on Sunday afternoon and Wednesday evening between late May and mid-September. The tours last between one and two hours; no advance reservations are necessary for most. Call ☎ 416-586-5513 for details, pick up a brochure at ROM (see the Things to See & Do chapter) or visit the museum Web site (www.rom.on.ca).

The Ontario Black History Society (Map 4; ☎ 416-867-9420), 10 Adelaide E, offers three-hour multicultural tours of Central Toronto every month. Tours highlight places where people of African descent lived, worked and made significant contributions to the evolution of the city, as well as abolitionist sites like the George Brown house. Call ahead to check dates and reserve tickets ($15 for adults).

Bus Tours

The reliable Gray Line (☎ 416-594-3310, 1-800-353-3484) runs basic two-hour, double-decker bus tours of central Toronto for $27, less for seniors and children. The hop-on, hop-off buses run every 30 minutes during the day from mid-April to mid-October.

Tours depart from the Metro Toronto Coach Terminal (Map 5) at 610 Bay. Tickets can be bought on the bus, or at the Gray Line desk in the Royal York Hotel. Passengers who book in advance can request pickups from downtown hotels or the HI hostel.

Olde Towne Tours (☎ 416-614-0999, 1-800-350-0398) uses pseudo-trolleys and double-decker buses for its hop-on, hop-off narrated tours around town. Hours vary seasonally, but tours operate year-round, costing $29/15 for adults/children. You can purchase tickets onboard or at Nicholby's Sports and Souvenirs, 123 Front St W, the bus departure point.

Boat Trips

Several companies run boat tours in and around the harbor and Toronto Islands roughly between May and September. Most boats depart from the Harbourfront beside Queen's Quay Terminal or at York Quay. For short harbor excursions, you can often just show up and buy a ticket from a makeshift ticket shack at the quay, though reservations by phone are recommended for brunch and dinner cruises. The Toronto Islands ferries (see the Boat section, earlier in this chapter) offer spectacular views of the city that are cheap by comparison.

The main operator is Mariposa Cruise Lines (☎ 416-203-0178, 1-800-976-2442). One-hour, basic narrated harbor tours depart several times daily and cost $15 for adults,

less for students, children and seniors. More leisurely (and expensive) dinner cruises include a buffet, cash bar and dancing.

Docked behind Harbourfront Centre, Leisure Cruise Lines (☎ 416-203-8711) offers daily one-hour cruises on its 50-foot yacht ($8).

The *Harbour Star* sets sail from York Quay for dinner cruises ($45 per person) to the strains of live classical music and with an award-winning chef. Reserve well in advance through Musique Aquatique Cruise Lines (☎ 416-410-0536, cruises@harbourstar .com), 264 Queen's Quay W, Suite 606.

If you'd like to 'sail on a "Tall Ship,"' the three-masted *Kajama* goes out one to three times daily between June and Labor Day. This authentic 1930s trading schooner rises 165 feet above the water and has a fully licensed bar. It's moored behind Harbourfront Centre, but the ticket kiosk is beside Queen's Quay Terminal. Tickets cost $16.95/ $10.95 adults/children – call ☎ 416-203-2322 for reservations.

Helicopter Flights

If your little rooftop bar tête-à-tête has ever been droned out by the whirring of helicopter wings, blame The Toronto Helicopter Company (☎ 416-203-3280, 1-888-445-8542). You, too, can be whisked away from Toronto's City Centre Airport for a six-minute trip over the downtown skyline for only $45 when you fly stand-by.

Things to See & Do

To tell the truth, Toronto is a very walkable city. Even reluctant pedestrians find themselves wandering from one different neighborhood to the next. The downtown area is clasped on almost all sides by a hodgepodge of bohemian, ethnic and historic neighborhoods, with the remaining southern edge crisply defined by Lake Ontario, one of the North America's Great Lakes.

Most out-of-towners start by taking long strides from downtown to the Harbourfront area, then up through Chinatown and over to Kensington Market and Little Italy, then back east through the museum district to Yorkville and down Yonge St. By the time these neophytes realize how many kilometers have passed under their feet, it's too late – they've already collapsed at the gargantuan Eaton Centre shopping mall.

Not to worry if your stamina gives out before this point though, since there are almost always subways, streetcars and (as a last resort) buses to whisk you back to where you started. Failing that, there's sure to be an outdoor café or pub for not going much of anywhere at all.

DOWNTOWN WALKING TOUR

Our walking tour is a biggie. If you don't stop anywhere, you could polish it off in 90 breathless minutes. But what's the point? You're better off carving out time for just those sites that most attract you – please feel free to pick and choose, making the tour a half-, all-day or even two-day affair. If you don't mind missing the Canadian National (CN) Tower (and really, no one should mind), start at the Theatre Block (King St) or Union Station. But on no account should you miss out on the Old Town of York. From there our tour takes on Bay St (Toronto's 'Wall Street') and the Eaton Centre on Yonge St, finishing at University Ave, the heart of government and law in Toronto, Ontario (otherwise known as just 'T.O.').

You'll find more things open the earlier in the day you start, as galleries, gardens and markets tend to close after 3 pm. Sites of particular interest are discussed in more depth in the following Downtown Toronto sections, and restaurants, bars and shops appear later in this book in their respective Places to Eat, Entertainment and Shopping chapters.

The Biggies

Even if we tell you not to, you'll probably feel obligated to go, so let's start at the **CN Tower** (☎ 416-360-8500, www.cntower.ca/). The highest freestanding structure in the

---

Highlights

- Cycling along the Harbourfront, then ferrying to the Toronto Islands and riding from Hanlan's Point beach to the lookout point on Ward's Island

- Touring the restored double-decker Elgin & Winter Garden Theatre Centre

- Soaking up the spices and smells of Kensington Market, then drinking fresh coconut milk on Chinatown's Spadina Ave

- Tripping through the Bata Shoe Museum

- Wandering along the Beach neighborhood's boardwalk at sunset on your way to the Art Deco Palace of Purification

- Ambling through the old town of York and the sedate St Lawrence Market, ending with a beer along the Esplanade

- Plunging into the flora of Allen Gardens conservatory or the junglelike ravines along Toronto's rivers

- Making your way through the PATH underground system and arriving at Eaton Centre's Trinity Square

- Indulging in late-night *mezes* (tapas) in Greektown after viewing a repertory film at the Music Hall cinema

- Escaping the city to Niagara Peninsula wine country and ending up at the glorious falls when the afternoon light is golden

THINGS TO SEE & DO

DOWNTOWN TORONTO WALKING TOUR

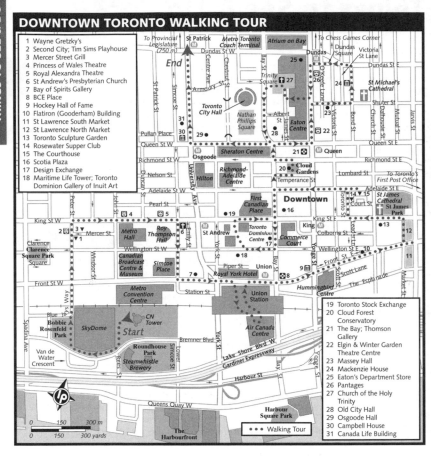

1 Wayne Gretzky's
2 Second City; Tim Sims Playhouse
3 Mercer Street Grill
4 Princess of Wales Theatre
5 Royal Alexandra Theatre
6 St Andrew's Presbyterian Church
7 Bay of Spirits Gallery
8 BCE Place
9 Hockey Hall of Fame
10 Flatiron (Gooderham) Building
11 St Lawrence South Market
12 St Lawrence North Market
13 Toronto Sculpture Garden
14 Rosewater Supper Club
15 The Courthouse
16 Scotia Plaza
17 Design Exchange
18 Maritime Life Tower; Toronto
   Dominion Gallery of Inuit Art

19 Toronto Stock Exchange
20 Cloud Forest Conservatory
21 The Bay; Thomson Gallery
22 Elgin & Winter Garden Theatre Centre
23 Massey Hall
24 Mackenzie House
25 Eaton's Department Store
26 Pantages
27 Church of the Holy Trinity
28 Old City Hall
29 Osgoode Hall
30 Campbell House
31 Canada Life Building

••• Walking Tour

world since 1976, this tower has become a symbol and landmark of Toronto. Its primary function is radio and TV communications. The top antenna had to be put in place by helicopter, making the tower 533m high. Glass elevators whisk you up the outside to observation decks at the top; for extra thrills, one deck has a glass floor, and the other is a windy, vertigo-inducing outside platform. On clear days you can see for about 160km. If it's hazy, however, you won't be able to see a thing.

Many visitors find the CN Tower a huge waste of time and money. During summer,

lines run up to two hours – going up *and* down. Entry just to the main observation deck is $16 for adults (plus $5 to get to the top deck), not including tax or the motion simulators and virtual-reality rides. A better deal is the 360 Revolving Restaurant (π 416-362-5411), because the elevator ticket price is waived; lunch, brunch or dinner starts at $30, and reservations are advised. The tower itself is open 8 am to 11 pm daily.

Built during the late '80s, when the city's economic outlook was bright, the **SkyDome** is technically awe-inspiring. It has the world's first fully retractable dome roof and can hold up to 67,000 people during mega-concerts or Toronto Blue Jays baseball games. High up on the exterior north face, look for the very human faces of Michael Snow's *Audience* sculptures looking right back at you.

Farther north, on Blue Jays Way, is **Wayne Gretzky's** (Key No 1), the restaurant owned by none other than 'The Greatest' hockey player who ever lived, according to Canadians. Walk around to the building's north side, on Mercer St, to see how No 34 thanks his fans with a huge wall-sized mural.

Catercorner from Wayne Gretzky's is **Second City** (Key No 2), the comedy club that trained many of Canada's great comics, including Gilda Radner, Dan Aykroyd and Mike Myers. Sharing its name with a comedy club in Chicago, the moniker dates from when each city played second fiddle in the past, Chicago to the Big Apple (New York City) and Toronto to Montréal (in the eyes of Montréalers, that is).

Just opposite Wayne Gretzky's is the eccentric-looking **Mercer Street Grill** (Key No 3). Cemented into the sidewalk in front of the restaurant is a western place setting with chopsticks. The back patio is adorned with a huge gigantic Hokusai woodblock print mural.

Theatre Block

Head north and make a right on King St to reach Toronto's theater district, called the Theatre Block, part of the larger Entertainment District.

A couple of blocks down and on your left, you'll pass Honest Ed's **Princess of Wales Theatre** (Key No 4), built for *Miss Saigon* in 1993; Princess Di herself attended the ceremonial opening.

About a block farther is the much-loved **Royal Alexandra Theatre** (Key No 5). Nicknamed the 'Royal Alex,' it was built by Toronto's youngest millionaire, Cawthra Mulock, in 1907. It was saved from demolition in the 1960s by 'Honest Ed' Mirvish, Toronto's discount-shopping king (see the Annex & Little Italy section, later), who restored its velvet and brocade Edwardian

luxury and put on productions of *Hair* and *Godspell* that woke up the entire district.

Across the street, that ugly donut (or inverted ballerina's tutu) is **Roy Thompson Hall**. Its controversial design has been called Neo-expressionist and 'deconstructionist.' It's a pity that no one has yet literally knocked it down. You may recognize the hall from the opening scene of the 2000 film *X-Men*. On the east side of the building, the Canadian Walk of Fame is a straggling line of concrete stars à la Hollywood with names that few will recognize, and even fewer that were born in Toronto.

The corner of King and Simcoe Sts you are now standing on was nicknamed 'Education, Legislation, Salvation and Damnation' in the 19th century because the Upper Canada College, Governor's House, church and a rowdy tavern faced off on opposite corners. Only salvation remains today at **St Andrew's Presbyterian Church** (Key No 6). Built in 1876, it's as much Scottish as it is Normanesque – note the twisted barley on certain interior columns and the grand French Classic–style organ decorated with Scottish thistle motifs.

Around Union Station

Passing the excellent **Bay of Spirits Gallery** (Key No 7) shop, you'll come upon the magisterial **Royal York Hotel**. It's just one of many grand chateaulike hotels built by the Canadian Pacific Railroad all across the nation to accommodate its passengers. Walk in the Front St entrance, turn around and look up above the doors to see a fresco landscape of Canadian history, from arctic Inuit natives to voyageurs in their canoes.

After 16 years of construction delays due to WWI and bureaucracy, the equally imposing Union Station finally opened in 1930. Ironically, this was long after the Royal York railway hotel had opened its doors. Designed by the great Montréal architects Ross and MacDonald, its classical revival style successfully signifies progress and prosperity. Enter the glorious ticket hall and take the escalators nearest the east wall down to the lower level. Hidden at the back are a set of gray doors that lead underground

to the **Air Canada Centre**, home of Toronto
Maple Leafs hockey and the NBA Raptors.
Events permitting, hourly guided tours
($9.50) take you where the players go, but
you'll enjoy the arena more if you can actually score tickets to a game.

Exiting Union Station onto Front street,
the impressive BCE Place (Key No 8) is
almost opposite. Its award-winning design
called for interior metal ribs, which look like
dinosaur bones, to support the weight of an
enormous glass atrium, filling the courtyard
of this postmodern office building with light.
Attached to it is the former Bank of Montréal building, a gorgeous, gray stone rococo
structure dating from 1886; it houses the
Hockey Hall of Fame (Key No 9; ☎ 416-360-
7765). This shrine gives fans all they could
ask for, and more. Try to virtually stop Wayne
Gretzky's winning shot or have your photo
taken with hockey's biggest prize – the one
and only Stanley Cup (or a replica). After
being overwhelmed with interactive history
exhibits and memorabilia, visitors unfamil-
iar with the game may come to an under-
standing of Canada's passion for this, the
fastest of sports. The museum is open 10 am
to 5 pm daily (until 6 pm in summer) and
charges an excessive $12/8 per adult/child.

Old Town of York

Continuing on Front St, many of the city's
oldest and best-preserved buildings come
into view. Established by Captain John Simcoe, the historic town of York was situated
in the southern portion of what is now
Toronto. It was bounded by Queen St, the
Esplanade, Victoria St and the Don River.

The **Flatiron (Gooderham) Building**
(Key No 10) was the headquarters of the
Gooderham distillery family starting in the
1890s. Resembling New York's Flatiron
Building, its unique triangular shape was
dictated by the angle at which the city's
grid system intersects the waterfront. The
famous trompe l'oeil mural on the building's western face mimics the restored 19th-
century warehouses with their cast-iron
facades on the other side of Front St.

Farther on, the **St Lawrence Market** (Key
Nos 11 & 12; see the Places to Eat chapter)

is actually two separate buildings. When the
South Market was refurbished in 1970,
workers uncovered Toronto's Old City Hall,
dating from 1845. The **Market Gallery**
(☎ 416-392-7604) upstairs is now the city's
exhibition hall, with rotating displays of
paintings, photographs, documents and historical artifacts (free, closed Monday and
Tuesday). On the north side of Front St, the
North Market is topped with a clock tower
and is considered one of the city's finest ex-
amples of Victorian classicism. After being
sadly neglected, it was at last cleaned up for
Canada's 100th birthday, in 1967. Heading
west on King St, the **Toronto Sculpture
Garden** (Key 13) doesn't contain much art
worth looking at, but it opens up grand
vistas of the downtown skyline.

Turning your gaze north, you'll see the
lovely gardens of venerable **St James Cathedral**, erected after the Great Fire of 1849
and graced by Tiffany stained glass, a grand
organ and the tallest spire in Canada.

Pay your respects to the city by strolling
up Toronto St, a narrow road full of elegant
triple-story office buildings built in the 19th
century. One now houses the **Rosewater
Supper Club** (Key No 14). Around the corner is **The Courthouse** (Key No 15), the site
of Toronto's last public execution. It's now a
bar & grill; check out the jail-cell bathrooms
in the basement.

Continue east if you'd like to step off the
set walking tour to check out Toronto's First
Post Office (☎ 416-865-1833), 260 Adelaide
St W. Dating from the 1830s, it is now a living museum. After writing your correspondence with a quill pen and ink, costumed
staff will seal your letters with wax and send
them postmarked 'York-Toronto 1833' for a
small fee (entry free).

Bay Street

Jumping a over a century and a half of
progress, walk west into the windy corridor
of Bay St, Canada's premier financial district. The dignified **Scotia Plaza** (Key No 16)
has 1930s style bas reliefs and old-fashioned
teller cages.

Farther south, the Art Deco **Design Exchange** (Key No 17) served as the original

Ferrying the Toronto Islands

Greeting visitors to Niagara

Surveying the Toronto skyline from Centre Island

JON DAVISON

The Flatiron (Gooderham) Building

SARA BENSON

Cabbagetown Bay & Gable architecture

CURTIS MARTIN

Experience postmodernity at BCE Place.

ANDRE JENNY

Romanesque Old City Hall with new friend

Four servings a day – even in Toronto!

Did someone say 'dolmas'? (Greektown)

Who could ask for anything more?

SARA BENSON

El Mocambo Club, Spadina Ave

NEIL SETCHFIELD

Doin' the Yonge St shuffle

RICK GERHARTER

Look out for Cabbagetown wildlife!

RICK GERHARTER

All the old timers get their fish here.

Toronto Stock Exchange starting in 1937; its opening pushed Toronto ahead of Montréal as the nation's investment center. The frontal 74-foot stone frieze depicts toilers in Canadian industry; inside are changing exhibits of very contemporary design.

The three stark, black skyscrapers of the **Toronto-Dominion Centre** were designed in the International Style and overseen by Ludwig Mies van der Rohe, the German prophet of the Modernist Movement in architecture. When IM Pei, who also designed Paris's Pyramide du Louvre, drew up plans for the **Commerce Court**, across the street, he was careful to make it one story taller. Much later a fourth Toronto-Dominion tower was added on the other side of Wellington St. It recently changed its name to the **Maritime Life Tower**, but the **Toronto Dominion Gallery of Inuit Art** (Key No 18) is still there on the ground and mezzanine floors, displaying Native carvings and sculptures in stone and bone (free, open daily).

Back on King St, inside **First Canadian Place** you'll find the FCP Network Gallery of contemporary Canadian art, also free for wandering. Next door, stocks worth $100 million are bought and sold each day at the high-tech **Toronto Stock Exchange** (Key No 19), which relocated here in 1987 during Toronto's boom years. There is no longer a trading floor, since everything is computerized, but the interactive Stock Market Place (☎ 416-947-4676) demystifies stock transactions and high-finance for small-fry capitalists (ie, kiddies), at a cost of $3 for them and $5 per adult; it's open 10 am to 5 pm weekdays.

Head east back to Bay St and turn left. Make a right on Temperance St, and you'll find a beautiful relief from high-powered Bay St: The **Cloud Forest Conservatory** (Key No 30) is an unexpected sanctuary in the downtown core. Built vertically as a 'modernist ruin,' it has exposed steel, creeping vines, a waterfall and a mural depicting construction workers (free, open 10 am to 3 pm weekdays). Walk through the park north to the Bay department store. On its 9th floor, the **Thomson Gallery** (Key No 21; ☎ 416-861-4572) has a small but elegant collection

of fine 19th- and 20th-century Canadian painting, including works by Emily Carr (admission $2.50, closed Sunday).

Yonge Street

Once a humble oxcart trail, Toronto's Yonge St is now the start of what *The Guinness Book of World Records* officially designates the 'longest road in the world'. (Later, look for the concrete sidewalk inscription and map testifying to this fact on the northeast side of Eaton Centre). The street follows the trail used by Natives and colonial traders portaging their canoes on their way north to avoid risking the exposed waters of the Great Lakes.

On Yonge St you'll see the **Elgin & Winter Garden Theatre Centre** (Key No 22), the last and only operating double-decker theater in world. Around the corner on Shuter St is **Massey Hall** (Key No 23), a Toronto landmark given to the city in 1894 by farm-machinery magnate Hart Massey. Orators, explorers and other famous people (including Mary Pickford and Oscar Wilde) have all appeared on its stage. The acoustics are superb, and that's why the Toronto Symphony Orchestra still occasionally plays here.

Loop around to the **Mackenzie House** (Key No 24), on Bond St, then take Dundas St back to Yonge. If you'd like to head north on Yonge St (going off the walking tour), you will find, at Yonge and Gould Sts, the Chess Games Corner. Here, through all kinds of weather, night and day, chess players and aficionados of every sort gather to duel and bet. It all began with the late 'open highway' Joe Smolij in 1977, who can

My knight can kick your knight's ass!

be found in *The Guinness Book of Records* as the world's fastest chess player.

If you head south on Yonge St, on your right you'll see the historic **Eaton's department store** (Key No 25), which spawned the modern **Eaton Centre**. Even though this shopping complex was completed in 1979, you would be forgiven for thinking it's still under construction, since no attention has been paid to the exterior whatsoever. Inside it's all sweetness and light, with trees and sculpted Canada geese by Michael Snow

What's Free?

In addition to Pay What You Can (PWYC) museum admission and theater performances, here's a quick day-by-day rundown of what to do when your wallet's running on empty:

Any Day (variable)
Second City improv nights
Cloud Forest Conservatory
Allan Gardens
CBC Museum and Glenn Gould Studio concerts
Visitors' gallery and tours of the provincial legislature
Grounds of Ontario Place – after 5 pm
Metro Toronto Police Museum
Toronto Dominion Gallery of Inuit Art
History of Contraception Museum

Tuesday
Bata Shoe Museum and Gardiner Museum of Ceramic Art – 1st Tuesday of every month
Casa Loma gardens – summer only, after 4:45 pm

Wednesday
Power Plant Art Gallery – after 5 pm

Friday
Royal Ontario Museum – after 4:30 pm

Weekends
Salsa lessons at El Convento Rico and Plaza Flamingo (see the Entertainment chapter)

Sunday
Afternoon yoga at the Sivananda Centre

(remember the SkyDome?) suspended from its immense glass galleria roof.

Farther on is **Pantages** (Key No 26), a classic 1920s vaudeville theater worth visiting just for its gorgeous lobby. Since hosting the long-running *Phantom of the Opera*, however, the theater has been empty, for the most part.

Enter Eaton Centre and exit out the west side, into **Trinity Square**, named for the **Church of the Holy Trinity** (Key No 27). When this Anglican church opened in 1847, it was the first in the city not to charge parishioners for pews, courtesy of an anonymous Englishwoman who was reportedly quite taken with the presiding bishop. Interestingly, this church is where Canada's Cowboy Junkies recorded their critically acclaimed *Trinity Sessions* in just 14 hours. It's a funky, welcoming cross between a house of worship and a drop-in center – everything a community-oriented inner-city church should be. Don't miss the wonderful Christmas pageant if you're in town in December.

University Avenue

Walk west to **Toronto City Hall**, which fronts Nathan Phillips Square. On the other side of Bay St is the **Old City Hall** (Key No 28), the definitive work of Toronto architect EJ Lennox, the same man who built Casa Loma (see the Annex & Little Italy section, later). He was chastised for inscribing his name just below the eaves of this Romanesque hall, which has a distinctive off-center bell tower and today houses legal courtrooms. Inside is a stained-glass-window allegory of justice.

Walk west of the twin city halls along Queen St, toward University Ave, to historic **Osgoode Hall** (Key No 29). When you next cross University Avenue, note the Japanese pedestrian signals that chirp like birds. From here you can drop in at **Campbell House** (Key No 30) or walk north to the monumental **Canada Life Building** (Key No 31). At the lobby security desk, pick up a weather card that explains the mysteries of the Beacon Tower on top. If it's flashing white, everyone knows that snow is on the way.

Our walking tour ends here, but the parliament buildings of the Ontario provincial legislature are clearly visible at the northern end of University Ave, a short walk away. If you're still raring to go after that, Heritage Toronto (☎ 416-392-6827), 205 Yonge St, stocks more walking-tour booklets with loads of historical background – you couldn't possibly exhaust them all. See also Walking Tours under Organized Tours in the Getting Around chapter.

DOWNTOWN TORONTO (SOUTH; Map 4)
SkyDome

At 1 Blue Jays Way beside the CN Tower, this dome-roofed sports stadium (☎ 416-341-2770) opened in 1989 with the world's first fully retractable dome roof. Made mostly of concrete, this feat of engineering moves at a rapid 71ft per minute, taking just 20 minutes to open completely. This certainly beats Montréal's Olympic Stadium, which opened once and failed to ever do so again.

Although far from eye-pleasing on the outside, the SkyDome's interior is striking. One-hour tours (a pricey $10.50) are offered on the hour between 10 am and 3 pm, events permitting. After watching a 10-minute introductory film, the tour sprints up to a box suite, takes in the view from the stands and press section, and briefly walks through a locker room (without athletes). Did you know that eight 747s would fit on the playing field and that the stadium uses enough electricity to light the province of Prince Edward Island?

A cheap seat to a Blue Jays baseball game or Argonauts football match is the least expensive way to see the SkyDome. When no game is on, the SkyDome's own Hard Rock Café runs as a regular sports bar; you can simply go in for a hamburger and a beer and have a look at the playing field. During games, tables with views must be paid for. For those with money (and lots of it), rooms overlooking the field can be rented at the SkyDome's own Renaissance hotel.

Canadian Broadcasting Centre

Apparently made of Lego blocks, the Canadian Broadcasting Centre (☎ 416-205-8605), 250 Front St W, serves as the headquarters for English-language public radio and TV programming across Canada. The French-language production facilities are in Montréal, which leaves the president, in a truly Canadian spirit of compromise, alone in an executive office in Ottawa.

One-hour CBC tours don't really take you much 'behind the scenes' and definitely aren't worth $7. However, the free CBC Museum, on the ground level, has attention-getting exhibits on the history of Canadian pop culture and a do-it-yourself video puppet theater (open 10 am to 5 pm weekdays, noon to 4 pm Saturday).

On weekdays between 6 and 8 am, you can join the audience of CBC Morning, which broadcasts live from the main lobby. Late-risers can take a peek at the radio newsrooms all day or attend a free concert in the world-class Glenn Gould Studio, where the soundtrack to *Schindler's List* was recorded (☎ 416-205-5555). Call ahead or check the Canadian Broadcast Centre's Web site (www.cbc.ca) for other special-events information.

Harbourfront

The Harbourfront area was once a run-down district of warehouses, factories and docklands along Lake Ontario. Once slated for redevelopment, Queen's Quay W gained galleries, cultural centers and outdoor entertainment venues, most of them springing up between Yonge St and Spadina Ave. However, construction has been allowed to run amok: much of the waterfront has been blighted by ugly condos. The lakeshore is still underutilized, but any further progress has been stymied by wrangling among governmental bodies and the 2008 Olympic Committee.

Nevertheless, on weekends the Harbourfront is quite popular for walks in the lakeshore breezes. Most people stroll down from Union Station on York St or take the 509 Harbourfront or 510 Spadina streetcars right along the quay. Parking in the area can be a headache, with daily (no hourly) rates of $10 or more.

Start your stroll at **Queen's Quay Terminal**, a refurbished 1927 warehouse filled with specialty arts-and-crafts shops, as well as the Premier Dance Theatre. Outside, vociferous ticket sellers hawk assorted harbor cruises (see the Getting Around chapter).

In an old power station closer to the water, the **Power Plant Art Gallery** hosts rotating exhibitions of contemporary North American art; it's open noon to 6 pm Tuesday to Sunday, until 8 pm Wednesday. Admission costs $4, but it's free on Wednesday after 5pm. It's behind the prestigious **du Maurier Theatre Centre**.

Throughout the summer, especially on weekends, **York Quay Centre** puts on world-music shows, ballet and opera performances and other special events, many especially for kids and most free. Some take place on the covered outdoor concert stage beside the lake; pick up a schedule of events at the information desk (☎ 416-973-3000) or box office (☎ 416-973-4000) inside. You can also visit the **Photo Passage** photography gallery and **Craft Studio**, a series of workshops where artists blow glass and mold clay; both are free and open daily.

Take the footbridge west over to the restored 1930s shipping warehouse that holds the kid-oriented **Pier Waterfront Museum** (☎ 416-338-7437, 1-888-675-7437). Energetic museum guides expound the trading history of Lake Ontario and all things nautical, including the lost art of iceboating. Admission is $5; it's open 10 am to 4 pm daily mid-March to October, later in peak season. For serious adult mariners, wooden boat–building classes are taught in the workshop.

Farther east, the Harbourfront Canoe & Kayak School (see the Activities section, later), in the Nautical Centre, rents boats.

Redpath Sugar Museum

At 95 Queen's Quay East, the Redpath Sugar Mill (☎ 416-366-3561) is a waterfront landmark. Inside the working industrial complex is a free museum featuring an educational film on production of the sweet stuff (teasingly titled *Raising Cane*), as well as equipment exhibits. Factory operations permitting, it's open 10 am to noon and 1 to 3:30 pm weekdays; call ahead to check. Enter by the Yonge St gate and follow the museum signs.

Fort York

Established by the British in 1793 to protect the town of York, as Toronto was then known, this fort (☎ 416-392-6907) was mostly destroyed during the War of 1812, when a small band of Ojibwa warriors and British troops couldn't stop the invading US fleet. The American troops went on to raze and loot the capital city but were kicked out after just six days. The fort was quickly rebuilt, and today, eight of the original log, stone and brick buildings have been restored.

In summer, men decked out in 19th-century British military uniforms carry out marches and drills and fire musket volleys. However, kids who visit much prefer running around the fort's embankments with wooden rifles – and they couldn't care less about the bits of history left inside, which, frankly, are missable. Admission costs $5/3.25 for adults/children, including tours given on the hour. The fort is open 10 am to 5 pm daily from late May to early September, closing at 4 pm in winter. It's on Garrison Rd, which runs off Fleet St W, east of Strachan Ave. Free parking is available, or take the No 511 Bathurst streetcar south to Fleet street and then walk west. Just look for the old Union Jack waving in the breeze.

Exhibition Place

For much of the year, Exhibition Place (see Map 2 for location) is bereft of visitors, apart from conventioneers or those headed to the Canada Sports Hall of Fame (free, open 10 am to 4:30 pm weekdays). However, for four weeks in August and September, the grounds are revived for their original purpose, namely the gargantuan Canadian National Exhibition (CNE). Millions of visitors pass under the Princes' Gate entrance every year to visit 'The Ex' (see Special Events, in the Facts for the Visitor chapter), with it's carnival rides and lumberjack competitions. The beaux-arts winged Victory statue over the gate has been there since the first exhibition, held in 1927 on the occasion of Canada's 60th birthday. To reach Exhibition Place, take the No 511 Bathurst streetcar south or the No 509 Harbourfront streetcar west from Union Station. Cyclists can get here via the Martin Goodman Trail, which runs along the lakeshore.

Ontario Place

This 40-hectare recreation complex (☎ 416-314-9900), 955 Lake Shore Blvd W, is built on three artificial islands offshore from Exhibition Place. Its spacious design and lakeside setting make it an attractive, easy way to escape downtown in summer, but the privilege of grounds admission costs $10 (free after 5 pm). For parents, there's a popular children's play area, where you can let them go nuts. Day passes entitle you to selected attractions and walk-up seating at the Cinesphere IMAX cinema, where 70mm films are shown on a six story-high curved screen. Passes are valid until 5 pm and cost $24.50/11 for adults/children (adults get away with paying just $15 for an evening pass after 5 pm). Additional attractions, such as the human-sized MegaMaze or the 700m-long flume water slide with simulated rapids and tunnels, must be paid for separately, the same goes for the HMCS *Huida*, a WWII destroyer moored outside the east entrance. In summer there are nightly concerts at the Molson Amphitheatre; a concert ticket permits grounds entry for the whole day.

The park is generally open 10 am to midnight mid-May to early September, but most attractions close by 9 pm. On rainy days, many of the activities, restaurants and rides do not operate. If you are driving, parking is a whopping $9.

DOWNTOWN TORONTO (NORTH; Map 5)
Elgin & Winter Garden Theatre Centre

This is the last operating double-decker theater in the world, a restored masterpiece right on downtown Yonge St. Built in 1913 as the flagship for a vaudeville chain that never really took off, the Winter Garden was eventually closed, while the downstairs

Elgin was converted into a movie house in the 1920s. After the advent of TV, cinemas across Canada began to close, and the Elgin lost customers, declining into a kung-fu and dodgy XXX cinema in the 1970s.

The Ontario Heritage Foundation saved both theaters from being demolished in 1981 and brought in a new production of *Cats* to spur public interest during its $29-million restoration effort: Bread dough was used to uncover original rose-garden frescoes, the Belgian company that made the original carpeting was contacted for fresh rolls, and the beautiful foliage hanging from the ceiling of the upstairs Winter Garden Theatre was replaced, leaf by painstaking leaf. With hanging colored lanterns and seats from Chicago's own Biograph Theater, it's a breathtaking sight.

Thoroughly entertaining public tours (☎ 416-314-2901) are worth every penny of the $7 ticket price. Tours are given Thursday at 5 pm and Saturday at 11 am by the same passionate volunteers who staff ongoing restoration efforts. If you're wondering where all the funding comes from, note the Eaton's Grand Staircase inside and the American Express box office from which you bought your ticket.

Mackenzie House

This gaslit Victorian home (☎ 416-392-6915), 82 Bond St, was owned by William Lyon Mackenzie, the city's first mayor and the leader of the failed Upper Canada Rebellion of 1837. It's well furnished with 19th-century antiques; note the brass door knocker, presented to Mackenzie in 1859 after his return from exile in America. In the basement is a working 19th century–style print shop. It's said that on certain nights the machines can be heard working. T-shirts printed with 'William Lyon Mackenzie: Rebel with a Cause' are sold in the adjoining gift shop. Admission to the house costs $3.50; it's usually open only in the afternoon (closed Monday).

Toronto City Hall

The distinctive, much-maligned new City Hall (☎ 416-392-7341) was Toronto's first jump into modernity. The twin clamshell towers, with a flying saucer–style structure between them at the bottom, were completed in 1965 to Finnish architect Viljo Revell's award-winning design. Frank Lloyd Wright called it a 'headmarker for a grave,' and in a macabre twist of fate, Revell died before construction was complete. When sculptor Henry Moore first offered to sell 'The Archer,' a piece located in the gardens, out of his own personal collection and at a low price, the city council (unbelievably) refused. You can pick up a self-guided-tour booklet of City Hall inside the lobby.

Nathan Phillips Square out front is a meeting place for skaters, demonstrators, office workers on lunch break and, in summer, concerts and special events. Canada's rock band Barenaked Ladies were once banned from playing here ('too scandalous,' said the mayor), but were invited back in a conciliatory gesture just last year. In winter the attractive fountain pool becomes a popular ice-skating rink (rental skates available). Don't feel intimidated if you are a novice – you won't be alone. Immigrants from around the world are out there gingerly making strides toward assimilation.

Osgoode Hall

This classical hall (☎ 416-947-3300) was built in stages during the Victorian era as a showcase for elite colonials, many of whom were lawyers. The building looks like a hybrid of an Italian Renaissance palazzo and Versailles. The peculiar wrought-iron 'cow gates' out front were put up to keep out wandering bovines, a common street problem in the 1860s. Inside the hall a grand staircase leads up to the Ontario superior courts and the Great Library, with miles of books, twisting rickety stairways and 40-foot-high vaulted ceilings. Free tours are given at 1:15 pm weekdays from July to early September by students of the Law Society of Upper Canada, whose members have been pacing the grounds for 160 years.

Campbell House

This formal Georgian mansion (☎ 416-597-0227), 160 Queen St W, from 1822 was one of the first brick buildings built in Toronto. It belonged to Chief Justice William Campbell, the same judge who presided over the famous Types Trial of 1826. It has been beautifully refurbished in 19th-century style by the Advocates' Society, which now uses the premises as its clubhouse. Startlingly, it took six hours to move the historic house from its original location, just 1.5km away. Tours ($3.50) are given continually year-round between 9 am and 4:30 pm weekdays, as well as noon to 4 pm on weekends in summer.

Queen Street West

Queen St W is mainly for shopping, but on the corner of John St there's a public video booth, the **Speaker's Corner**. For a loonie ($1), anyone can step inside and record themselves doing or saying pretty much anything. Later, the most creative and controversial segments are broadcast on City TV's *Speaker's Corner* program, airing Sundays at 2 and 7:30 pm. On Friday nights, club kids decked out in hipper-than-thou gear wait in front of the adjacent glassed-in studios of MuchMusic, the equivalent of MTV; glimpse the lucky ones inside dancing on the show *Electric Circus*, which broadcasts Fridays at 9 pm. At other times, you might see pop stars dashing into their limos – if one is expected, Toronto fans line up à la Beatlemania. Next door, the Chum City TV store is worth a peek for its mini-museum in back, running continuous loops of Marilyn Monroe's television appearances. Finally, on the west side of the building (look up), a City Pulse news truck spinning its wheels crashes out of the City TV studio walls.

Art Gallery of Ontario

Though not the Louvre, the collections of the Art Gallery of Ontario (AGO; ☎ 416-979-6648), at 317 Dundas St W, are excellent, and unless you have a lot of stamina, you'll need more than one trip to see it all. Highlights include rare Québecois religious statuary, First Nations and Inuit carvings, and major Canadian works by Emily Carr and the Group of Seven (see Arts in the Facts for the Visitor chapter). The museum is best known for its Henry Moore sculpture

Gallery Hopping

If you'd like something that feeds your mind, but you can't bear to concentrate on another museum, take in Toronto's adventurous art-gallery scene for an afternoon (except Sunday or Monday, when most galleries are closed).

Start by joining the moneyed set at Yorkville's contemporary and Native art galleries. The airy **Isaacs/Inuit Gallery** (Map 6), 9 Prince Arthur Ave, and **Feheley Fine Arts** (Map 6), 14 Hazelton Ave, have exquisite prints and Inuit carvings that must cost about 5% of the annual budget of Nunavut, Canada's newest arctic province. The **Guild Gallery** (Map 6; ☎ 416-921-1721), 118 Cumberland St, displays works in glass, pottery and wood by contemporary Ontarian craftspeople and hosts arts-related events. Abstract and emerging art reigns at **ArtCore** (Map 6), 33 Hazelton Ave, and **Gallery One** (Map 6), 121 Scollard St. For a taste of the subcontinent, visit **Gallery 7 & India Arts Centre**, at 118 Scollard St.

The old lithograph factory (Map 4), 401 Richmond W St W, downtown, has been converted into a multilevel arts space with an artists' café and floors full of galleries. Especially worth a look is the contemporary photography at **Gallery 44** and the multidiscipline, political shows at **A Space**. Lying somewhere around the building you'll find the city's free bimonthly *Slate* gallery guide, for further explorations.

Jane Corkin Gallery (Map 5), 179 John St, is Toronto's prestigious showplace for vintage and contemporary prints, especially during the World Photography Festival, in May. A respite from the hurly-burly W Queen St W scene, **Stephen Bulger Gallery** (Map 9), 700 Queen St W, has well-curated exhibitions of social-documentary photography. You may want to head a block or two east to the **Queen West Tattoo Museum** (Map 9), 602 Queen St W, where tacky movie stills and body-art photos lead to an actual tattoo parlor.

Those looking for a more international angle can drop by the Alliance Française, the Goethe-Institut, the Italian Cultural Institute or the Japan Foundation for excellent (and usually free) exhibitions of thought-provoking cultural photography and other arts media. For locations, see Libraries & Cultural Centers, in the Facts for the Visitor chapter.

---

pavilion; outside are benches with sit-down listening stations, one of which recounts the controversy over the city's acquisition of Moore's work (see the Toronto City Hall entry earlier).

The AGO is open 11 am to 6 pm Tuesday to Friday, until 8:30 pm on Wednesday, and 10 am to 5:30 pm on weekends and holidays. The suggested donation is $6 for adults. Tickets are required for special exhibitions, usually $8 to $12, and include admission to permanent collections. For schedule information regarding free gallery tours and Cinematheque Ontario films in Jackman Hall (see the Entertainment chapter), check at the information desk or the museum's Web site (www.ago.net).

Looking out onto its own park, **The Grange** is a restored Georgian house that's actually part of the AGO and is included in the admission price. Authentic 19th-century furniture and staff in period dress present life in a 'gentleman's residence' of the time, staying in character without so much as a snicker. The Grange is open shorter hours than the AGO, usually noon to 4 pm Tuesday to Sunday, until 8:30 pm Wednesday.

Museum for Textiles

Obscurely situated with no walk-in traffic, this museum (Subway: St Patrick; ☎ 416-599-5515) will enrapture anyone with the slightest interest in handmade textiles and tapestries. Exhibits draw from Latin America, Africa, Europe, South-East Asia and India, as well as contemporary Canada; the Indonesian ikat collection is particularly fine. Admission is $5, or Pay What You Can

(PWYC) after 5 pm on Wednesday; open 11 am to 5 pm Tuesday to Friday, until 8 pm Wednesday, and noon to 5 pm weekends. The museum can be found (look hard) at 55 Centre Ave.

Baldwin Village

A short stroll north of the AGO, Baldwin St makes a shady retreat from the city's heat and noise. As evidenced by the Yiddish sign at No 29, the village has Jewish roots. But the definite bohemian air comes from counterculture US exiles who decamped here after immigrating during the Vietnam War era. The spillover from nearby Chinatown makes things even more interesting, and in summer the eclectic restaurants and outdoor cafés are full to bursting (see the Places to Eat chapter).

Chinatown

Toronto's principal Chinatown area is right in the center of the city. It originally ran along Dundas St W, but its busiest thoroughfare nowadays is Spadina Ave. A brilliant vermilion **twin dragon gate** next to the Spadina streetcar stop just north of Dundas St marks the epicenter. The whole area looks more like Little Saigon or Bangkok every year, as Vietnamese and South-East Asian immigrants continue to.

There are, of course, piles of Asian restaurants here, but there are also pungent grocery stores, herbalists, bakeries and places selling mysterious items recognizable only to the initiated. Vendors often set up along the already cramped sidewalk space in summer; just wander down and buy a fresh coconut or some spiky rambutan.

There's a smaller pocket of Chinese merchants and restaurants around Gerrard St E and Broadview Ave in East Central Toronto (Map 10). Most of the immigrants here seem to have just stepped off the boat (or plane), and almost everything is in Chinese.

YORKVILLE & UNIVERSITY OF TORONTO (Map 6)

Once Toronto's smaller version of Greenwich Village or Haight-Ashbury, the old countercultural bastion of Yorkville has become the city's trés glamorous shopping and gallery district, done up with glitzy restaurants, nightspots and outdoor cafés for eyeing the passing parade of Jaguars, Bentleys and classic convertibles. Long gone are the penny-pinching rooming houses and bohemian cafés where Joni Mitchell and the Lovin' Spoonful got their starts, but atmospheric **Old York Lane** gives you just a glimpse of old times.

The busiest streets are Yorkville Ave, Cumberland St, and Hazelton Ave, all just north of Bloor St. Nudged in between art galleries on Hazelton Ave, the stately **Toronto Heliconian Club** rises in Carpenter Gothic Revival style, with a unique carved rose window and wooden spire. It originally belonged to the Olivet Congregational Church (1875) but was taken over by the Heliconian Club, an association for women in the arts and letters, in 1923.

At 34 Yorkville Ave, the 19th-century **Firehall No 10** is still in use. It bears the coat of arms from Toronto's old town hall, symbolically depicting the former councilors'

SARA BENSON

Carpenter Gothic Revival for the Heliconians

occupations. Its neighbor is the **Toronto Public Library – Yorkville Branch**, one of hundreds of bold 'Carnegie Classical' libraries built by philanthropist Andrew Carnegie in the early 1900s across North America.

Royal Ontario Museum

The multidiscipline ROM (Subway: Museum; ☎ 416-586-8000) is Canada's largest museum, filling up five floors to cover natural science, ancient civilization and art. The Chinese temple sculptures and Gallery of Korean Art are some of the best anywhere in the world. Kids will be mesmerized by the dinosaur rooms and the replica of an immense bat cave found in Jamaica.

Next to the front staircases (not the escalators), leading up to European period rooms and Egyptian mummies on the 3rd floor, are four towering crest poles carved by First Nations tribes in British Columbia. The largest (85m) was shipped from the west coast by train, then lowered through the museum roof, leaving only centimeters to spare.

That said, the ROM is not nearly as impressive as it sounds, and for most adults, a quick walk-through suffices. After 4:30 pm on Friday, admission is free. Otherwise admission costs $12/6 for adults/children. The museum is open 10 am to 6 pm Monday to Saturday, until 9:30 pm on Friday, and 11 am to 6 pm Sunday. For special programs, lectures and concerts, check the Web site (www.rom.on.ca).

Children's Own Museum

That dome squatting beside the ROM at 90 Queen's Park Ave is a kids' museum (☎ 416-542-1492). It's geared exclusively toward fun, interactive learning for children under 8 years old. There are play areas, such as the garden and hands-on construction sites; a wall of musical instruments; and an art workshop for those budding Emily Carrs. Admission is $4.75 per person, large or small, but PWYC Friday after 1 pm. The museum is open 10 am to 5 pm daily.

Gardiner Museum of Ceramic Art

This excellent museum (☎ 416-586-8080) is opposite the ROM at 111 Queen's Park Ave. It has quite an extensive collection spread over two floors and several millennia of ceramic history: pre-Columbian, Italian Renaissance majolica, English 17th-century tavern ware and the renowned Bell collection of blue-and-white Chinese porcelain. On Sunday afternoons you can drop in at the Clay Pit for hands-on pottery demonstrations. Admission costs $5 for adults, less for students and seniors. It's open 10 am to 6 pm daily, until 8 pm Tuesday and Thursday, and closes at 5 pm on weekends. The first Tuesday of every month is free.

Bata Shoe Museum

Designed to resemble a stylized lidded shoebox, this quirky museum (Subway: St George; ☎ 416-979-7799), 327 Bloor St W, has much more to offer anyone than you might imagine. Kids and adults (of both sexes) gawk at the 19th-century chestnut-

COURTESY OF BATA SHOE MUSEUM

These boots aren't made for walkin'.

crushing clogs from France and famous footware belonging to Elton John, Indira Gandhi, even Pablo Picasso. Over 10,000 pedi-artifacts stored here were hunted down in every corner of the globe by Sonja Bata, of the same family that founded Canada's well-known Bata Shoes company.

Beginning with a replica set of footprints almost four million years old, the permanent exhibits cover the evolution of human footwear, from the gruesome to the gorgeous. Rotating exhibitions are thoughtfully curated and often have featured selections from the museum's immense collections of Canadian Inuit and circumpolar tribal footwear. On the 3rd floor, you can peek through glass windows at curators effecting shoe restoration.

Admission costs $6/2 for adults/children and is free the first Tuesday of every month. It's open 10 am to 5 pm Tuesday to Saturday (until 8 pm Thursday) and from noon to 5 pm Sunday. If you miss out on visiting, the Web site (www.batashoemuseum.ca) lets you view some of the museum treasures.

Provincial Legislature

The attractive, pinkish sandstone building sitting in Queen's Park, just north of College St at University Ave, is the seat of Ontario's provincial legislature. The parliamentary building dates from 1892, and there are usually a few hospital employees picnicking on the lawn or some stray demonstrators writing up sandwich boards and picketing the front entrance.

Free tours (☎ 416-325-7500) are given frequently on weekdays, daily in summer, but schedules vary, so call first. For some homegrown entertainment, head for the visitors gallery when the legislative assembly is in session (roughly, October to December and February to June). It's free, but security regulations are in full force. You may not smoke, write, read or applaud (who would?) while the honorable members discuss such pressing issues as Ski-Doo (snowmobile) safety.

University of Toronto

On University Ave, just north of College St, is the principal campus of the prestigious University of Toronto, or just 'UT' for short. It's Canada's largest university and has been a guardian and wellspring of Canadian literature in English, counting Margaret Atwood among its alumni.

Free walking tours of the historic campus buildings start from the Nona Macdonald Visitors Centre (☎ 416-978-5000), 25 King's College Circle, at 10:30 am, 1 pm and 2:30 pm on weekdays between July and August, with special theatrical walking tours led by actors at 11:30 am on Saturday. Student tour guides will tell you all about the haunted love triangle involving the stone masons who worked on **University College** and point out how the old campus cannons aim toward the provincial legislature buildings, which are only a stone's throw (or one good shot) east of campus. Next to **Hart House** is the **Soldiers' Tower** memorial to students who gave their lives during the world wars. Farther west, the **UT Art Centre** is a contemporary art gallery (free, open noon to 6 pm Tuesday to Friday and, except during summer, noon to 4 pm Saturday). Across Hoskin Ave the ultraconservative **Trinity College** is worth a peek for its traditional quadrangle and the **Anglican chapel** designed by Sir Giles Scott, the man responsible for Britain's ubiquitous red telephone booths. The cathedral-like chapel has a modern altar that challenges traditional ideas of religious art.

Metro Toronto Police Museum

The police museum (☎ 416-808-7020), inside the impressive Toronto police headquarters at 40 College St, has a small but diverting collection of equipment, uniforms and crime-related paraphernalia from 1834 to the present day. Visitors can sit in the patrol car and flash the lights (but not the siren). This is also the place for wannabe sleuths to learn how DNA can be traced from a simple cigarette butt.

The display of major firepower confiscated from the streets of Toronto certainly gives one pause. More macabre are the exhibits of evidence taken from noteworthy cases, for example the personal possessions of the last man hanged in Canada (in 1962) or the Boyd Gang, a group of bank robbers who escaped from the Don Jail twice before being caught for good (third time's a charm). The police museum is open daily; free.

Church Street

Toronto's gay village, referred to simply as Church St, stretches along its main, pulsing artery from Isabella to Alexander Sts. The hot spot is around Wellesley St, where you'll find quite a few cafés, restaurants and nightclubs (see Lesbigay Venues, in the Entertainment Chapter). Next to the 519 Community Centre, in Cawthra Square Park, is the restrained **AIDS Memorial**. Plaques inscribed with the names of people who have died of AIDS (listed by year starting with 1981) are affixed to pillars in the ground. What's chilling is the number of spaces left set in the ground for more columns to fill in years to come.

Farther south at the intersection of Carlton St stands historic **Maple Leaf Gardens**, for years the home of Toronto Maple Leafs hockey since their opening game against the Chicago Black Hawks in 1931 (the Hawks won). Over the years, Elvis Presley, Chubby Checker and the Beatles all played concerts here, too. But the Leafs have moved to the Air Canada Centre and now only use the gardens as a practice venue. After rumors that this piece of history was to be torn down, the gardens are instead being redeveloped into – you guessed it – a shopping and entertainment complex.

THE ANNEX & LITTLE ITALY (Map 8)

West of Spadina Ave and the UT campus, The Annex is predominantly a student neighborhood, overflowing with pubs, pan-global restaurants, organic grocery stores and the cheapest discount shopping in the city. If it's culture you're after, there's a Tibetan Buddhist temple, classical and early music concerts (see the Entertainment chapter) and even the one-room **Ukranian Museum of Canada** (☎ 416-923-3318, 620 Spadina Ave), with its collections of embroidered Ukranian headdresses and Easter eggs ($2; open afternoons, closed Monday).

The main drag of The Annex is Bloor St W, though Harbord St also has a few scattered restaurants and art shops. North of Bloor St, the area is mainly Caribbean, and to the west, there's **Koreatown** and multiethnic **Bloor Village**.

Though you'll find student hangouts as far south as College St west of Euclid Ave, also on College St is Little Italy, an established trendsetting area full of outdoor cafés, bars and small restaurants that are almost always changing hands (the clientele is notoriously fickle). However, the farther west you go, the more traditional and old-world it becomes, with bakeries and fine *ristoranti*. There's another Italian area called **Corso Italia** on St Clair Ave W, west of the Dufferin St intersection. Here you'll find the real Italian cinemas, smoky espresso cafés and pool halls.

Mirvish (Markham) Village

As you approach the corner of Bloor and Bathurst Sts, you may think you're in Las Vegas, but it's just zany Honest Ed's, Toronto's most colorful, gaudy discount-shopping emporium (see the Shopping chapter). Giant signs say things like 'Don't just stand there, buy something' and 'Only our floors are crooked!' Hardly subtle, but you won't believe the lines outside the door before opening time.

With the money he made, beloved Ed Mirvish established a major reputation as a theater impresario/entrepreneur (see the Downtown Walking Tour, earlier). The revival of **Markham St**, an artists' lane of shops and galleries running along the west side of the store, south of Bloor St, is mostly the work of him and his son.

Casa Loma (Map 3)

Literally the 'House on a Hill,' this medieval-style castle-cum-mansion (☎ 416-923-1171) juts up above The Annex proper. The eccentric 98-room mansion was built between 1911 and 1914 for Sir Henry Pellat, a wealthy financier whose fortunes came from his exclusive contract to provide the city with electricity. He later lost everything he had in land speculation during the

Depression era, which resulted in foreclosure and forced Sir Henry and his wife to move out. The castle briefly reopened later as a hotel, but its famous swingin' nightclub attracted far more patrons than the hotel ever did guests, and it too failed. The charitable Kiwanis organization bought the castle and have operated it as a tourist site since 1937.

Self-guided audio tours (available in eight languages) lead you through the sumptuous interior. The rugs are done in the same patterns as Windsor castle. The conservatory where the Pellats did their entertaining is lit by an Italian-made chandelier with electrical bunches of grapes. It is said that the original castle kitchen had ovens big enough to cook an ox.

Casa Loma's towers offer views of the city that rival the CN Tower, while an 800-foot-long underground tunnel connects it to the former stable buildings across the street. After a long walk, there's nothing much to see here apart from the Spanish floor tiles and wooden horses. It might thrill you to know, however, that the stables were used by the government as a secret laboratory for wartime research into anti-U-boat technology.

In summer, the 2.5 hectares of restored gardens behind the castle are open to the public (free) on the first Monday of each month and every Tuesday from 4 pm to dusk.

Casa Loma is open 10 am to 5 pm daily (last entry 4 pm). Admission costs $10 and on-site parking is $2.30 an hour ($7 maximum). If you're uncommonly lucky, you may find a spot in the surrounding neighborhood; drive up Spadina Ave from Bloor St and follow the signs. A better alternative is to walk north from Dupont subway station to Davenport Rd and up the scenic Baldwin Steps.

Spadina House (Map 3)

Just east of Casa Loma, this gracious mansion (☎ 416-392-6910), 285 Spadina Rd, is a Canadian take on Art Nouveau. Built in 1866 and still lit by working gaslights, the impressive interior contains fine furnishings and art collected over three generations. The Edwardian and Victorian gardens are beautiful in spring or summer and perfect for a stroll (or a snooze). The house is open for tours in the afternoons only ($5); it's closed Sunday and Monday.

KENSINGTON MARKET & WEST QUEEN STREET WEST (Map 9)

The first Jewish merchants in Toronto came in the early 1900s and settled in Kensington Market, bounded by College St, Spadina

Spadina, Spadina?!

Spadina: that great thoroughfare where Chinatown grocers double park, the same winding road that leads up the ancient shorecliffs of glacial Lake Iroquois to castlelike Casa Loma. But how, visitors ask, do you pronounce Spadina?

Historically, this has been a vexed question – ever since the early 1800s, when Dr William Baldwin first laid out Spadina Ave measuring 'two chains wide' (132 feet). That was double the usual width, as befitted the main link between muddy downtown and the exclusive neighborhood above Bloor St that would come to be comprised of Sir Henry Pellat's Casa Loma, the personal residence of EJ Lennox (the 'Architect of Toronto') and the exclusive society of first families, like the Austins. While the rich and affluent called it 'Spuh-**dee**-nuh Road', down beneath in the bowels of the city regular folk called it 'Spuh-**die**-nuh Ave.'

Nowadays the only holdouts for the aristocratic pronunciation are the staff at the Spadina House museum. But if you find your tongue tied, just think of the old streetcar drivers who used to chant 'Spuh-DEE-nuh, spuh-DIE-nuh! Spuh-DEE-nuh, spuh-DIE-nuh!' as they rolled around the dividing line at Spadina Circle.

Ave and Dundas St W. They built **Anshei Minsk Synagogue** in 1930. This Russian Romanesque masterpiece at 10 St Andrews St is undergoing restoration and should be a real gem when work is complete (see Religion, in the Facts about Toronto chapter).

In the 1940s and '50s this historic Jewish quarter was transformed by post-WWII immigrants from Hungary, Italy, Portugal and Ukraine. In the 1970s, waves of Chinese arrived, followed by Latin Americans, East and West Indians, Koreans, Vietnamese and Thai. It still draws more new immigrants every day, along with plenty of bohemians, old-school punks and anarchists – this is multicultural Toronto at its most authentic. For more descriptions of the marketplace, see the Places to Eat chapter.

Many of the city's other bohemians and more impecunious artists have moved south to W Queen St W, roughly (and we mean rough – it's an unruly neighborhood) between Spadina Ave and Bathurst St, and beyond. Along here you'll find a range of creative, upstart restaurants, secondhand junk markets, cool clubs and old-world fabric stores. The local goths, vampires and Edwardians also parole the area since the closing of Sanctuary bar has left them homeless.

South of College St, based along Dundas St W, is **Portugal Village**. Many of the houses are decorated with traditional painted ceramic tiles, and the bakeries, fish shops and markets are enticing. The old men sitting inside the macho espresso sports bars, however, don't appear to have moved much since the day they arrived from the old country.

EAST CENTRAL TORONTO (Map 10)

In the east end of town along Danforth Ave – roughly speaking, east of Broadview Ave as far as Coxwell Ave and beyond – is a large **Greektown**. Often called The Danforth, this has become one of the city's most popular restaurant districts; it is hopping late into the night, with a few smoky men's cafés and busy fruit, vegetable and flower stores open during the day.

Also out this way is **Little India**, with various specialty stores, women in saris and the scent of spices in the air coming from the numerous inexpensive restaurants. It's along Gerrard St E, just one block west of Coxwell Ave.

Allan Gardens

The highlight of this dilapidated city park (☎ 416-392-1111) is the early-20th-century domed greenhouses filled with huge palms and flowering trees from around the world. The central conservatory, called the Palm House, dates from 1909 (free, open 9 am to 4 pm weekdays, 10 am to 5 pm weekends). Limited free parking is available off Horticultural Ave. On public transit, take the No 506 Carlton streetcar or walk over from College station on the Yonge-University subway line. After dark, the entire place is unsavory enough to be not recommended, and that includes even taking a shortcut through the park.

Cabbagetown & Rosedale Walking Tour

The district east of Parliament St to the Don River was settled by Irish immigrants fleeing the potato famine of 1841. It became known as Cabbagetown because the sandy soil of the area provided ideal growing conditions for cabbage. Since the 1970s there has been considerable gentrification of this once-rundown area, whose denizens range from poor to quite comfortable. Today it has possibly the richest concentration of fine Victorian architecture in North America, and it's worth a stroll to peek at some of the beautifully restored houses and their carefully tended gardens.

Start at the corner of Winchester and Metcalfe Sts, two short blocks north of the No 506 Carlton streetcar line. Formerly St Enoch's Presbyterian Church, the **Toronto Dance Theatre & School** (Key No 1), is a soaring red-brick Romanesque Revival building (1891) with a distinctive weather vane. South along Metcalfe St at No 37 is an **Italianate Villa** (Key No 2) once belonging to the president of the Brilliant Sign Company. In 1910 when an apartment complex was built next door, he transferred all of the finest details, such as classical Ionic columns and carved stone lions, to the Metcalfe St front, increasing its movie-like effect.

Walk south to **Trinity Mews** (Key No 3), originally part of the Trinity College Medical School (1859). Duck into its courtyard, patterned with bricks, for the best views of its red- and yellow-brick construction, nicely contrasting with the black-roofed, pink-brick **Spruce Lane Townhouses** (Key No 3) next door.

Cut east, then walk north on Sackville St to No 377, the **Shields House** (Key No 4). It's identical to every mansard-roofed 2nd Empire building in the neighborhood, except for its distinguished gray stone facing – talk about keeping up with the Joneses. At the end of the block, turn right toward **No 320 Carlton St** (Key No 5), a plump example of the architectural style Toronto is best known for, the Bay & Gable house (a large bay window on the ground level and pointy Victorian gable rising above).

Head east and loop through the working class–style **Geneva Ave Cottages** (Key No 6) and walk up Sumach St next to Riverdale Park. On the left at No 384 is the **Witches' House** (Key No 7), nicknamed for its quintessential gingerbread-house appearance and the gargoyle on its front face. At the corner is **Winchester Café** (Key No 8), serving take-out lunches and tempting ice cream and pies. You can't miss the hand-painted 'Salon de Thë' sign (closed Monday and Tuesday).

Turn right and go as far as the **Riverdale Farm**, the original Toronto Zoo where prairie wolves used to howl at night and scare Cabbagetown kids. It's run as a working farm museum now, with two barns to wander through and waterfowl and animals, some of which may permit a pat or two (free). On the north side of Winchester St, a road leads through the cemetery gates to the gothic **Necropolis Chapel** (Key No 9). Many of the remains of Toronto's earliest colonists were transferred to this cemetery in the early 1850s because the old potter's field (near Todmorden Mills; see Map 3) burial ground was contaminating the town.

Continue north to Wellesley St, turning left to come upon a sampler of all the different Cabbagetown styles. The most hidden, yet well-known, buildings are the **Alpha Ave Cottages** (Key No 10) and **Wellesley Cottages** (Key No 11), with picket fences, all originally built for workers in the 19th century and now occupied by urban professionals.

The white Victorian home at **No 314 Wellesley St** (Key No 12) is a whimsical delight of terra-cotta and carved ornamentation, including a full serpent carved under the highest gable. Turn right on Parliament St, and it's just a few steps north to St James Cemetery and **Chapel of St James-the-Less** (Key No 13), reminiscent of an English countryside church. The squat structure (1858) has a deep spire and is set appealingly on an uneven rise. It has justifiably been called one of the most beautiful buildings in Canada.

Continue north on Parliament St, turning right onto the continuation of Bloor St and heading east toward **Castle Frank subway station**. The station was named after Castle Frank, the summer colonial residence of Toronto's founder, Lieutenant Governor John Simcoe, and his artistic wife, Elizabeth. Unfortunately, the majestic house that once stood here on the banks of the Don River burned down almost two centuries ago.

To the north is Rosedale, one of the city's wealthiest areas for nearly a hundred years. Laid out in the 1870s by Edward Jarvis, it was not at first a success (too isolated, people said), but it came into its own after his death in 1907.

From the Castle Frank station, turn left and walk up Castle Frank Rd, stopping to view the terra-cotta picture-frame ornamentation on the **James Ramsey House** (Key No 14) and the shaped hedges of the stately white Georgian home at **No 65** (Key No 15). Farther north, look carefully at **No 43** (Key No 16), where each 'clinker brick' (misshapen seconds) is of a different hue. Just opposite, where Castle Frank Rd begins to twist around, is **No 42** (Key No 17), a white country manor with profuse gardens.

Farther north, next to the redeveloped **Hawthorn Gardens** (Key No 18), with its

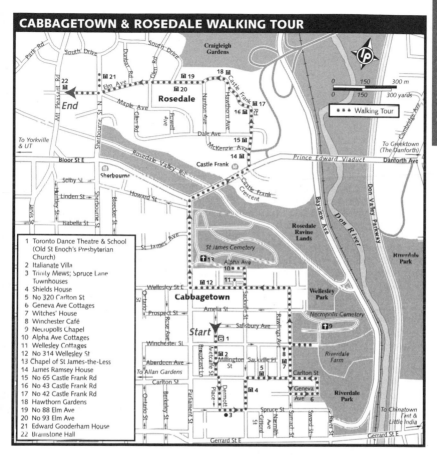

CABBAGETOWN & ROSEDALE WALKING TOUR

1 Toronto Dance Theatre & School
  (Old St Enoch's Presbyterian
  Church)
2 Italianate Villa
3 Trinity Mews; Spruce Lane
  Townhouses
4 Shields House
5 No 320 Carlton St
6 Geneva Ave Cottages
7 Witches' House
8 Winchester Café
9 Necropolis Chapel
10 Alpha Ave Cottages
11 Wellesley Cottages
12 No 314 Wellesley St
13 Chapel of St James-the-Less
14 James Ramsey House
15 No 65 Castle Frank Rd
16 No 43 Castle Frank Rd
17 No 42 Castle Frank Rd
18 Hawthorn Gardens
19 No 88 Elm Ave
20 No 93 Elm Ave
21 Edward Gooderham House
22 Bramstone Hall

restored coach house, is a sign pointing 'To Craigleigh Gardens.' A short detour here takes you into a small and elegant old park edged by the impressive back gardens of some of Rosedale's finest mansions.

Castle Frank Rd leads to Elm Ave, where nearly every house is listed by the Ontario Heritage Foundation as being of architectural or historical significance. They are all most impressive, but particularly noteworthy are the two ornate faces of **No 88** (Key No 19), which won an architecture prize in 1921, and **No 93** (Key No 20) for its ornamental iron porch. Turn north onto Sher-

bourne St, toward the charmingly unkempt **Edward Gooderham House** (Key No 21) at No 27. This Georgian home was built for the same distillery clan that had its downtown offices in the Flatiron Building (see the Downtown Walking Tour, earlier).

From here, backtrack and walk to the western end of Elm Ave. These are the original houses of Rosedale, where a group of Victorian manors has been joined together as a private school, **Bramstone Hall** (Key No 22). If you return to Sherbourne St, it's a 10-minute walk south to Sherbourne subway station, on the Bloor-Danforth line.

THE BEACH (Map 11)

To residents, The Beach is a rather wealthy, mainly professional neighborhood along Queen St E at Woodbine Ave, down by the lakeshore. To everyone else, it's part of 'the beaches' – meaning the area, the beaches themselves and the parkland along the lake.

The sandy beaches are good for sunbathing and picnicking, and the 3km boardwalk, which edges the sand, is perfect for strolling (or strutting, as the case may be), but the polluted water of Lake Ontario inhibits swimmers (just listen for beach-closure announcements on the evening news). Kew Beach is the most popular section, and the boardwalk goes through here. At the west end, in Woodbine Park, there's an excellent Olympic-size public swimming pool. The **Silverbeach Boathouse** doesn't have boats but does rent beach-volleyball and badminton equipment, sand toys and board games (open July to early September). There's also a paved recreational path (part of the Martin Goodman trail system) for cycling and in-line skating (see the Getting Around chapter for rental shops).

Enjoying a grand command of the lakeshore, the **RC Harris Filtration Plant** (☎ 416-392-2932), 2701 Queen St E, is a modern Art Deco masterpiece, both inside and out. Its costly construction during the Depression era rubbed residents the wrong way, so they disparagingly dubbed it the 'Palace of Purification,' as recounted in Michael Ondaatje's novel *In the Skin of a Lion*. The great hall looks like the factory in Charlie Chaplin's *Modern Times* and has in fact appeared in countless films (most recently *Scary Movie*). One-hour technical tours of the wonders of modern filtration will at least get you in the door (free, 10 am, 11:30 am and 1 pm every Saturday).

There are quite a few places to eat nearby along Queen St E (see the Places to Eat chapter). To get to The Beach from downtown, take the 501 Queen streetcar east; the journey takes about 30 minutes.

TORONTO ISLANDS (Map 12)

Once upon a time, there were no Toronto Islands; there was only an immense sand bar, stretching 5½ miles out into the lake from the foot of present-day Woodbine Ave. The Mississauga Indians called it the place of 'trees standing in water;' early colonials who flocked here to take advantage of the cooler lakeshore breezes called it 'the Peninsula,' a name later taken on by the premier resort hotel built here. Then on April 13, 1858, an immense storm cut through the sandbar, swallowed the hotel and created 'the Gap' (now known as the Eastern Channel), forming Toronto's jewel-like islands. The cool breezes are great on a hot, sticky day, and cycling along the islands' paved paths and boardwalk on the southern shore isn't a bad way to spend some time.

From the foot of Bay St near the Westin Harbour Castle hotel, catch a ferry to Hanlan's Point (on the west side of Centre Island), Centre Island (meaning Centre Island Park, in the middle of the island) or Ward's Island. These quick cruises are as good as harbor tours, and it doesn't much matter which ferry you take, seeing as all the islands are interconnected by bridges or footpaths, except that you'll have to go to Centre Island Ferry Terminal first if you plan to rent a bicycle (see the Getting

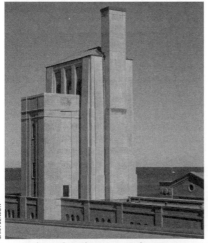

Palace of Purification on Lake Ontario (RC Harris Filtration Plant)

Around chapter). For general information on Toronto Islands, call Toronto Parks and Recreation (☎ 416-392-8195).

At the extreme west end of Centre Island is Toronto City Centre Airport and **Hanlan's Point**, named after world-champion sculler 'Ned' Hanlan who lived here until his death. From the 1830s to 1940s, the sport of ice-boating atop the frozen lake was at its peak; it's hard to believe, but Toronto's winters nowadays are too mild for it. Following the paved paths past picnic tables and barbecue pits brings you near **Hanlan's Point Beach**, the best on the islands. Popular especially with gay men for years, the 'clothing optional' status of this beach was finally legalized by the city council in 1999. Civic-minded island volunteers distribute 'naked-beach etiquette' flyers to new arrivals.

To the southeast, **Gibraltar Point** was selected by Captain John Simcoe as the most easily defensible point in the harbor, promptly building a British fort here in 1800. It was destroyed just 13 years later during the American raid on York. Inland, the **Gibraltar Point Lighthouse**, built in 1809 with gray limestone from Queenston near Niagara, was the first of its kind on all of the Great Lakes and used sperm oil to light its lamp. It stands all of 52 picturesque feet tall and is thought to be haunted by its first keeper, JP Rademuller, who disappeared mysteriously in 1815. Years later, human bones were dug up close by, supporting the theory that he was murdered by soldiers for not sharing his bootleg liquor.

Ferries also dock at Centre Island Ferry Terminal, meaning central Centre Island Park, which has the most amusements and hosts all of the special events, like the Dragon Boat races in June. Next to the ferry terminal is the Island Paradise Restaurant and a bridge leading to **Olympic Island** with its outdoor stage, where Caribana concerts are held. Head past the information booth and first-aid station to **Centreville Amusement Park** (☎ 416-203-0405), which is quaintly old-fashioned and is open in summer from 10:30 am to 8 pm daily, weather permitting. It only costs 60¢ per ride ticket. Behind the park is **Far Enough Farm** (free).

Head south over the bridge past the Iroquois Coffee shop toward the splashing **fountains** and by an authentic **hedge maze**. Near the south shore are locker rooms, snack bars, bicycle rental and a pier leading out into the lake. To the east is a **boathouse**, where canoes and paddleboats can be rented, and **St Andrews-by-the-Lake (The Island Church)**, a petite Anglican house of worship dating from 1884. It holds heart-warming traditional Christmas celebrations each year (and a good thing, too, since the winter winds over here are pretty cold).

Centre Island has hundreds of visitors each weekend, but no residents. In the 1960s the city began steadily evicting all of the 'sandbar bohemians' who had been living here for more than a generation. The remaining residents on other islands struggled for over 20 years to keep their homes and unique way of life. It all boiled down to a dramatic standoff on July 28, 1980, after which the city granted 99-year leases for year-round residents under a land trust administration arrangement.

Once you see the small artistic communities living on **Algonquin Island Park** and **Ward's Island** for yourself, you may be jealous. They've got peace, little pollution and incredible skyline views of the city. They also have The Rectory (☎ 416-203-6011), 102 Lakeshore Ave, a cozy art gallery café that serves weekend brunch on the boardwalk (reservations recommended, open Friday to Monday between May and August).

At the west end of Ward's Island is a **frisbee-golf course** and **children's play fort**. Take the boardwalk until you can go no farther east and cut back onto 1st St. At the corner of Channel Ave is a gorgeous flower garden framing perfects views of the Toronto skyline. From here, it's a short distance back to the Ward's Island Ferry Terminal.

HIGH PARK (Map 13)

The city's biggest park (but that's not saying too much), is High Park, a popular escape for a little picnicking, cycling, in-line skating or sitting in the flower gardens and watching the sunset. Some parts are left as natural woods, but outdoorsy folk should skip this park in favor of Toronto's wilder ravines (see the Riverside Parks section, later).

Near the north entrance, off Bloor St W, the **Sports Complex** has tennis courts and an outdoor swimming pool (free). The main road winds around south through the park, with other roads branching off. A branch to the east takes you to **The Dream in High Park** stage (see the Entertainment chapter). Farther south are the refreshing **Hillside Gardens** overlooking **Grenadier Pond**, where people fish in summer and skate in winter.

The road continues downhill past the **Animal Paddocks** (a small children's zoo) to **Colborne Lodge** (☎ 416-392-6916), a Regency-style cottage built in 1836. Once belonging to the Howards, the founders of High Park, it still contains many of the original furnishings, including Ontario's first indoor flush toilet. Admission is $3.50, and it's open noon to 5 pm daily except Monday in summer, with reduced hours in spring and fall. From January to April it's open weekends only.

The park's north entrance is off Bloor St W at High Park Ave, near High Park station, on the Bloor-Danforth subway line. If you exit from the south past Colborne Lodge, walk down to Lake Shore Blvd and catch any streetcar back east to downtown.

AROUND TORONTO
Ontario Science Centre
Where can you climb a rock wall, travel the Information Highway into virtual reality and race an Olympic bobsled, all in one day? Answer: at this excellent museum (Map 3; ☎ 416-696-3127) containing over 800 totally interactive, high-tech science exhibits and live demonstrations that will wow most kids, and even some adults. It's worth driving by just to admire the structure, designed by the innovative architectural firm of Moriyama & Teshima (see Architecture, under Arts in the Facts about Toronto chapter). You won't want to miss the beaver pond out back, either.

Admission is $12 for adults, less for youth, families or seniors. Combined discount tickets with OMNIMAX films (double features!) are available. The museum is open 10 am to 5 pm daily; on weekends there are hundreds of kids running around like mad. It's located in a small ravine on the corner of Eglinton Ave E and Don Mills Rd. By public transit, take the No 34 Eglinton East bus from Eglinton station (not Eglinton West), on the Yonge-University subway line. Parking costs $7.

Historic Sites
The following are our picks from Toronto's myriad outlying historic sites. Admittedly, one is probably enough for anyone who isn't a total colonial-history buff.

Dating from 1848, the **Enoch Turner Schoolhouse** (Map 10; ☎ 416-863-0010), 106 Trinity St, is a restored one-room classroom where kids are shown what the good old days were like. The wealthy brewer Enoch Turner opened it as Toronto's first free school, where children of poorer citizens could learn the three Rs. Visiting is free but is only permitted when school tours are not scheduled. It's a 20-minute walk east of downtown on King St E.

Near the Don River at 67 Pottery Rd, **Todmorden Mills** (Map 3; ☎ 416-396-2819) was the location of an important 1794 sawmill, turned gristmill, and then paper mill. There are historical exhibits inside the Brewery Gallery, where eager guides await to show visitors around the old millers' houses and the petite Don Train Station, relocated here in 1969. Nature paths start near the bridge and wind back to secluded wildflower gardens. Admission is $2.25; it's open daily (except Monday) from May to December. From Broadview station on the Bloor-Danforth subway line, take any bus to Mortimer Ave and walk west. There is parking, which is free – a rarity in Toronto, as you know by now.

Built in 1832 by an Irish military captain of the same name, **Montgomery's Inn** (Subway: Islington; ☎ 416-394-8113) is a fine example of Loyalist architecture and has been faithfully restored to the late 1840s era. Staff in period dress answer questions and serve afternoon tea between 2 and 4:30 pm. Admission is $3; it's open afternoons daily at 4709 Dundas St W, near Islington Ave in the city's west end.

A successful surveyor and politician built the Georgian-style **Gibson House** (Subway: Sheppard; ☎ 416-395-7432) after his return from exile in the USA, which resulted from his role in the Upper Canada Rebellion of 1837. Costumed workers offer tours of the house between 11 am and 3 pm, as well as cooking demonstrations on summer weekends and holidays ($2.75; open 9:30 am to 4:30 pm Tuesday to Friday, noon to 5 pm weekends). It's in the far northern part of the city at 5172 Yonge St, north of Sheppard Ave.

The city's top historical attraction for families, **Black Creek Pioneer Village** (☎ 416-736-1733) recreates rural life in 19th-century Ontario. Workers, once again in period costume, demonstrate country crafts and skills using old-fashioned tools and methods, and one of the barns holds a large toy museum and woodcarving collection. Admission costs $9/5 per adult/child; it's open 10 am to 4:30 pm daily, May to December. Traditional 'Christmas Remembered' celebrations start in mid-November. The village is at the corner of Steeles Ave and Jane St, a 40-minute drive northwest from downtown. Parking costs $5. From Downsview subway station, the northern terminus of the Yonge-University line, there are several buses. The most convenient is the No 84 Sheppard westbound to Jane Ave. Then, transfer to the Jane No 35 bus northbound.

Mount Pleasant Cemetery

North of Moore Ave, between Yonge St and Bayview Ave, this cemetery (Map 3; ☎ 416-485-9129) is the final resting place of many of Toronto's brilliant and best (or at least richest) citizens. Here you'll find the graves of Glenn Gould, the world-famous classical musician from the Beach community; Timothy Eaton, founder of Eaton's department store; Titanic survivor Arthur Godfrey Peuchen; and Foster Hewitt, Canada's 'Voice of Hockey,' the sportscaster who coined the phrase, 'He shoots, he scores!' The most arresting sight is the castlelike Massey mausoleum.

Historical maps are available from the cemetery office near the south gate, off Mt Pleasant Rd, which cuts through the middle of the cemetery. If you're not driving, take the Yonge-University subway line north to Davisville station, then walk about 10 minutes east along the north side of the cemetery to the north gate, at Mt Pleasant Rd.

History of Contraception Museum

This small-scale contraception museum is really just a series of intriguing display cases put together by Janssen-Ortho Inc (☎ 416-449-9444). A video narrates humanity's earliest, fumbling attempts at contraception, from amulets to crocodile dung (don't ask). Visitors also can see Dr. Condom's original designs, dating from the era of King Charles II, and a collection of 350 IUDs – anything from butterflies to fishing lines. The museum is free, but call to check opening hours, since the collection is often on tour. Janssen-Ortho is at 19 Green Belt Dr, east of Don Mills Rd and just north of Eglinton Ave.

Riverside Parks

Though short on city parks, Toronto does have some substantial nature reserves in the numerous ravines formed by rivers and streams that empty into Lake Ontario.

Outside Old Mill subway station, on the Bloor-Danforth line, is the start of the two-hour **Humber River Discovery Walk**. The walk loops south to Lake Ontario and Humber Bay, much of the way through woodland, then back north past a 1700s French settlement site. This last section follows Riverside Dr, the old 'Carrying Place' trail used by Native tribes and French traders when portaging canoes from Lake Ontario to the upper lakes of northern Canada.

The **Don River Valley** ravine walk begins behind Castle Frank subway station (Map 3). Follow the signs down into the urban jungle – it's a veritable forest in there. You can walk for hours and hours north, past the Ontario Science Centre and Wilket Creek Park, all the way to the flower-filled Edwards Gardens, on the corner of Lawrence Ave E and Leslie St.

Tommy Thompson Park

Often still known as the Leslie St Spit, this artificial landfill site (Map 3) is managed by the Toronto & Region Conservation Authority (☎ 416-667-6299). It extends out into the lake farther than the Toronto Islands and has unexpectedly become a phenomenal wildlife success. It was designed to both improve and develop shipping facilities but within a few years became the second-largest nesting place in the world for ring-billed seagulls, as well as for terns and other birds.

The area, a narrow 5km-long strip, is open to the public usually only on weekends and holidays in summer. Schedules of free guided walks, which often have an ornithological or photographic angle, are posted at the front gate. At the far end (named Vicki Keith Point, after a local long-distance swimmer), there is a lighthouse and views of the city.

The park is on the corner of Unwin Ave and Leslie St. No vehicles are permitted, but many people use bicycles – the Martin Goodman Recreational Trail runs by in both directions. Call the conservation authority for information on shuttles from nearby TTC bus stops.

Scarborough Bluffs

A few kilometers east of the Beach neighborhood, these cliffs of glacial deposits (commonly known as till) tower over the lakeshore. When Elizabeth Simcoe came here in 1793, she named this spot Scarborough after the town in Yorkshire, England, also famed for its cliffs.

If you want to be atop the cliffs (and you do), there are several parks that will give you access to footpaths, sweeping views of the bluffs and panoramas of Lake Ontario, as well as ways of getting down to the water. From Kingston Rd (Hwy 2), turn south at Cathedral Bluffs Dr to reach an excellent vantage point, Cathedral Bluffs Park. It's the highest section of the bluffs (at 98m) and once belonged to the Sisters of St Joseph, whose property extended from Kingston Rd to the lake. These bluffs were not named after the former convent, but

because of geology: at the top of the cliffs, erosion has created oddly beautiful formations resembling cathedral spires, and simultaneously revealed full profile evidence of five different glacial periods.

Below, in the lake itself, landfill has been used to form **Bluffers Park**, a boat-mooring and recreational area for walking. Access to Bluffers Park is from Brimley Rd, running south off Kingston Rd just west of Cathedral Bluffs Dr. From the Victoria Park subway station on the Bloor-Danforth line, take the Kingston No 12 bus. The park is a 10-minute walk south of the nearest bus stop. A 15-minute drive east of the bluffs is the quirky **Guild Inn** (see the Places to Stay chapter).

ACTIVITIES
Outdoor Sports

For cyclists (and in-line skaters), the Martin Goodman Trail is the place to go. This recreational trail stretches from The Beach along the Harbourfront to Humber River, in the west end (see Riverside Parks, earlier). If you fancy a longer trek, it links to the Lake Ontario Waterfront Trail, which stretches 325km from Hamilton to Trenton. Ask at the Ontario Tourism office for a map and pamphlet of sights along the way. On Toronto Islands, the boardwalk on the south shoreline and all of the interconnecting paved paths are car-free zones for cycling or skating. For more information on equipment rentals and recommended routes, see the Getting Around chapter.

In winter there are good, free places to skate at Toronto City Hall and Harbourfront, both with artificial ice and skate rentals. If it's been quite cold, there are natural ice rinks at Grenadier Pond, in High Park, and Riverdale Park, in Cabbagetown, which also has toboggan runs overlooking the Don Valley Parkway.

Golfers may have already heard of Glen Abbey Golf Club (☎ 905-841-3730), 1333 Dorval Dr, a 40-minute drive west of downtown via the QEW, past Hwy 407 and in the suburb of Oakville. It was the first to be designed solely by Jack Nicklaus, and the pros play here during the Canadian Open.

Water Sports

Free swimming can be found at the pool in High Park or at the Gus Ryder Pool (known as Sunnyside pool), on Lake Shore Blvd, south of the park. The pool at Christie Pitts, west of The Annex, has water slides, and there's an Olympic-sized pool in Woodbine Park, at The Beach.

The Harbourfront Canoe & Kayak School (Map 4; ☎ 416-203-2277), 283A Queen's Quay W, rents crafts for paddling around its 1½-acre pond or going out to Toronto Islands. There's also an on-site sailing school for people with disabilities.

Windsurfing rental is available at the Ashbridge's Bay area, near the western edge of the Beach boardwalk.

Indoor Sports

Near Leslieville, the Toronto Climbing Academy (Map 10; ☎ 416-406-5900), 100A Broadview Ave, has 50 different indoor routes. Day rates are $12, plus $5 for shoes and harness rental. Rates are a bit higher at famous Joe Rockhead's Climbing Gym (Map 3; ☎ 416-538-7670), 29 Fraser Ave, north of Exhibition Place. It's owned by Canadian climbing champ Joe Bergman.

Massage & Alternative Therapies

The Shiatsu Depot (Map 8; ☎ 416-323-1818), 547 College St, gives 15-minute shiatsu tune-ups ($11). Students at the Sutherland-Chan Clinic (Map 3; ☎ 416-924-1107), 330 Dupont St, just west of Spadina Rd, will apply their healing hands for one hour for only $29, by appointment only.

Clinic Ineed (Map 6; ☎ 416-944-8055), 128½ Cumberland St, is a one-stop shop for acupuncture, reflexology and traditional massage. Daily specials offer 20% off selected services.

COURSES
Language

Those coming to Canada to study English should first shop around with reliable language schools like Berlitz (Map 6; ☎ 416-924-2280), 94 Cumberland St, or GEOS (Map 5; ☎ 416-599-2120), 415 Yonge St.

Tool around the Toronto Islands in style.

Other independent schools in Toronto include the St George Business & Language School (Map 6; ☎ 416-929-5553), 208 Bloor St W, for ESL and business English. For information, visit the Web site at www.stgeorgeschool.com.

One advantage of studying French in Toronto is that instructors do not use Québecois, a dialect many French citizens would have trouble comprehending at all. Alliance Française has well-qualified instructors, a language lab and immersion programs, or you could also check with the Centre Francophone de Toronto (for locations of both, see Libraries & Cultural Centers, in the Facts for the Visitor chapter).

Cooking

Toronto's greatest chefs really do teach at Great Cooks (Map 9; ☎ 416-703-0388, grtcooks@idirect.com), 787 Queen St W, where, if you can afford to pay $90 for an evening of instruction, the magic of Canoe's Anthony Walsh or Chiado's Manny Vilela can work its way into your own fingertips. The 'Hands-on Basic Knife Skills' sounds a touch criminal, but a schedule of other milder courses and sedate gourmet-restaurant tours is listed on the Web site, at www.greatcooksinc.com.

The bakery Wanda's Pie in the Sky (Map 6; ☎ 416-925-7437), at 7A Yorkville Ave, teaches come-as-you-are pastry classes twice a month on Sunday mornings ($75 for three hours).

THINGS TO SEE & DO

The Big Carrot (Map 10, ☎ 416-466-2129), 348 Danforth Ave, hosts evening vegetarian cooking classes taught by none other than the published author of the *Complete Idiot's Guide to being Vegetarian in Canada*.

More famous culinary schools are found in Niagara's wine country and Stratford (see the Excursions chapter).

Art & Dance

Many Toronto museums offer hands-on workshops in their areas of expertise, such as the Gardiner Museum of Ceramic Art, the Museum for Textiles, and Toronto's First Post Office Museum (papermaking). Specialty stores, like The Japanese Paper Place or Clay Design, which has its own on-site pottery studio, also offer classes (see the Shopping chapter).

If you've ever wanted to explore belly-dancing or improve your salsa steps, the studios of Arabesque Academy (Map 6; ☎ 416-920-5593), 625 Yonge St, employ Middle Eastern and South American dance specialists to teach you. Its Web site (www .interlog.com/~dancenet) also has excellent listings for multicultural events.

Meditation & Yoga

If it feels like the urban jungle is closing in, the Zen Buddhist Temple (see the arrow on Map 8, ☎ 416-658-0137), 86 Vaughan Rd, near Bathurst St and St Clair Ave, offers introductory meditation retreats and Sunday practice sessions that are free to all. Or drop by the Sivananda Yoga Centre (Map 8; ☎ 416-966-9642), 77 Harbord St, for free introductory one-hour yoga classes on Sunday afternoons.

Places to Stay

In any season other than the deep-freeze Arctic winter months of January to March, reservations in Toronto are absolutely necessary. From May through Labour Day, and beyond that for as long as the weather holds, decent places to stay will be full, night after night. Even the undesirable ones will have 'No Vacancy' signs on Friday and Saturday nights. If it's during Caribana, Pride or the International Film Festival, rooms will be booked out months in advance. For those who blithely assume they can scavenge out a decent room, let us repeat: you need reservations.

As if this dismal spectacle weren't enough, accommodation in Toronto isn't cheap, or even reasonable. While $50 may get you a spot in a tidy little B&B in old Montréal, it won't even get you a room in a dumpy motel that's within a half-hour radius of downtown Toronto.

There are decent, even great (but packed) hostels charging around $20 a night for dorm beds. But for visitors who would like to close their own door at night, there are no rays of sunshine, especially for single travelers who get almost no breaks on room rates. The most basic tourist homes and B&Bs, even those not serving breakfast, start at $50 per night, rising well over $70 for stylish, historic abodes serving full, hot breakfasts.

Motel rooms are no bargain, averaging $60 before taxes for questionable rooms in somewhat questionable neighborhoods, far from downtown. The cheaper chain hotels like Howard Johnson or Days Inn have rates starting near $100, as do Toronto's older independent high-rise hotels, but that at least puts you in the heart of the city. All the amenities (TV, radio, telephone) are guaranteed and the sheets will be freshly laundered.

At top-end and luxury hotels, you'll pay upwards of $150, but at last you're getting real value for money. All these establishments have swimming pools, fitness rooms, saunas, pubs, bars and fine restaurants, as well as concierges who can assist your every whim. Opt for one of Toronto's original and historic establishments, such as the Royal York or King Edward; the civilized atmosphere will envelop you the moment you walk through the sparkling lobby doors.

If you think you can't afford hotel rooms like these, try Last Minute Travel (www .lastminutetravel.com), which advertises great bargains on downtown Toronto hotel rooms, especially weekend package deals.

Some tourist homes (the small ones), guesthouses and B&Bs don't charge GST for rooms but hotels certainly will (see Taxes & Visitor Refunds in the Facts for the Visitor chapter). At most hotels rates fluctuate wildly from day to day, even hour to hour, and many places charge double or triple the off-peak rates during summer and on holidays. Always ask if tax is included and about discounts for students, HI cardholders, seniors, CAA/AAA members or multiple-night stays.

CAMPING

There are several camping and RV grounds within 40km of central Toronto. Unless otherwise stated, campgrounds are open May until September or October, weather permitting. Rates quoted are for unserviced sites and include tax; note that these often will be higher on Canadian holiday weekends.

Next to Wild Water Kingdom amusement park, ***Indian Line Campground*** *(☎ 905-678-1233, 1-800-304-9728, 7625 Finch Ave W)* is part of Claireville Conservation Area (Map 1; ☎ 416-667-6299). It's just southeast of the intersection of Steeles and Finch Aves, and 1km west of Hwy 427 north of Pearson airport. It has a swimming pool, reservoir, playground and 240 sites costing $19 per night. Take either branch of the Yonge-University-Spadina line north to York Mills or Yorkdale station ($2), then a GO Transit Brampton bus bound for Hwy

27/Wild Water Kingdom as far as Darcel Ave ($3.10).

Within the city limits, **Glen Rouge Park** (☎ 416-392-2541) is off Kingston Rd (Hwy 2), just east of the Sheppard Ave E and Hwy 401 interchange. It's near the lakefront and the Metro Zoo, at the eastern border of Toronto and the town of Pickering. The 124 sites are clean and surrounded by woodlands ($22 per night). Special backpacker sites are $14. From downtown, take a GO Transit train to Rouge Hill station then a GO Transit bus north to the campground.

Open year-round, **Milton Heights Campground** (☎ 416-878-6781, 1-800-308-9120, 8690 Tremaine Rd) is a 45-minute drive west of Toronto. Take Hwy 401 to Hwy 25 north, then turn left at Campbellville Rd and left again onto Townline Rd. Sites costs $24 for two people, and there are laundry facilities, a heated outdoor pool and pets are allowed. The Ontario Agricultural Museum is next door, and it's a short drive from Crawford Lake and Mountsberg conservation areas.

HOSTELS

Hostels are open year-round, but be aware that less reputable places may pull the rug out from under you and renege on booked rooms or overstuff the corridors with extra bunk beds at busy times. The better hostels offer kitchen facilities, common lounges, laundry and Internet access and staff who dispense travel advice and arrange day trips.

In a great location just south of Chinatown, the independent **Global Village Backpackers** (Map 4; ☎ 416-703-8540, 1-888-844-7875, 460 King St W) was formerly the Spadina Hotel where Jack Nicholson, Leonard Cohen and the Tragically Hip once stayed. It's a big, brightly-colored place that travelers rave about, and not just for the handy on-site bar and TravelCUTS office. It's well-run, the 24-hour reception staff are pros and dorm beds cost $24, doubles $60 and quads $27 per person; discounts for ISIC and HI cardholders.
Web site: www.globalbackpackers.com

The super-friendly **Canadiana Guesthouse & Backpackers** (Map 4; ☎ 416-598-9090, 1-877-215-1225, canadiana@inforamp

.net, 42 Widmer St) is in two quiet, charming Victorian houses tucked inside the Entertainment District. The small, air-conditioned hostel has a few dozen dorm beds for $25 and private rooms for $60. Although they fill up regularly, you're more likely to find an empty bed here than elsewhere.
Web site: www.canadianalodging.com

A cut above the basic hostel standard is **Hostelling International (HI) Toronto** (Map 4; ☎ 416-971-4440, 1-877-848-8737, 76 Church St), which won the HI Canadian-Hostel-of-the-Year award in 2000. It gets thumbs up for its central location and for recent renovations that include: a rooftop deck, an kitchen and laundry facilities and electronic key locks for added security. A bonus is the air-conditioning. Beds in larger dorms (eight to 10 people) cost $18.85 for hostel members, $22.50 in smaller dorms, and $67.20 for couple and family rooms; non-members add $4.28.
Web site: www.hostellingint-gl.on.ca/toronto.htm

The oldest independent hostel in Toronto is **Leslieville Home Hostel** (Map 10; ☎ 416-461-7258, 1-800-280-3965, 185 Leslie St) in an east-end residential neighborhood, 20 minutes from downtown via the 501 Queen streetcar, on the way to The Beach. This homey, chilled-out hostel can accommodate up to 40 people in dorm beds ($17) or private singles/doubles ($39/49).
Web site: www.leslieville.com

At modest **Havinn** (see the arrow on Map 8; ☎ 416-922-5220, 1-888-922-5220, 118 Spadina Rd) you get a bed in a co-ed room with one or two others for $25, including continental breakfast. It's simple and clean and there are limited kitchen facilities and free parking. Private rooms are also available.

For women only, the **YWCA** (Map 3; ☎ 416-923-8454, ywcagen@ywcator.org, 80 Woodlawn Ave), is in Rosedale, just south of St Clair Ave and east off Yonge St. The friendly reception desk is open 24 hours and dorm beds cost $22, singles/doubles are $48/62. Continental breakfast is included and there's an inexpensive cafeteria. Discounts for stays of a week or longer are offered.

As a last resort when every other hostel bed is full, no-frills ***Marigold International Travellers Hostel*** *(Map 3; ☎ 416-536-8824, 2011 Dundas St W)* has about thirty bunk beds and two couples rooms for $23 per person, which includes morning coffee and donuts. Though painting and other improvements are in the works, the tiny rooms and common areas remain grim. From downtown take the 505 Dundas St or 506 College St streetcars west for 20 minutes (longer on weekends) past Lansdowne Ave and over the bridge.

Most other hostels, serving transient workers, new immigrants or down-on-their-luck clientele, are not recommended.

UNIVERSITY ACCOMMODATIONS

The traveler's favorite is ***Neill-Wycik College Hotel*** *(Map 5; ☎ 416-977-2320, 1-800-268-4358, 96 Gerrard St E)*, near Ryerson Polytechnic University, operating from early May to late August. There are laundry facilities, a student-run cafeteria for breakfast and incredible views from the rooftop patio. The building isn't air-conditioned and there are no fans, so be prepared to sweat it out in mid-summer. Private bedrooms with telephones are in apartment suites that share a kitchen/lounge and bathroom. Staff at the 24-hour reception desk charge $35 for singles, $52 for twins or doubles and $59 for family rooms, plus tax. These rates drop respectively to $29/42/48 for students, seniors or HI cardholders.

Set in beautiful grounds near the museums, ***Victoria University*** *(Map 6; ☎ 416-585-4524, accom.victoria@utoronto.ca, 140 Charles St)* opens its doors from early May to late August, charging $42/60 for singles/twins, less for students and seniors. Reduced monthly rates work out to $29 per night. Full complimentary breakfasts are served in the old-world dining hall.

The University of Toronto Student Housing Office (Map 6; ☎ 416-978-8045, housing.services@utoronto.ca), 214 College St, rents rooms in college residences from early May to late August by the day, week or month. The Innis Residence on the St George campus is very central, at the edge of the lively student Annex neighborhood with easy access to Kensington Market and Chinatown. Rooms cost from $45 per person and include breakfast and maid service.

Also at UT, ***Campus Co-op*** *(Map 6; CCRI; ☎ 416-979-2161, inquiries@campus-coop.org, 395 Huron St)* has over 30 houses scattered around The Annex. It's a total pot luck, though, as to whether you get into a sedate shared Victorian or frat-type animal house (pets are allowed). Rates vary from $300 to $600 per month, depending on room size, but all come furnished with shared kitchen and bath facilities. There's a one-month minimum stay and you should apply a few months before summer starts. Web site: www.campus-coop.org.

In North York, ***Hospitality York*** *(☎ 416-736-5020, 4700 Keele St)* rents out dormitory and hotel-quality rooms at York University (Map 1) during the summer and at other times of year for short and long-term stays. It's a long haul north of downtown, but bonus facilities include swimming pools, a fitness center and jogging trails. Web site: www.yorku.ca/hospitality

B&Bs & TOURIST HOMES

Generally speaking, tourist homes and guest houses don't serve breakfast. The cheaper B&Bs will put out coffee and toast or cold cereal, while the stylish establishments will stuff you silly with eggs, fruit, pancakes and the like. A 'single' usually means for one adult, a 'double' for two people.

B&B Associations

B&B associations check, list and usually book rooms in the participating members' homes. When you indicate your preferences, all attempts will be made to find a particularly suitable host. If you're in town and want to check last-minute availability, they may be able to help during normal business hours. There is no need to go to the agency – a telephone call should get things sorted.

The Downtown Toronto Association of B&B Guest Houses *(☎ 416-410-3938, bnbtoronto@globalserve.net, PO Box 190, Station B, Toronto M5T 2W1)* specializes in

PLACES TO STAY

rooms downtown, mainly in renovated Victorian houses. Prices start at $45/55 for one/two people in simple guest rooms.
Web site: www.bnbinfo.com

The oldest association in town is Toronto B&B Registry (☎ 705-738-9449, fax 705-738-0155, beds@torontobandb.com, PO Box 269, 253 College St, Toronto M5T 1R5). They have about 20 members in central Toronto, The Annex, Little Italy and The Beach costing from $55 with shared bath for one person up to $160 for four-person suites.
Web sites: www.torontobandb.com

Bed & Breakfast Homes of Toronto (☎ 416-363-6362, PO Box 46093, 777 Bay St, Toronto M5G 2P6)) has listings and brochures for residential-area B&Bs, anything from those in modest family homes to deluxe suites. You'll find full descriptions with photos for its members, as well as other associations and independent B&Bs, at this excellent Web site: www.bbcanada.com.

Downtown Toronto (North; Map 5)

The cheery **Les Amis** (☎ 416-591-0635, 31 Granby St) is run by a Parisian couple who offer full vegetarian breakfasts and futon beds in air-con singles/doubles for $65/80. French and Spanish are spoken, and it's gay-friendly. The only drawback is that access to Granby St is off Church St, near familiar prostitute haunts.

Yorkville & University of Toronto (Map 6)

Gay-owned and operated, **Dundonald House** (☎ 416-961-9888, 1-800-260-7227, dundonal@idirect.com, 35 Dundonald St) has been voted a Church St community favorite. The gorgeous red brick house has striking black gables, stained glass, well-tended front and back gardens, a sauna and a gym. As if that isn't enough, aromatherapy and shiatsu services and bicycle rental is offered. Rates for no-frills rooms start at $65/$100 for a single or twin beds and soar to $175 for a double room with bay windows and private balcony.

More subdued, **Immaculate Reception** (☎ 416-925-3799, 34 Monteith St) is set back (but only three minutes on foot) from the hoopla of Church St, beside Cawthra Square Park. Sunny common areas and tasteful simple air-con rooms in this restored 2nd Empire townhouse cost $85/$115 for shared/private bath, including a 'gourmet' breakfast. Make sure your reservation is for this particular house, and not the owner's secondary establishment.

Tucked in a residential area is **Daniel's Musical Hideaway B&B** (☎ 416-929-2715, 118 Isabella St), so named because the host is an operatic baritone and music teacher. The elegant yet modern building has romantic rooms from $85 to $125, some with kitchens, private baths, jacuzzis or fireplaces. Two doors east is **The Mulberry Tree** (☎ 416-960-5249, multree@istar.ca, 122 Isabella St). Indeed, two of the three rooms, which cost $85 to $110, are painted a mulberry color. Full hot breakfasts are served.

Parking is free at either and there's a health club just around the corner charging $12 for day-use.

The Annex & Little Italy (Map 8)

Like an upscale hostel, **Global Guesthouse** (☎ 416-923-4004, singer@inforamp.net, 9 Spadina Rd) has a great location just north of Bloor St. This old-fashioned brick home has beautiful carved gables and a balcony. Good-value rooms fill up quickly and cost $52/62 including daily cleaning, cable TV, telephones and free parking. For a private bath, add $10.

When it's lit up at night, elegant **Casa Loma Inn** (☎ 416-924-4540, 21 Walmer Rd) is almost as breathtaking as its namesake. The 23 non-smoking rooms inside the red-brick Victorian building are equipped with fridges, microwaves, TV and air-con, but rates of $90 to $120 don't include breakfast.

Amblecote (☎ 416-927-1713, 109 Walmer Rd) is an early 20th-century Arts & Crafts–style home set on beautiful grounds. Non-smoking singles cost $70 to $95, doubles $90 to $125. Some cozy rooms have antique beds.
Web site: www.amblecote.com

Artistic **Feathers B&B** (☎ 416-534-2388, 132 Wells St) is airy and relaxed, with Japanese dolls and Indonesian puppets sometimes on display. Simple singles start at $55, with rates creeping up to $85 for doubles with private baths, including a continental breakfast with fruit and yogurt. Dutch and French are spoken.

Recommended by many travelers, *Terrace House* (☎ 416-535-1493, *52 Austin Terrace*) boasts North African rugs, full hot breakfasts and business services. Rooms with shared/private bath cost $80/95. It's a 10-minute walk west of Casa Loma, or take the No 7 Bathurst bus to Austin Terrace and walk east 1½ blocks.

East Central Toronto (Map 10)

Many of Toronto's best B&B values are those in historic Victorian houses in Cabbagetown. *Aberdeen Guesthouse* (☎ 416-922-8697, *aberdeen@aol.com, 52 Aberdeen Ave*) has three beautiful air-conditioned rooms, all with shared bathroom, costing from $80/90 single/double. Breakfast is fabulous, it's gay-friendly and there's a shady back garden. In a cream-colored, stately Victorian house with high stencil-like gables, *Lavender Rose B&B* (☎ 416 962-8591, *franjeu@sympatico.ca, 15 Rose Ave*) is very alluring. There's even a piano on the premises. Expect to pay $95 to $125 for a cozy, cheerful non-smoking room. Weekday breakfasts are continental, but on weekends the spread is lavish.

On the edge of Greektown is spotless *Allenby* (☎ 416-461-7095, *223 Strathmore Blvd*). The Greenwood subway stop is practically at the door. In summer, prices for simple rooms are $45/55 with continental breakfast, dropping even lower the rest of the year. All guests share bathrooms and kitchen facilities.

If you simply must partake of Rosedale luxury, the 5-star *Robin's Nest* (☎ 416-926-9464, *nest@pathcom.com, 13 Binscarth Rd*), in a stately restored 1892 heritage home (it looks like a mansion), is your best shot at feeling like a million bucks. Rooms start at $105/$140 in the low/high season, but the Tree Tops room with mansard ceilings, an antique chesterfield and views of the formal garden is worth the extra money.

Other Neighborhoods

For unforgettably unique accommodation, take the ferry over to *Toronto Island B&B* (*Map 12;* ☎ 416-203-0935) on Centre Island. Rooms in this white lakeside house cost $58 including full breakfast and the use of bicycles. It books up quickly throughout the summer season, so call ahead.

At *Beaches B&B* (*Map 11;* ☎ 416-699-0818, *174 Waverly Rd*), the warm, personable hostess Edith (as seen on BBC!) welcomes children and has three cats in residence. The loft room ($95) has a double bed built into a bay window that opens onto a deck. The 'Jungle' and 'Secret Garden' room (with private entrance, kitchenette and bathroom) cost less. Healthy breakfasts are included and there's a minimum two-day stay between June and October.

With a jungle of a front garden almost obscuring it from sight, lovely *Beaconsfield* (*Map 3;* ☎ 416-535-3338, *38 Beaconsfield Ave*) is like a Victorian boutique hotel. Rooms range from $65 to $95, or $199 for the 'Mexican' suite with private bath and living room. Full breakfasts are served.

West of downtown is the simple *Candy Haven Tourist Home* (☎ 416-532-0651, *1233 King St W*) on the 504 King streetcar line; look for front porch with the sign right beside McDonald's. It's been around for decades and is quaintly old-fashioned. Rooms with a shared bathroom (no breakfast) are just $45. Farther west near Roncesvalles Ave is the *Grayona Tourist Home* (*Map 3;* ☎ 416-535-5443, *1-800-354-0244, 1546 King St W*). It's a renovated old house run by a friendly and reliable Australian. Singles/doubles with shared baths cost $60/80 (no breakfast). Every room has a fridge, telephone and, often, a TV. More expensive rooms, which are good for families (there's even a cot), have cooking facilities. Smokers will be politely but firmly shown the door. It's about 7km from downtown, and the streetcar stops practically at the door.

Though traffic on the front road whizzes by, *Tudor House* (*Map 3;* ☎ 416-440-1922, *tudorhse@home.com, 71 Oriole Parkway*) is a special treat if you won't be going to Stratford (Ontario, that is). The owners are art lovers who offer guided tours of the Art Gallery of Ontario for guests. Rooms cost $95 to $115 per night including a full breakfast. It's quite far north of downtown, south of Kilbarry Rd and across from Upper Canada College.

HOTELS

Unlike, say Montréal, you can't say Toronto and budget hotels in the same breath.

Toronto does have an abundance of modern mid-range and top-end hotels downtown and a good number around Pearson International Airport. Many offer discounted weekend packages, but daily rates fluctuate with demand and the season. Unless otherwise stated, rates do not include tax and apply to peak summer months.

Airport

The *Sheraton Gateway* (☎ *905-672-7000, 1-800-565-0010*) attached to Terminal 3 couldn't be more convenient. All rooms are soundproof, some have views, and weekend rates are normally $99 per double, rising to the normal weekday corporate rate of $230. The hotel has a 24-hour indoor swimming pool and fitness room.

There are plenty of other options in the vicinity, but they don't offer better deals than the Sheraton, except perhaps on weekdays. Strongly recommended by travelers, the *Delta Toronto Airport* (☎ *416-675-6100, 1-800-268-1133, 801 Dixon Rd, Etobicoke*) has spacious rooms, excellent facilities, and sits beside a private 18-hole golf course. Rooms rates range from $109 to $289. The *Travelodge Toronto Airport* (☎ *416-740-9500, 1-800-578-7878, 445 Rexdale Blvd*) is one of the cheapest, costing from $99/119 for singles/doubles. Both hotels operate airport shuttles ($5).

Downtown Toronto (South; Map 4)

On York St and convenient to Union Station, the *Strathcona* (☎ *416-363-3321, 1-800-268-8304, strathcona@sprint.ca, 60 York St*) is an old familiar face. Recently and thoroughly renovated, it offers all the usual amenities and yet, for the downtown area, is

reasonably priced from $119. Ask about special B&B packages.

At the waterfront, the *Westin Harbour Castle* (☎ *416-869-1600, 1-888-625-5144, 1 Harbour Square*) is popular with conventioneers and families. It's near the bottom of Yonge St, directly opposite the Toronto Islands. The revolving restaurant offers good views over the city and Lake Ontario. Standard rooms cost from $129 to $269, some with full lake views. Weekend and long-stay discounts are available.

The SkyDome's *Renaissance Toronto Hotel* (☎ *416-341-7100, 1-800-468-3571, One Blue Jays Way*) has rooms starting at $229 in summer, dropping to $195 in the off-season, but only 70 of the most expensive rooms overlook the playing field.

The serene *Novotel Toronto Centre* (☎ *416-367-8900, 1-800-668-6835, 45 The Esplanade*) is gracefully perched near the waterfront at Scott St, steps away from the St Lawrence Market. European visitors should not let themselves be thrown: unlike its namesake chain in France, this distinguished Novotel is done in grand French Renaissance style with an impressive lobby. Luxury rooms start at $129/159 in the low/high season and are worth every loonie.

Among the city's top-end hotels, the *Royal York* (☎ *416-368-2511, 1-800-663-7229, 100 Front St W*) is one of the most historic (since 1929) and has accommodated rock stars and royal guests. It was built opposite Union Station by the Canadian Pacific Railway, and its mock chateau style adds character to Toronto's otherwise bland modern skyline. Rooms mix richness with style from $189 to start, and rates rise depending on demand. Visit www.cphotels.ca and link to the Royal York homepage for special Internet package deals.

One of the best small downtown hotels is the *Hotel Victoria* (☎ *416-363-1666, 1-800-363-8228, reception@hotelvictoria.on.ca, 56 Yonge St*). Refurbished throughout, it maintains old-fashioned features like its fine lobby. The 24-hour reception desk warmly welcomes everyone, even backpackers arriving in the middle of the night (with reservations, of course). Rates are $125 to $169 for rooms with telephones, cable TV and perhaps coffeemakers and fridges.

Theatergoers could not be better placed than at *Holiday Inn on King* (☎ 416-599-4000, ☎ 1-800-263-6364, 370 King St W), looking as if it had been airlifted straight off Waikiki beach. The brilliant, white resort-like hotel has a seasonal rooftop pool that enjoys views of the CN tower. Superior service for rooms with either lake or skyline views costs $159/189 in the low/high season. Visit www.hiok.com to pick up some great Internet-only deals.

Other top-end hotels centrally located near City Hall deliver exactly what you'd expect. Most are practically interchange-able, as the Hilton and Westin proved when they simply swapped their respective estab-lishments in the late '80s They include the *Sheraton Centre* (☎ 416-361-1000, 1-800-325-3535, 123 Queen St W) and the *Hilton* (☎ 416-869-3456, 1-800-445-8667, 145 Rich-mond St W). Rates at either start around $200 to $250.

The glorious *Le Royal Meridien King Edward* (☎ 416-863-9700, 1-800-543-4300, 37 King St E), also known as the 'King Eddie,' is Toronto's oldest hotel (1903). The Beatles, Teddy Roosevelt and the Duke of Windsor have all stayed here. It has had ups and downs, but no one can deny now that the Meridien group has turned it into a showpiece: baroque plaster, marble, luxuri-ant carpeting and etched glass. Standard rooms are well-priced from $215 (including twice-daily maid service), almost 50% less on selected weekend nights.

Downtown Toronto (North; Map 5)

East of Eaton Centre is the modest high-rise *Bond Place* (☎ 416-362-6061, 1-800-268-9390, 65 Dundas St E), a pleasantly affordable hotel with old-fashioned charac-ter. Rates of $129 to $150 in summer are still good value, dropping to $89 in winter. At the *Marriott Eaton Centre* (☎ 416-597-9200, 1-800-228-9290, 525 Bay St), rates start at around $200 to $250.

The unbeatable *Delta Chelsea* (☎ 416-595-1975, 1-800-243-5732, 33 Gerrard St W)

Hotel Hijinks

The SkyDome hotel became instantly notori-ous when, during one of the first Blue Jays baseball games, a couple in one of the up-perfield side rooms – either forgetfully or rakishly – became involved in some sporting activity of their own with the lights on, much to the crowd's amusement. Such a perform-ance was later repeated at another game. After that, the hotel insisted on guests signing waivers that stipulated there would be no more such free shows off field.

is Toronto's largest, and arguably best-value hotel. Families will enjoy the engaging arts and games centers, children's swimming pools and inexpensive babysitting services. Business travelers are privileged with ex-press check-in and executive services. Singles/doubles start at $119/139 during low season, or $189/209 during peak season. The ground floor is chock-a-block with onsway pubs and eateries, including Bbb33 bistro+brasserie (see the Places to Eat chapter). You could also have breakfast in the Deck 27 skyline lounge, which stays opens from the afternoons until midnight.

Far more opulent, the *Metropolitan* (☎ 416-977-5000, 1-800-668-6600, 108 Chest-nut St) has an inviting atrium and pleasant rooms, but travelers say the service remains iffy. Standard doubles cost $310, but promo-tional B&B and weekend packages may be available. While you're at it, make reserva-tions for the chef's table at Hemispheres (☎ 416-977-9899), the hotel's high-flying restaurant, which has engaged star Toronto chefs since its inception.

Yorkville & University of Toronto (Map 6)

The cheapest accommodation in ritzy York-ville is at the *Howard Johnson Inn* (☎ 416-964-1220, 1-800-446-4656, 89 Avenue Rd), beside Hazelton Lanes shopping center. Standard rooms with the usual features cost $109 to $169, including continental break-fast. Central *Days Inn* (☎ 416-977-6655,

1-800-329-7466, 30 Carlton St) has rooms for $109/$139 in low/high season. It's a fairly reliable chain that has other locations around the city.

Hidden on its own city half-block, the ***Courtyard Marriott*** *(☎ 416-924-0611, 1-800-343-6787, 475 Yonge St)* with all its greenery has guests feeling less weary the moment they step inside. Unfortunately the quality of service runs from bad to incompetent and standard rooms are high-priced at $160 to $245.

The luxurious European-style ***Sutton Place Hotel*** *(☎ 416-924-9221, 1-800-268-3790, res@tor.suttonplace.com, 955 Bay St)* is popular with visiting dignitaries and international film festival stars. Placed throughout are elegant antiques and tapestries, gilded mirrors and chandeliers. A room and a perfect pillow upon which to lay your head will cost $149 to $320.

Small, but popular for its location just midway between Yorkville and the Eaton Centre, ***Comfort Hotel Downtown*** *(☎ 416-924-1222, 1-800-228-5050, 15 Charles St E)* charges $100 to $199 for standard rooms. It's nicely placed off Yonge St, but only worth the money when discount rates are offered.

The ***Park Hyatt*** *(☎ 416-925-1234, 4 Avenue Rd)* has an impressive circular drive with fountains and a rooftop skyline lounge. Rates start at $170/$225 in low/high season. The pricier ***Hotel Inter-Continental*** *(☎ 416-960-5200, 1-800-327-00200, 220 Bloor St W)* is further west, just opposite the Royal Conservatory of Music.

To the east, the ***Marriott Bloor-Yorkville*** *(☎ 416-961-8000, 1-800-267-6116, 90 Bloor St E)* provides A+ service and quite good rooms starting at $145, extra for in-room Nintendo. The café's large-scale murals, painted in tribute to Matisse, are well known.

Some of the costliest rooms in town are found at the glamorous ***Four Seasons*** *(☎ 416-964-0411, 21 Avenue Rd)* in the heart of Yorkville. Prices start at around $350 a night, and everyone here always looks quite comfortable, thank you. It offers upscale boutiques, art galleries, five-star French

Provençale cuisine at Truffles restaurant and a unique indoor-outdoor pool. Top marks go to the excellent concierge staff as well.

Finally, the ***Windsor Arms*** *(☎ 416-971-9666, 1-877-999-2767, 18 St Thomas St)* is the most opulent piece of history on the accommodation market, whether you're staying the night or just dropping in for tea. Built in 1927, the exquisite neo-gothic building boasts stained glass and a grand entryway. Faultless service and surroundings come with a price tag of $295, rising to $2000 for the most decadent suites.

East Central Toronto (Map 10)

The ***Howard Johnson Selby Hotel & Suites*** *(☎ 416-921-3142, 1-800-387-4788, 592 Sherbourne St)* is a turreted Victorian mansion; dating from 1880, it's a designated city heritage site. Formerly a girls' school, it became a residential hotel in 1915. Ernest Hemingway lived here during the 1920s when he worked as a cub reporter for the *Toronto Star* before heading to Paris. Newly upgraded singles/doubles cost $100/120. The high-ceilinged suites with fireplaces in the original mansion cost $200. The hotel's long-standing bar is gone, but construction is ongoing, so it pays to ask for a quiet room. All prices include continental breakfast and health club privileges; parking privileges can be added for a fee. Rates go up $20 or more in summer and during special events. It's worth asking for discounts on weekdays and for longer stays.

Other Neighborhoods

The main house of the ***Guild Inn*** *(☎ 416-261-3331, 201 Guildwood Parkway)* is an Arts & Crafts–style mansion dating from 1914, set in serene lakefront parklands with walking trails. An artists colony was formed here in 1932, and in the front garden there's a collection of sculptures, Ionic columns and gargoyles rescued from condemned and half-destroyed city buildings in the 1950s. The attached hotel is aging, but it's wondrously uncrowded and the slightly faded rooms cost $85. Afternoon tea is served on the patio, and there's an outdoor swimming pool and tennis courts. The inn is east of

Scarborough Bluffs, a 45-minute drive from downtown. Take Kingston Rd (Hwy 2) and exit at Guildwood Pkwy, which winds around to the front gates. On public transit, take the No 116 Morningside bus from Kennedy subway station. Alternatively, the Guildwood Go Train station is a 2km walk north of the inn. You can park here and commute downtown.

On the other side of town and not far from the southern gates of High Park, the *Four Points Sheraton Lakeshore* (Map 3; ☎ 416-766-4392, 1-800-463-9929, 1926 Lake Shore Blvd) has invested well in multi-million dollar renovations that have really spruced things up. Standard rooms cost from $99 to $189, and the hotel has a spa, exercise rooms and easy access to paved recreational paths along the lakefront. It's a bit isolated, though, about 8km west of downtown. Take the No 501 streetcar west to Windermere Ave, get off and walk south under the overpass. You can't miss this brightly lit, salmon-pink hotel.

At the western end of The Beach, *Days Inn Toronto East* (Map 11, ☎ 416 691 1177, 1-800-329-7466, 1684 Queen St E) has a prime location, just a short jog or walk from the lakefront. Promotional rates for huge rooms dip as low as $109/123 for singles/doubles, but peak prices of $200 or more are far more than anyone should fork out for unhelpful service. It's a 20-minute ride from downtown on the 501 Queen streetcar.

MOTELS

For such a large city, Toronto is rather short on motels, so in summer they are often full. They are universally overpriced, so insist on seeing what you get before checking in.

Downtown your only option is the *Executive Motor Hotel* (Map 9; ☎ 416-504-7441, 621 King St W), which has 85 motel-quality rooms at surprisingly high-prices, around $134.40/$85.50 in the high/low season, including free continental breakfast and parking. The 504 King streetcar stops nearby.

There are two other main districts for motels and individual accommodations scattered outside the city limits. On the west side of town, a shrinking motel strip can be

found on Lake Shore Blvd W, just west of Park Lawn Ave. This district isn't too far from the downtown area, about 12km from Yonge St, and No 501 streetcars run the whole way. The waterfront offers cool breezes in summer and good views of the city and islands.

The motels range from decrepit to borderline acceptable and are fast being squeezed out by multi-million dollar condominiums. The safest of the cheapies is the *Rainbow Motel* (☎ 416-259-7671, 2165 Lake Shore Blvd W), where very clean, not altogether seedy singles/doubles cost $40/55. The *Silver Moon* (☎ 416-252-5051, 2157 Lake Shore Blvd W) has rooms with TV and telephones starting at $75, including tax. Farthest west, with the yellow sign, the *Beach Motel* (☎ 416-259-3296, 2183 Lake Shore Blvd W) has well-kept rooms starting at $89. All three are close to Humber Bay Park.

Nearby, but a definite step up is the *Queensway Motel* (☎ 416-252-5821, 638 The Queensway). It's away from the main routes

Guild Inn, former artists colony

and may have rooms when others are full. The management is excellent and singles/doubles are $75/85. From Lake Shore Blvd, take Park Lane Rd north and turn left at The Queensway; it's five minutes farther down on the right.

A couple of respectable motels can be found along Dundas St (Hwy 5), west of Hwy 427, just over the city limits in the suburb of Mississauga. From Lake Shore Blvd, head north up Hwy 427 towards Pearson airport. Just past the border sign is the *Super 5 Motel* (☎ *905-624-6424, 2171 Dundas St*) costing from $75 double.

The other main motel district is on Kingston Rd, much farther from the center in the east end. It starts immediately east of Brimley Rd. Many of these motels are now used by the government as overflow welfare accommodation and are not recommended unless you're in a bind, and even then you may want to think twice. The *Manor Motel* (☎ *416-261-7184, 2740 Kingston Rd*) has passable rooms with telephone for $65, tax included. Bare bones shelter can be found at the *Avon* (☎ *416-267-0339, 2800 Kingston Rd*).

On public transit, take the Bloor-Danforth subway line east to Warden station, then catch any bus going along St Clair E.

APARTMENT HOTELS

Although many apartment hotels are geared toward the corporate client and business executive, they can be reasonably priced. Safe and secluded on its one-way street, the modern *Grange Apartment Hotel* (*Map 9;* ☎ *416-603-7701, 165 Grange Ave*) has small studios with kitchenettes, cable TV and air-con costing $90 for up to two people, $6 more for a third. No minimum stay is normally required. Its twin, the busy *Alexandra Apartment Hotel* (*Map 9;* ☎ *416-504-2121,*

1-800-567-1893, 77 Ryerson Ave) isn't nearly as inviting.

Just minutes from Church St, the high-rise *Cromwell* (*Map 6;* ☎ *416-962-5670, 55 Isabella St*) is gay-friendly (watch for the loud balcony parties) and central, though the location can be iffy at night. The minimum rental is three days, and small studios start at $80 per night. The aging *Town Inn* (*Map 6;* ☎ *416-964-3311, 1-800-387-2755, 620 Church St*) has a pool, tennis courts and sauna. Rates for studios with attached kitchens and full amenities are $140/170 weekdays/weekends, including a small breakfast.

At the top end, *Cambridge Suites Hotel* (*Map 4;* ☎ *416-368-1990, 1-800-463-1990, 15 Richmond St E*) offers two-room suites with microwaves, fridges, separate phone and fax lines and a penthouse health club. Daily rates vary between $170 and $410, including deluxe complimentary breakfast and the *Globe & Mail*.

Finding an Apartment

If you're just moving to Toronto and looking for something more permanent, free weeklies like *Now* and major newspapers have classifieds listings. Also, various renters' guides are available free: Look for them in downtown news boxes. Bulletin boards in hostels and neighborhood coffee shops around Kensington Market, West Queen St W and Church St have advertisements for roommates and subletters. You could also check under Real Estate Agencies in the Yellow Pages.

Be forewarned that renting an apartment in Toronto is not cheap. Many of the city's older buildings are being converted to condominiums and that puts a real squeeze on affordable housing. The cheapest monthly rents are comparable to long-term university accommodation.

Wayne Gretzky, 'The Greatest' hockey player who ever lived, immortalized at his restaurant

AIDS Memorial, Cawthra Square Park

Chinatown: Shinytown at night

Prehistory lives at the Royal Ontario Museum.

Hockey stars live on at the Hockey Hall of Fame.

Look out for Loyalists at Fort York.

Ahoy! Pirates at the Harbourfront!

Urban oasis

JON DAVISON

The ever-effervescent Niagara Falls

SARA BENSON

Slow – Mennonite crossing

ANDRE JENNY

Lake Ontario

NEIL SETCHFIELD

Maid of the Mist, Niagara Falls

Places to Eat

America calls itself a 'melting pot,' but Canadians prefer the term 'mixed salad' for themselves. The metaphor is never more apt than when it describes Toronto's internationally-flavored restaurant scene. What chefs at five-star Michelin restaurants are finally admitting, Torontonians have known since the '70s, when waves of immigration started bringing the world to their forks and fingertips, namely that fusion is the future of food.

So it's no surprise to find miso or Thai lemongrass sprinkled across the contemporary bistro menus here, but keep in mind the lingering British influences, too. A pint with lunch and afternoon high teas are still much-loved traditions. Near Yorkville, the **Duke of York** *(Map 6; ☎ 416-964-2441, 39 Prince Arthur Ave)* is the classic pub for Sunday night roast beef dinners ($10.95), traditional ploughman's lunches, savory pies and yes, bangers and mash.

While Toronto's weather is certainly no more balmy than other Great Lakes cities like Detroit or Chicago, residents savor every last ray of summer by dining out: on rooftops, in shady backyards and on jostling sidewalk patios.

With such a feast of tables and cuisines to choose from, the one sour note is taxes. A hamburger and beer priced at $9.95 on the menu will actually cost you $13, including tip (see the Money section in the Facts for the Visitor chapter), by the time you get out the door. Visitors can stretch their budgets by eating well at lunch, when most restaurants charge about half as much for a meal as at dinner – often for exactly the same menu.

Unless stated otherwise, all of the restaurants listed in this chapter are open daily for lunch and dinner, though some may close for a few hours in the afternoon or take days off in winter. Reservations are strongly advised for higher-priced restaurants; without them, try for an early or late seating, say before 5 pm or after 9 pm.

FOOD
Groceries & Markets

Grocery stores are found in every neighborhood. Downtown, the indoors **St Lawrence Market** *(Map 4; ☎ 416-392-7219)* has a sedate atmosphere – at times there are classical musicians playing. The range and quality of produce and imported foods is superb; just walk around and graze on **Carousel Bakery** goods, Montréal-style bagels from **St Urbain** or the **Mustachio** chicken sandwiches that locals say are 'about as big as your head.' Cast furtive glances at **Caviar Direct** and the illegal (ie, unpasteurized) French cheese sold by vendors at the back. Market hours are 8 am to 6 pm Tuesday to Thursday, 8 am to 7 pm Friday, and 5 am to 5 pm Saturday, when Toronto's historic farmers' market (since 1803) is also held in the North Market.

West of Chinatown, **Kensington Market** (Map 9) is an explosion of Italian butchers, West Indian roti shops, Middle Eastern groceries, fruit markets and home-spun bakeries. It's hot, hectic and fragrant – just the opposite of the St Lawrence. Market shops are open daily, but are busiest Saturday morning when new immigrants and old-world families keep things spinning. **My Market Bakery** *(172 Baldwin St)* sells Portuguese buns, focaccia and lots of desserts like gooey Vancouver-born Nanaimo bars. Its sister shop **Cheese Magic** *(182 Baldwin St)* has cranberry stilton and more gouda than you can shake a stick at. Sandwiched in between, **European Quality Meats & Sausages** *(176 Baldwin St)* hangs bratwurst and *debrezeni* in its streetfront windows.

Other ethnic groceries and organic bulk-food stores abound. (All of the following are also on Map 9.) Portuguese **Casa Acoreana** invites shoppers to 'Come in and go nuts with our nuts!' while cheerful **El Buen Precio** steps to a Latin American beat. For halal meat and falafel, visit **Akram's Shoppe**. Finally, get your ginseng on St Andrews St at the **Chinese International Herb Co**.

Vegetarian

Major health-food stores and bulk and organic groceries are your best bet for vegetarian, vegan and non-dairy eats (including hot and cold take-out delights). The grandmother of them all, co-op *Big Carrot Natural Food Market (Map 10;* ☎ *416-466-2129, 348 Danforth Ave)*, runs a holistic dispensary inside its big Carrot Common

(www.thebigcarrot.ca). *Baldwin Natural Foods (Map 5; 20½ Baldwin St)* and *Noah's Natural Foods (Map 6; 322 Bloor St W; 667 Yonge St)* are both central. In Kensington Market, you'll recognize *Essence of Life Organics (Map 9; 52 Kensington Ave)* by the rice cakes stacked up out front.

When dining out, Indian and Asian restaurant menus almost always turn up meat-

C'est What, Eh?

When traveling you want to try the local cuisine. Except in Canada, what's there to try? A bit of charred moose? A maple syrup pie? Once upon a time there was only Québecois cuisine, but all that has all changed. Of course, be careful not to think Yukon Gold potatoes are anything more than just plain potatoes, or that seafood labeled as being from Prince Edward Island is necessarily anything special. Real Canadian nouveau cuisine combines unusual, fresh (often organic) local ingredients with twists of classic French style and daring borrowings from Asian fusion techniques. In essence it's a bit like California cooking, but fleshed out with meaty northern game and continental sauces.

Many say the definitive Toronto dining space is still *Canoe (Map 4;* ☎ *416-364-0054, 66 Wellington St W)*, and what a space it is, situated on the 54th floor of the Toronto-Dominion Bank Tower. On weekdays, you can enjoy full views of the lake and Toronto Islands while indulging in Canadian regional haute cuisine like maple-barbecued sweetbread or Alberta beef with black truffle bread pudding ($35). If chef Anthony Walsh isn't there, he's probably at Auberge du Pommier (see the Other Neighborhoods section in this chapter), the classic French training ground where so many of Toronto's best kitchen geniuses laid their groundwork.

In the Colonnade (Map 6), understated *Patriot* (☎ *416-922-0025, 131 Bloor St W)* is the new home of experimental chef David Chrystian, whose work once graced the tables of Cafe Societa (see the Little Italy section in this chapter). Patriot's pure Canadian menu almost overdoes it (everything seems to have maple in it), but is reasonably priced for such gourmet fare: Ontario spring lamb and other mains for less than $20, followed by an Ontario sour cherry dessert and Niagara ice wine. Or, you could just trust in the chef's $25 prix fixe menu. Patriot is open daily, except Sunday lunch.

Oro (Map 5; ☎ *416-597-0155, 45 Elm St)* was revamped in the mid-'90s as a showpiece for the contemporary Canadian food creations of chefs Dario Tomaselli and Chris Klugman. The menu reveals much more Asian flavoring, successfully grazing the outer limits of creativity with hoisin-and-tangerine-glazed pork chops or tea-smoked Chilean bass ($40), all served with top-notch elegance. If you can get past the limos waiting outside, it's open weekdays and for dinner on Saturday.

With such stiff competition in the gourmet scene, many of Toronto's top hotels have revamped their own offerings in recent years including spare, fresh *Tundra (Map 4;* ☎ *416-860-6800, 145 Richmond St W)* at the Hilton. Chris Klugman ended up at the Delta Chelsea's *Bb33 bistro+ brasserie (Map 5;* ☎ *416-585-4319)*, where the more formal bistro offers a 'tastes of the season' Canadian menu, complemented by a casual brasserie serving a reasonable buffet ($23). At either you can taste Klugman's homegrown herbs and the warm sourdough of his chosen local bakeries.

If you want to be your own chef, taste test the select Canadian cookbooks listed in the Facts for the Visitor chapter.

free choices. Two all-vegetarian faves are *Juice for Life* (see The Annex section in this chapter) and organic *Kensington Natural Bakery* (Map 8; 460 Bloor St W) for yummy rice flour shakes ($3.50), nondairy cookies and cakes. Farther north, budget *Annapurna* (Map 3; ☎ 416-537-8513, 1085 Bathurst) serves South Indian food and pan-global tofu dishes with an emphasis on the macrobiotic, all amidst leafy ferns and cream-colored walls (closed Sunday).

Not high on ambiance, cafeteria-style *Le Commensal* (Map 5; ☎ 416-596-9364, 655 Bay St, entrance on Elm St) sells fresh salads and hot main dishes for $1.59 per 100g. Some dishes border on bland and have been under the heat lamps too long, but you can't fault the immense selection for people with all sorts of dietary restrictions. The dessert buffet ($1.89/100g), sweetened with maple syrup and fruit nectars, is very tempting.

For more advice on restaurants, cooking classes and the vegetarian food fair in September, contact the Toronto Vegetarian Association (☎ 416-544-9800), PO Box 2307, Toronto, ON M4P 1E4. Web site: www.veg.on.ca

Fast Food

In summer, street vendors are everywhere, selling mainly hot dogs (regular, veggie or spicy Italian sausage that lingers with you for days) or ice cream. On the east side of the UT Robarts Library (Map 6), brain-weary students refuel at *Wokking on Wheels*. Any of two dozen different stir-fry dishes ($5) could feed two people (or one very hungry backpacker).

As in most Canadian cities, fast-food joints are never lacking in Toronto. American standards such as Pizza Hut and McDonald's rub shoulders with Canada's own *Mr Sub*, *Pizza Pizza*, *Mr Greek*, *Harvey's* (looking suspiciously like the American Hardee's), *Wrap n' Roll* and the family-style *Swiss Chalet*.

Equally ubiquitous are 24-hour *Coffee Time*, where two bucks buys a big ol' coffee and maple-iced donut, and *Tim Horton's* donut shops, named after the late, great Canadian hockey player. For gourmet brew,

don't bother with *Second Cup* or *Timothy's World Cafe*; even Torontonians admit they don't measure up to *Starbucks*.

DOWNTOWN TORONTO (SOUTH; Map 4)

Near the SkyDome, *Wayne Gretzky's* (99 Blue Jays Way), as in the hockey legend, is a festive pub, bar and restaurant with pastas and burgers that get the job done. Most people come here because their kids beg them, or because they're on a hockey pilgrimage.

A real downtown delight is *Accolade* (☎ 416-597-8142, 225 Front St W), where there is in fact no menu. Instead Chef Michael Potters dreams up unique 'tasting menus' with light, classic French accents. His breathtaking creativity blooms in the starters, such as eggplant pancakes with marinated salmon and truffle vinaigrette, on through magnificent mains, ending with Ontario ice wine and bittersweet chocolate *bombe*. Reservations are mandatory and weekday lunches start at $25. Dinner is served daily, except Sunday, starting at $55 for four courses, $100 including exquisite wine pairings. The only drawback (and it's a biggie) is its unfortunate location inside the lobby of the Crowne Plaza convention hotel.

Inside BCE Place, *Marche Mövenpick* (☎ 416-366-8986) is an innovative market-style restaurant. Fill up your tray with treats (great fun for kids) like Atlantic salmon with sweet mustard sauce or Swiss rösti, but watch the price tags since most items are over $8. You can smell the signature maple ice cream a mile away. It's open 7 am to 2 am weekdays, until 4 am on weekends. There's a smaller branch called *Marchelino Mövenpick* inside Eaton Centre (Map 5).

Stylish *Nami* (☎ 416-362-7373, 55 Adelaide St E) is profoundly Japanese: kimono-clad matrons, intense sushi chefs and a sleek black lacquer interior. A filling meal will cost $25 minimum. The name means 'wave' – look for the neon version outside (closed Sunday).

Next door at the *Courthouse* (☎ 416-214-9379), off-work traders digging into steaks ($13 to $28) ignore the grisly fact that

Brunch Hunt

Torontonians are single-minded in their search for the perfect brunch. If you've overlooked this combination late breakfast-lunch meal in the past, indulge yourself. Wake up late (past noon but before 4 pm, please) and try pancakes with fresh Ontario peaches and maple syrup, or smoked salmon with cool jazz at *Sassafraz* (see the Yorkville section in this chapter). For elegant contemporary brunches, *Agora* at the Art Gallery of Ontario has skylights and sculpture, while *Latitude* in The Annex (see that section, in this chapter) serves spicy Latin brunches, heavy on salsa, eggs, cornmeal and sangria.

More eclectic *Bella's Bistro* (Map 9; ☎ 416-967-1078, 320 College St) hosts the Bella! Did Ya Eat? Jewish brunch with live klezmer and Yiddish music ($14.95). If you've woken up with a headache, cure it with comfort food at *Insomnia* (see The Annex), *Hello Toast* (see Other Neighborhoods) or *Azul's* Hangover Helper brunch (see the West Queen Street West section). The *Bedford Ballroom* (see Bars in the Entertainment chapter) has nostalgic brunch menus under $7, such as small boxes of cold cereal with cafeteria-sized cartons of milk.

▣▣▣▣▣▣▣▣▣▣▣▣▣▣

Toronto's last public execution took place here. Macabre humor aside, the 19th century building is superb and the grilled meats and seafood are done just right. Best of all, the downstairs bathrooms are actually set amidst old jailhouse cells, one of which is an ice-wine cellar; the other holds a prisoner mannequin.

At the King Edward Hotel, *Café Victoria* (☎ 416-863-4126, 37 King St E) serves wonderfully gourmet pre-theater set meals for $31 including tax, coffee and dessert, every day between 5 and 7 pm.

Intimate *Sarkis* (☎ 416-214-1337, 67 Richmond St E) comfortably enjoys its prestige without attitude. Famous Toronto chef Greg Couillard dreams up seasonal menus of brave fusion that goes all over the

map – East Asia, India and the Pacific Rim. The tiny dining space reflects the mix with European oil paintings and a petite Japanese rock garden nestled at the back. To sit in the very lap of luxury, reserve the sofa table by the front window. Hours vary, but lunch is served a few days per week and dinner every day except Sunday.

Ever wonder where bike couriers go when they're on standby? They gather outside *Spread*, on Temperance St, and gulp $1 self-serve coffee.

Entertainment District

For pre-theater dining, there's a line-up of places on King St, just west of John St and the Theatre Block. Although most give indifferent service and serve worse food, people keep coming.

One saving grace is *N'Awlins* (☎ 416-595-1958, 299 King St W), where even if the food (mains $12 to $20) leans more toward Italian than Deep South, service is courteous and prompt and the live jazz is free (dinner daily).

The cavernous *Peel Pub* (☎ 416-977-0003, 276 King St W), which originated in Montréal, has great prices at any meal, like $5 daily specials, and cheap beer, but it feels like an empty barn. It's open 6:30 am to 2 am daily, with 9¢ wings on Sunday.

Keep heading west to find a real prize, *Asakusa* (☎ 416-598-9030, 389 King St W). On the menu are sushi and sashimi standards, noodles and authentic appetizers, averaging $10 for lunchtime main dishes. But that's a real bargain considering that the Japanese chef-owner worked for three decades in Tokyo's top hotel kitchens – it's worth the long wait (closed Monday lunch).

There are a clutch of other new restaurants (some ferociously passè even as they open) to be found in this fickle, expanding galaxy south of Queen St W, often referred to as the Entertainment District. Largely drawing a suburban crowd, the fact that there's a Hooters here really says it all.

Independent *Fez Batik* (☎ 416-204-9660, 129 Peter St) is of an entirely different breed. Flower murals are painted over the exterior walls and the patio sprawls. A tame menu of pasta and meat main dishes for $11 to $20 belies the crazy come-on (closed Monday).

Perfect for families, *Alice Fazooli's* (☎ 416-979-1910, 294 Adelaide St W) features crab and Italian fare with a huge wine list to help wash it down, about $25 all told at dinner.

For those with less money or who are in need of a smoked-meat sandwich in a small, busy, Jewish-style deli, check *Zupa's* (☎ 416-593-2775, 342½ Adelaide St W). You'd have to be an alligator to get your mouth around one of these mega-sandwiches ($6). It's open 6 am to 7 pm, with an all-day breakfast for $2.85 (closed Sunday).

DOWNTOWN TORONTO (NORTH; Map 5)

Beneath the Top O' the Senator (☎ 416-364-7517, 249 Victoria St) jazz club is a classic *steakhouse* with semi-private curtained booths (closed Monday). An adjacent '30s luncheonette, the *Senator Diner* has good weekday breakfast deals before 11:30 am and cheap burgers, fries and greasy spoon stuff into the early afternoon.

Queen Street West

Tiger Lily's Noodle House (☎ 416-977-5499, 257 Queen St W) is so plush it seems to embody one of its dishes, the 'love nest' (a stir-fry with walnuts over noodle cake, $12). The creative dim sum brunch and rich Vietnamese coffee bring people back again and again.

Long-established *Le Select Bistro* (☎ 416-596-6405, 328 Queen St W) gets by on its $23.95 prix fixe French menu and the cute bread baskets that hang above patron's tables. Call after hours to hear the crazy, triumphant answering machine message.

Chinatown

The city's large Chinatown is home to scores of restaurants. Cantonese, Szechuan, Hunan and Mandarin food are all served.

Refined *Ten Ren's Tea* (☎ 416-598-7872, 454 Dundas St W) is where you come for rare Chinese import blends, or if you're hoping for a little ginseng.

Always bustling, *Furama Cake & Desserts Garden* (248-250 Spadina Ave) bakes lotus seed cakes, almond cookies and curried buns and sells them for less than $1. That same loonie will buy a *bánh mí* (Vietnamese sub sandwich) with meat or tofu filling at shops like *Kim Thanh* (336 Spadina Ave).

Clean, bright and jam-packed, *Goldstone Noodle House* (☎ 416-596-9053, 266 Spadina Ave) is easily identified by the barbecued ducks (a house specialty) hanging in the window. Humongous helpings of Hong Kong noodle or rice dishes with grease-free meats or veggies cost only $3.25 to $7.50. On the 2nd floor of Hsin Kuang shopping center, *Bright Pearl* (346-8 Spadina) is a Cantonese-style banquet hall popular for weekend dim sum.

Longstanding *Lee Garden* (☎ 416-593-9524, 331 Spadina Ave) offers an unusually varied Cantonese menu with dishes from $8 to $12. It's open 4 pm to midnight daily – join the queue. Authentic *Sang Ho* (☎ 416-596-1685, 536 Dundas St W) has seafood aquariums: House specialties like shellfish crab with garlic and pepper go for $10, rarer marine delicacies cost $20 to $30. It's worth the wait.

Swatow (☎ 416-977-0601, 309 Spadina Ave) has an extensive menu covering cuisine

PLACES TO EAT

from (where else?) Swatow, on the coast of China's Kwangtung province. Swatow cuisine was once nicknamed 'red cooking' because it uses potent fermented rice wine. Try the house noodles for $10 (cash only) at almost any hour, since it stays open (amazingly) 11 am to 4 am daily.

As some Chinese restaurateurs pack up and leave for the suburbs, Thai and Vietnamese kitchens take their place. *Phổ' Hu'ng* (☎ 416-593-4274, 350 Spadina Ave) features an awesome array of Vietnamese soups ($5.50 to $8) that come with fresh greens. Featuring intestine, tendons and blood, certain dishes may be a touch too authentic for some but are delicious. A fairweather bonus is the patio.

Baldwin Village

A secretive street that not many out-of-towners get to is Baldwin St, just west of McCaul St. Outdoor Italian joints like *John's Italian Caffe* (☎ 416-537-0598, 27 Baldwin St) predominate, but Asian and African places also flourish.

Kowloon (☎ 416-977-3773, 5 Baldwin St) has knockout $4.50 weekday lunch specials – Thousand Year Egg and Pork Congee, and dim sum items that one person could order three of (under $3.10 each). You can safely skip the dying British Columbia crabs in the tank by the door, however. *Konichiwa* (☎ 416-593-8538, 31 Baldwin St) is a super-friendly, super-cheap Japanese diner with an outdoor patio and *donburi* (rice bowls) for under $7, as well as sushi and Sapporo beer (closed Sunday).

On this most secret of streets, a romantic hideaway like *Mata Hari Grill* (☎ 416-596-2832, 39 Baldwin St) makes perfect sense. Authentic Malaysian dishes such as fiery beef *rendang* and Nyonya (Straits Chinese) Chicken Kapitan curry average $11 at dinner. The short list of hard-to-find Belgian and German beers is a bonus. It's open for lunch Tuesday to Friday and dinner daily except Monday. For traditional Moroccan and Mediterranean cooking, try the cushions of *Casbah* (☎ 416-597-1366, 45 Baldwin St) (dinner only, closed Sunday).

YORKVILLE & UNIVERSITY OF TORONTO (Map 6)
Yorkville

All-natural *Greg's Ice Cream* has been made in the basement of 200 Bloor St W for 18 years. 'Flavors of the moment' (roasted marshmallow, if you're lucky) are $2 per scoop. Upstairs is a branch of Chinatown favorite *Phổ' Hu'ng* (see the earlier entry).

Mövenpick's *La Pêcherie* (☎ 416-926-9545, 133 Yorkville Ave) has people raving about its seafood. The daily-changing menu (most mains under $20) is written on a chalkboard that the staff hoist over to your table before they launch into mouthwatering descriptions of how the fish are prepared. Vegetarian dishes can be made to order and the atmosphere is smart, but friendly enough for families.

Why bother with nonfat yogurt when you can enjoy a double scoop of coconut cream ($4.25) from delicious *Summer's Ice Cream (101 Yorkville Ave)*? It's open noon to midnight daily.

Little Tibet (☎ 416-963-8821, 81 Yorkville Ave) cashes in on Tibetan trendiness, but the *momo* are plumper than the standard. Although some items look suspiciously Chinese, the Se-Sha Te (sautèed zucchini, mushrooms and choice of meat, $8.95) comes recommended. There are plenty of vegetarian options on the menu, too.

Wanda's Pie in the Sky (☎ 416-925-7437, 7A Yorkville Ave) has fantastical dessert creations like the Avalanche Cake and exceptional Ontario sour cherry and Niagara peach pies. Before the sugar rush, $6 gets you a filling half-sandwich with soup or salad.

With celebrity photographs autographed by Mike Myers (Yum! Yum!) and Robin Williams (L'chaim!), delightful *Sassafraz* (☎ 416-964-2222, 100 Cumberland Ave) feels so very much like LA. The indoor garden courtyard is as sun-drenched as the sidewalk tables. Weekend jazz combos serenade late brunches (11:30 am to 5 pm) and dinners ($20 to $30, served until 2 am!). Don't forget a pitcher of excellent sangria.

Equally fascinating people-watching can be had more cheaply next door at *Lettieri (94 Cumberland Ave)*, an Italian chain coffee shop with sandwiches and pastries (try the cannoli).

Okonomi House (23 Charles St W) is one of the only places in Toronto, let alone North America, serving *okonomiyaki*, a savory Japanese cabbage pancake filled with meat, seafood or veggies. This regional specialty is so immediately likable that Toronto's cops regularly stop by the grill for take-out ($6).

Patronized by Toronto film festival stars, *Bistro 990 (☎ 416-921-9990, 990 Bay St)* upholds French standards with classic dishes like duck in blackberry *jus* ($25) and meticulously made desserts. It's open weekdays and Saturday for dinner.

Yonge & Church Streets

Yonge St itself, though busy night and day, is not one of Toronto's prime restaurant districts. It is swamped with bland fast-food franchises and cheap take-out counters.

There are wonderful exceptions, however. *Spring Rolls (☎ 416-972-7265, 687 Yonge St)* leads the South-East Asian explosion. Its brick interior is adorned with statues of Chinese warriors and the Buddha. It's worth the extra dollar or two you'll spend on items from a flawless and extensive pan-Asian menu. Vietnamese *pho, bún* or vegetarian *pad thai* with tom yum soup will impress, and most dishes are under $8.95.

Expansive, very purple *Zyng Asian Market & Noodle Cafe (730 Yonge St)* is a build-your-own noodles place. Combine Vietnamese pho with Szechuan or Japanese miso sauce, all for less than $8.

At the hole-in-the-wall *Papaya Hut (513A Yonge St)*, there's homemade vegetable soup, sandwiches and a vast array of fruit drinks and smoothies. New Yorkers will recognize it as a long-lost twin to Manhattan's Gray's Papaya, right down to the silver kegs.

Kathmandu Kathmandu (505A Yonge St) is the only Indian food in sight here. A homemade mango lassi and tandoori chicken with naan for takeout is only $3.99. It's just a nook really, but the Indian breads ($2) and spread of curries ($6 to $8) are the real thing.

Ethiopia House (☎ 416-923-5438, 4 Irwin Ave) is packed and popular. Hot veggie *wot* options ($7.95) and meats like *gored-gored* spiced beef ($11) are plopped onto moist *injera* bread, naturally. Neighbor *Zyweic (☎ 416-924-0716)* serves 'Royal Polish' cuisine like kielbasa and potato pancakes ($8 to $15), plus beer on its ample patio.

Over the past 40 years, the popularity of *Carman's (☎ 416-924-8697, 26 Alexander St)* steakhouse has waxed and waned, but the profuse flower garden out front and the Alexander Wood homestead (notice the stained glass) will make you gasp. With your steak you get nine famous side dishes

High Tea

For traditional Victorian afternoon tea, the *Windsor Arms (Map 6; ☎ 416-971-9666, 18 St Thomas St)* has all the accoutrement: tinkling ivories, starched tablecloths and an airy tea room. Full tea (and they mean big) costs $32, or cream tea just $20. Daily sittings are at 1:30 and 3:30 pm. Just as luxurious, *Cafe Victoria (Map 4; ☎ 416-863-9700)*, at the King Edward Hotel, serves Buckingham Palace shortbread amidst palm trees and Victorian-print chairs from 2:30 to 4:30 pm ($18). Reservations are advised at either.

For afternoon tea with a twist, nouveau *Pangaea (Map 6; ☎ 416-920-2323, 1221 Bay St)* serves blends from former Asian and African outposts of the Empire, along with buttermilk-sunflower scones, between 3 and 4:30 pm daily except Sunday ($15).

Mixing with Masterpieces

Toronto's first homegrown, star chef was Jamie Kennedy, who has come down from the mountain of Scarmouche (see Other Neighborhoods, this chapter) to rule over the *JK ROM* (☎ 416-586-5578) penthouse at the Royal Ontario Museum (Map 6). An ever-changing lunch menu of nouveau Canadian cuisine is well done (all under $20) with by-the-glass wine pairings from a formidable cellar list.

At the Art Gallery of Ontario, equally contemporary *Agora* (Map 5; ☎ 416-979-6612) is exquisitely placed in its own sunny atrium, surrounded by sculptures. Elegant continental-inspired mains (around $20) are served like works of art. Reservations are recommended, especially for weekend brunch (closed Monday).

If it's just a quick bite you're after, *à la Carte* (☎ 416-586-8080) is tucked away upstairs in a quiet nook at the Gardiner Museum of Ceramic Art (Map 6). The caterer's kitchen serves weekday lunches for under $15, featuring the likes of apple-wood smoked salmon and Ontario whitefish.

(including mini-baklava). Dinner for two will be over $100.

Farther east, on Church St in the gay village, the restaurants are more worried about image ('Is his patio bigger than mine?') than passing any taste tests. Busy *Zelda's* (☎ 416-922-2526, 542 Church St), however, has a winning combination of good, standard North American food (chicken, salads etc for $10), reputable drinks and prime outdoor seating. Those with rich boyfriends should suggest a trip to swish *Byzantium* (☎ 416-922-3859, 499 Church St) to try creative mains like roast salmon with pineapple salsa ($30) laid out on linen-clad tables (dinner daily).

THE ANNEX & LITTLE ITALY (Map 8)
The Annex

If you're very hungry and cash-poor (like most students) *Cora Pizza* (656A Spadina) is open daily until at least 2 am. Gourmet slices, like the 'Cha-cha-cha' with chicken, roasted red peppers and mozzarella ($3.75), are enormous; juice costs just 50¢ more. *Basha Sandwich Bar* (300 Bloor St W) serves up the tastiest, full-to-bursting falafel and chicken schwarma sandwiches around. *Harbord Bakery* (115 Harbord St) is a fresh, joyful, noisy place. Get your challah, blintzes and rugelach here, as well as fruit-filled croissants and tarts. Just down the

street, *Harbord Fish & Chips* (☎ 416-925-2225, 147 Harbord St) shakes its fries with style, and large fried portions of haddock or halibut go for $7. You can get it all wrapped up in newspapers for takeout or sit down outside while your laundry spins across the street at Coin-o-Rama.

The intimate wine bar at *Latitude* (☎ 416-928-0926, 89 Harbord St) hides a tree-draped back patio. The Uruguayan chef takes good care of his Latin fare, sprinkled with Asian influences, and there's always fried yuca or plantains available on the side. Don't miss brunch or the *tres leches* cake, soaked in liquors and three kinds of cream (closed Monday).

Real Thailand (☎ 416-924-7444, 350 Bloor St W) must have T.O.'s tiniest patio, laid out with artificial turf reminiscent of mini-golf courses. But the food is authentically spicy, service is smilingly prompt and lunch specials are $6.95. Thai standards such as *tod mun plan* fish cakes and spicy beef and chicken *larb* salads are on the menu, and there's sticky rice with mango and coconut milk for dessert.

Sleek *Mumbo Jumbo* (☎ 416-531-5777, 527 Bloor St. W) opens only for dinner, when a short menu of 'oversized' dishes for sharing ($7.50 to $25) runs the gamut of world influences, proven by Prince Edward Island mussels steamed in sake. Almost a sister in invention, *Goldfish* (☎ 416-513-

0077, 372 Bloor St W) puts its diners inside a veritable fish bowl of aqua-colored front windows. Mouth-tingling mains such as Cornish hen with lemon and raisin couscous ($26) are half the price at lunch.

Why people take to the tiny patio at *By the Way (☎ 416-967-4295, 400 Bloor St W)* and forsake the cozy booths inside is a small mystery. This comfortable bistro has a proven fusion menu with main dishes for $10 that are worth every penny. Service is A+ and the excellent wine list has Niagara ice wines and vintages from as far away as Oregon and Australia.

For an affordable meal at almost any time of day (or night), there's *Future Bakery & Café (☎ 416-922-5875, 483 Bloor St W)*. It stays busy serving up budget dishes like cheese crêpes with sour cream, or all-you-can-eat perogies and sauerkraut on Wednesday night, followed up with bowls of café au lait and glorious pie.

Juice for Life (☎ 416-531-2635, 521 Bloor St W) is a city fave for its strictly vegetarian fare and absence of earnestness. The wholesome *and* tasty menu includes veggie burgers, creative salads, 'Free Tibet' rice bowls and 'Khao San' soba noodles. There is also a vast array of high-priced smoothies, shakes and 'vital fluids' to cure what ails.

No-frills *Country Style Hungarian Restaurant (☎ 416-537-1745, 450 Bloor St W)* has an institutional feel, but the chicken paprikash, cold cherry soup and real ghoulash are under $10 and the dessert crêpes (cottage cheese, walnut etc) are cheap and sweet.

You'll always have company at *Insomnia (☎ 416-588-3907, 563 Bloor St)*, no matter how late, since this eclectic café is open until 2 am weekdays and as late as 5 am on weekends. Roll in early the next day for brunch – don't miss 'Heaven on Earth' (wild berries, cream cheese and French toast for $7.95).

For some truly wacky (and kinda tacky) Cajun places, go to Mirvish Village, near Bloor and Bathurst Sts. *True Grits (☎ 416-536-8383, 603 Markham St)* is a bordello-like 'soul shack' with a balcony and picnic-style tables. The short menu includes red beans, fried chicken and jambalaya, all under $15, served on paper plates (dinner daily except

Monday). Its well-mannered cousin *Southern Accent (☎ 416-536-3211, 595 Markham St)* is just down the street (dinner daily).

West of Honest Ed's, Bloor St W merges into Koreatown, where the sushi shops and barbecue grills show a pan-Asian influence. Stand outside *Hodo Kwaja (656 Bloor St W)* and watch the machines pump out tiny little walnut cakes (30¢ each). Much farther west, *Rikishi (☎ 416-538-0760, 833 Bloor St W)* is a Japanese oasis of bamboo and indigo textiles. Sushi and *bentō* box meals ($15) are complemented by a vegetarian menu of *yūdōfu*, pickled plums and mountain vegetable *temaki* (hand rolls).

Little Italy

Based along College St, Little Italy is one of the hottest spots for eating and meeting, or just perusing the old-world bakeries and fine *ristoranti*.

Dark and delicious as the coffee it brews, *Kalendar Koffee House (546 College St)* is an intimate place offering things such as delicious pastry-wrapped 'scrolls,' naan-based pizzas and ginger-carrot soup, as well as pastas, salads and generous desserts, all under $10.

Trendsetters come and go but sparkling *Bar Italia (☎ 416-535-3621, 584 College St)* remains a places to be seen, as well as relax. The happily crowded front patio leads inside to a spacious bar and restaurant. An excellent Italian sandwich or lightly done pasta with lemon gelato and a coffee afterward will come to $25.

Family-owned *Café Diplomatico (☎ 416-534-4637, 594 College St)* is justifiably busy from 8 am until late every day. Perhaps too busy, since it's almost impossible to catch a server's eye. When you do, order a mix-and-match pasta ($9) like the heavenly soft gnocchi. The cappuccino is particularly good (try the *coretto* with a shot of sambuca). For the best *tartufo, zabajone* and specialty desserts in town, head farther west to the *Sicilian Ice Cream Co (☎ 416-531-7716, 712 College St)*, also known as the *Sicilian Sidewalk Café*.

The name may be hard to swallow, but *Supermodel Pizza (772 College St)* only refers to the motto that 'our crust is as thin as a super model.' Inventive, melt-in-your-mouth slices, such as perfect eggplant with olives and roast peppers, cost $3.75, and don't forget to treat yourself to locally-produced Jones soda pop.

Famed chef David Chrystian has left the kitchens of *Cafe Societa* (☎ 416-588-7490, 796 College St). Still the weekday prix fixe ($27) and weekend tasting menus ($75, including paired wines for each course) emphasize seasonal nouveau Canadian cuisine, like BC Albacore in sweet pea sauce or Nunavik caribou, finishing with maple-almond ice parfait or artisan cheese plates. The wine list harbors delights from New Zealand and Australia.

A personal favorite is *Ristorante Grappa* (☎ 416-535-3337, 797 College St), where warm salads, gnocchi with fruit topping and grilled veal with marsala are complemented by (what else?) grappa. Service is flawless and the rustic interior is several notches above standard. Pastas and *secondi* average $15 to $25, but look for the board listing unusual specials.

For top-end Portuguese, there's venerable *Chiado* (☎ 416-538-1910, 864 College St). Start with lobster-shrimp bisque, then indulge in second courses like roast pheasant in Madeira wine and citrus sauce, followed up by *natas do ceu* dessert in almond liqueur. Portuguese specialty dinners for two are just $40. Reservations are advised (dinner daily).

KENSINGTON MARKET & WEST QUEEN STREET WEST (Map 9)
Kensington Market
Louie's Coffee Stop has been on the corner of Augusta Ave and Baldwin St since 1965. Jazz floats lightly out to the streetside stools, an oasis in this hectic marketplace. Italian sodas, fruit and espresso shakes and regular coffee are just $1. *Jumbo Empanadas* (☎ 416-977-0056, 245 Augusta Ave) has real Chilean empanadas ($3), and the corn pie with beef, olive and egg ($6) always sells out early.

'Nothing here is just ordinary' says the man behind the counter at *Moon Bean Cafe* (30 St Andrews), and that's true. Though a bit short on elbow room, this café nevertheless has fine organic coffees, all-day breakfasts for $3 and 'Bite Me' vegan cookies.

Vanipha (☎ 416-340-0491, 193 Augusta Ave) is a basement hole-in-the-wall that cooks up authentically spicy northern Thai and Lao cuisine. It's considered one of the best in the city, but hours are erratic.

Lifted straight out of New Orleans, *Southern Po' Boys* (see Jazz, Swing & Blues in the Entertainment chapter) has authenticity, an in-house tarot reader and red-and-white checked tablecloths. The Cajun menu is regrettably underspiced (and a bit over-priced for mains around $20), but the supper club atmosphere created by the piano player encourages lengthy lingering over unbeatable Mardi Gras house cocktails.

West Queen Street West
The desserts made at *Dufflet's Pastries* (☎ 416-504-2870, 787 Queen St W) appear on the plates of Toronto's most prestigious top-end restaurants. There are a couple of cute tables at the bakery for biting into tasty little temptations like sugar cookies or tarts for $2 each. The chocolate cakes are unreal and almost justify the utterly aloof attitude of the staff (but the 'I Dream of Jeannie' background music is inexcusable).

Just as sweet, *Vienna Home Bakery* (☎ 416-703-7278, 626 Queen St W) has the kind of checked tiles that grandmothers have on their kitchen floors. Take a seat at the short luncheonette counter for hearty home-cooked favorites like steaming hot soup. Its only open 10 am to 7 pm, Wednesday to Saturday.

All along Queen St are Indian roti take-out shops where you can get a monster-sized wrap for $5. *Gandhi* (554 Queen St W) has dirt-cheap vegetarian roti ($2.50), too. *New York Subway* (520 Queen St W) has built its reputation on budget burritos filled to bursting, like the potato-and-bean combo ($4).

With a thrown-together look perfect for a bohemian coffeehouse, *Java House* (537 Queen St W) has an amazing worldwide selection of tea on its shelves. Outside under the jungle mural, neighborhood types take their caffeine fixes and slurp stellar fresh fruit shakes ($2.50). The menu is all over the Asian map, with generous servings under $5.95.

Off-duty Toronto chefs eat at *Terroni* (☎ 416-504-0320, 720 Queen St), a southern Italian import grocery and traditional deli with a long line of counter stools and a back patio for dining. Wines, wood-oven pizzas and *panini* for under $10 approach perfection.

Many trendier Queen St eateries come and go, but hot spot *Gypsy Co-op* (☎ 416-703-5069, 817 Queen St W) stays on, serving contemporary food with a twist, like black ravioli in pumpkin sauce ($12) and green salads with lemon-sesame vinaigrette ($10; closed Sunday and lunch Monday).

An unassuming storefront on a none-too-savory corner, *Azul* (☎ 416-703-9360, 181 Bathurst St) shyly hides its glory. Who would know that their motto is 'Damn fine food. Kickass cocktails'? Or that the ultra-creative menu lives up to its promises? Dinners are a steal at $8 to $18 (those marked with !#%? are spicy), and on weekends you can show up for the Hangover Helper Brunch. The 'Decadence' plate (lobster scrambled eggs with truffle oil, caviar blinis and other ecstasies for $32) must be pre-ordered by Friday.

Romantic and warm *Citron* (☎ 416-504-2647, 813 Queen St W) has dark wood booths and an ever-evolving menu that

Late-Night, All Night

Never fear, Cinderella, there's always good foraging after midnight in Toronto. You can depend on Greektown's most stylish and traditional restaurants to stay open until midnight or later, and on Spadina Ave, Chinatown's glaringly lit noodle shops stay open practically all night. At Queen St W, the people at the *McDonald's* (Map 9) walk-thru window get even odder as its 3 am closing time approaches. Meanwhile ravers and stoners are cleaning out the shelves of *Sugar Mountain* (Map 9, 571 Queen St W) candy store. Up at College and Bathurst Sts, UT students are keeping *Sneaky Dee's* (Map 8; ☎ 416-603-3090, 431 College St) alive until 4 am on the weekends, downing pitchers of Upper Canada with enormous platters of Mexican food ($10). Sneaky's exterior sign is so colorfully trashy, though, you may not feel much like eating.

When even these trusty standbys shut down, hungry night owls turn to Toronto's 24-hour diners. Across the street from Sneaky's, *Mars* (Map 8; 432 College St) is a diner qua diner with bar stools and plenty of chrome. Waitstaff know regulars by name and the homemade eggnog and butter muffins are famous, but it's only open around the clock from Thursday through Sunday morning. Legend has it that classic *Fran's* (Map 6; 20 College St) has never closed since the day it opened its doors in the 1940s. The chain *Golden Griddle* (Map 4; 111 Jarvis St) has sugary pancakes and North American family-style favorites. If you roll in very late (or early, by regular folks' reckoning), you can catch Saturday farmers or antique vendors on Sunday setting up across the street.

But you can't do better than delicious *Mel's Montreal Delicatessen* (Map 8; ☎ 416-966-8881, 440 Bloor St W), run by one of the daughters from Canada's largest family, as you'll find out when you read the newspaper clippings under the table tops. Completely appetizing full meals might include Montreal smoked meat, a bit of French toast made with challah bread or egg-white-only omelets, and all are thoroughly recommended.

Dark and romantic, *7 West Café* (Map 6; 7 Charles St W) is the perfect post-club stop for couples who've just hooked up. Even though the food is no great shakes, lovers tête-à-tête over table wines by the glass (last call 3 am on weekends), knowing that it's never too late or too crowded here to whisper in somebody's ear.

almost never misfires. Try the warm pear salad ($6) and the chicken supreme ($16). It's especially laid-back at Sunday brunch; try the French toast stuffed with lemon ricotta. The list of bottled beers includes Québecois microbrews.

EAST CENTRAL TORONTO (Map 10)

At the edge of downtown, *Montreal Bistro & Jazz Club* (☎ 416-363-0179, 65 Sherbourne St) doesn't put food in second place. Heavily-influenced Québecois cuisine like seafood cocotte, with British Columbia smoked salmon or Prince Edward Island mussels to start, will total $35 or more (closed Sunday and lunch Saturday).

Far more scenic than you might expect from a chain, *The Keg Mansion* (☎ 416-964-6609, 515 Jarvis St) steakhouse is actually inside the historic Massey Mansion. For an affordable steak ($20) with some class, this sets a standard. Dinner is served only until 11 pm, but the upstairs bar stays open late.

Cabbagetown

So very arty and self-consciously cool, *Jet Fuel* (519 Parliament St) is a hangout for east-end gentrifiers who like to jeer at the beautiful people of Yorkville. If their attitude gets you down, scurry off to *Now Cafe* (533 Parliament St) for all-day Flintsones breakfast combos or gourmet soup-and-sandwich lunches for less than $9.

The quaint bungalow housing *Rashnaa* (☎ 416-929-2099, 307 Wellesley E) is full of wonderful menu surprises, like South Indian devil curry and Sri Lankan String Hopper Rotty. The prices are unbeatable: $8 or less for main dishes and a dollar or two for appetizers like deep-fried lentil dumplings with coconut chutney. Don't you dare miss the traditional desserts like *vatalapam*, a honey and cardamom spiced custard pie. All this, and lassis and air-conditioning, too.

An oasis of sunshine, very French *Provence* (☎ 416-924-9901, 12 Amelia St) seems to pop up out of nowhere. Regulars know that the $15 prix fixe lunch is a steal, especially when it comes with Grand Marnier

brulee for dessert. Superior dinners with patio seating under the stars will cost $45 minimum.

Greektown (The Danforth)

Most of the places in the Greek area along Danforth Ave, east of the city center, get very busy on summer nights, when there's quite a festive air about. Casual, cheap souvlaki houses and upscale *mezes* (Greek tapas) restaurants abound, and some places serve until the very wee hours.

North of the main drag, romantic *Café Brussel* (☎ 416-465-7363, 786 Broadview Ave) is a Belgian exception. Mussels are served any of 32 ways, from Tahiti to Provençale ($16.95 per kilo with *frites*). European, Québecois and Belgian microbrews are on hand. It's open for dinner Tuesday to Saturday and Sunday brunch.

The pub *Dora Keogh* (☎ 416-778-1804, 141 Danforth Ave) serves amazing Irish fare from Yer Ma's Kitchen, an open country-style kitchen at the back of the bar. The salmon, potato and green onion cakes with chili sour cream are especially yummy ($6.95). Handwritten menus are put out in the bar from 5 pm till whenever the kitchen runs out of food, but you're safe if you're in before 9 pm (closed Monday). Next door *Allen's* (☎ 416-463-3086) pub reputedly has the best burgers and sirloin around.

Travelers who've been to Asia will be endeared to *Silk Road Cafe* (☎ 416-463-8660, 341 Danforth Ave). The photos hanging up were taken by the owner himself in India and Tibet, though he now concentrates his creativity on pan-Asian Chinese cooking – take your noodles Shanghai, Bangkok or Singapore style ($8 to $10) with Japanese beer, sake or plum wine (open daily except Sunday and Monday during lunch).

A good, bustling, family-owned place – just look for the queue – is *Astoria* (☎ 416-463-2838, 390 Danforth Ave), started by a pair of brothers from Sparta. Standard entrees cost $10 to $15 and you can get tender spanokopita to go.

Inside a former movie house, *Myth* (☎ 416-461-8383, 417 Danforth Ave) serves the most chic mezes on the strip, with pool tables and lots of high-ceilinged glamour. Small portions are dear at up to $13, but the balsamic-glazed octopus with smoked eggplant and artichoke compote might be the best you'll ever have. The crowds stay packed in here from the early evening until 4 am on weekends.

Popular *Ouzeri* (☎ 416-778-0500, 500A Danforth Ave) presents more sensibly priced mezes and sophisticated seafood mains. Fresh sardines in mustard sauce with a Greek salad and a cold beer will cost around $20. There's live traditional Greek music on Tuesday night.

Comfortable *πΑΝ* (☎ 416-466-8158, 516 Danforth Ave) serves very well-prepared meals with traditional Greek flavorings, like stuffed quail with green grape sauce ($15; dinner daily).

Since the 1960s, *Ella's* (☎ 416-463-0334, 702 Pape Ave) has carried on the tradition of the Greek standards. It's elegantly decorated with attentive, tablecloth service. Favorites like lamb and souvlaki plus the catch of the day lie on the 'Poseidon' platter for two ($46). Amazingly the main dishes are half-price during 'happy hours' from 3 to 6 pm and again after 9 pm until midnight.

At the tail end of the strip, *Acropole Bakery* (713 Danforth Ave) has famous baklava, honey balls and other sweets.

Little India

There are Indian restaurants scattered around Toronto, but for a wallet-friendly place with a side order of cultural experience, you can't beat Little India, trailing along Gerrard St E just west of Coxwell Ave.

Madras Durbar (1386 Gerrard St E) is a tiny, tattered, exclusively vegetarian place that serves South Indian dishes. The *thali* plate and *masala dosa* are real taste sensations ($5). Note there is another restaurant down the street with the same name (just like in India).

The long-established *Bar-Be-Que Hut* (☎ 416-466-0411, 1455 Gerrard St E) is plusher than most, overwhelmingly friendly and there's live music Friday to Sunday nights. From the selection of meat and vegetarian dishes, the half-chicken tandoori or

sizzling curry pots are just $9. The assorted naan, paratha and kulcha breads are a few dollars each.

The self-appointed 'Home of Halal Food' is *Lahore Gate* (☎ 416-406-1668, 1365 Gerrard St E), a *tikka* house with fish masala and chicken kebabs for under $10, as well as an outdoor patio where Muslim families gather for live music (open noon to midnight daily).

After dinner, pop into one of the shops for a *paan* made to order. With or without tobacco, this is a cheap, exotic mouthful. Or stop by *Punjab Foods & Sweets* (1448 Gerrard St E) for homemade sugarcane juice and Indian sweets. *Chaat Rendez-Vous* (1438-A Gerrard St E) has *kulfi*, roti and various *chaat* (usually shredded fresh fruit covered in tamarind sauce, sugar and salt).

THE BEACH (Map 11)

At its most crowded on summer weekends when good weather brings out the beach bum in everyone, the long Queen St E drag between Woodbine Ave and Victoria Park is full of gourmet restaurants, some that flop and some that fly. There are also enough fish-and-chips shops and beachfront hot dog vendors to keep budgeteers well fed.

Down at the east end, simple *Antoinette* (☎ 416-698-1300, 2455½ Queen St E) does no-fuss Italian fare well, including patriotically tri-color gnocchi and black-pepper angel hair pasta, with everything under $15 and tartufo for dessert (dinner daily except Sunday). Farthest east, *Otabe* (☎ 416-693-8994, 2326 Queen St E) is a super-authentic Japanese kitchen with *shoji* screens and sunlight. Vegetarian bentō and sushi platters cost $12, or try any of the authentic appetizers (same hours). Just down the street from the Fox cinema, *The Remarkable Bean* (2242 Queen St E) is a comfortable coffeehouse with still-in-the-pan homemade desserts.

Back in the busy, bustling west end, the choices are bewildering. Long-running *The Beacher Café* (☎ 416-699-3874, 2162 Queen St E) has a large outdoor patio and the look of an old seaside house. Egg and pancake brunches are especially good, and at other times the burgers, salads and seafood are reasonable ($12). *Akane-ya* (☎ 416-699-0377, 2214A Queen St E) has exquisite Japanese bentōfor two ($40) and sushi (dinner daily).

Since 1965, *Meat on the Beach* (☎ 416-690-1228, 1965 Queen St E) delicatessen has been a one-stop picnic haven stocked with fresh baked bread, pasta salads and meats and cheeses. The window displays show off M&M cookies and rum balls, all amazingly cheap. You could also take your sweet tooth to the *Nutty Chocolatier* (2179 Queen St E).

You'll have to squeeze in past your neighbor's elbows at *Jamaica Sunrise* (☎ 416-691-2999, 1959 Queen St E). The jerk chicken sandwiches on cocoa bread cost $10 and the Montego Bay ackee a bit more. Across the street, *Lion on the Beach* (☎ 416-690-1984, 1958 Queen St E) is an expansive pub that spills out onto the sidewalk (lyin' on the beach, get it?). Pub grub like bangers and mash and rainbow trout keep everyone satisfied and the beer list is respectably long.

OTHER NEIGHBORHOODS

It's almost a truism that Toronto doesn't have any Mexican food worthy of the name. Except *Jalapeño* (Map 9; ☎ 416-216-6743, 725 King St W), that is, where superb regional Mexican specialties like chicken mole poblano, as well as cactus and seafood dishes (around $15 each), are served in authentic surroundings by personable staff. The sangria and daily lunch special for $7 are outstanding. Occasionally there's live mariachi music on weekends.

Far west of the Annex in Bloor Village, *The Queen of Sheba* (Map 8; ☎ 416-536-4162, 1198 Bloor St W), just west of Dufferin Ave, is a long-running Ethiopian restaurant that's a pilgrimage place for students. With platters for two at $25, it's worth the trek.

Sprinkled along Queen St E in Leslieville on the No 501 streetcar line to The Beach community, the *Real Jerk* (Map 10; ☎ 416-463-6055, 709 Queen St E), at Broadview Ave, is a Toronto classic for jerk chicken or oxtail and goat curries, all $5 to $10. It's open until 1 am on weekends and feels a lot

like a beach bar with its reggae beats, tropical interior and Jamaican flags.

Or part the curtains and enter *Hello Toast* (Map 10; ☎ 416-778-7299, 993 Queen St E), an artsy new-fangled diner that's best at weekend brunch when $10 buys you 'Eggs Benny' or pancakes soaked with maple syrup and fresh fruit (closed Monday).

The spicy Little Portugal area, to the west of Ossington Ave on Dundas St W, offers nothing so much as espresso sports bars loaded with machismo. Travelers recommend *Lanterna Wine Bar & Grill* (☎ 416-516-4211, 1574 Dundas St W). Portuguese seafood dinners for around $30 are served daily. If that leaves you short of cash, the custards and orange sponge cake at *Brazil Bakery* (1566 Dundas St W) cost just pennies (open daily until midnight). Both places are just west of Sheridan Ave.

It's worth the trek out to Corso Italia, centered on St Clair West for *Jolly Italian Cafe* (Map 3; ☎ 416-656-1963, 1256 St Clair Ave W). It hides a spacious interior worthy of a Fellini set, plus a flower-bedecked patio in summer and a surprising menu, including fusilli with artichoke hearts, olives and lemon ($12). The coffees are nearly perfect and true to its name, the staff are always in a good mood. *La Bruschetta* (☎ 416-656-8622, 1317 St Clair Ave W) cooks up standard Umbrian cuisine uncorrupted by fusion or fuss, with pasta and meat main dishes under $20. You can admire the plates autographed by famous stars on the walls while you down a grappa (closed Sunday).

You don't have to go quite that far north, however, to reach *Scaramouche* (Map 3; ☎ 416-961-8011, 1 Benvenuto Place), tucked away on a hilltop off Avenue Rd and offering stunning views of the downtown skyline. It's a tried and true place for top-end French cuisine dusted with tasteful invention. Don't forget your gold card (dinner daily except Sunday).

Like a poor country cousin amongst the big moneyed places on Yonge St around Eglinton Ave, there's *Five Doors North* (☎ 416-480-6234, 2088 Yonge St) inside a barely converted 'Future Furniture' store. The quality Italian cooking is offered up at unbelievably low prices: Daily pasta specials cost only $5 (dinner daily except Sunday). Equally casual *St Louis Bar & Grill (☎ 416-480-0202, 2050 Yonge St)* has half-price specials on ribs and wings on selected weekdays and live R&B and classic rock (no cover) from Thursday to Sunday nights.

After deluxe renovations in mosaics and sculpted metal, sleek *North 44 (Map 3; ☎ 416-487-4897, 2537 Yonge St)* continues to hold its own and in 1999 was again voted one of North America's top tables. Contemporary and continental main courses ($30 to $50) are paired with selections from a mind-boggling international wine list (17 pages, excluding bibliography) that can also be enjoyed at the piano bar upstairs (dinner daily except Sunday).

Off on its own farther east, the independent *JOV Bistro (Map 3; ☎ 416-322-0530, 1701 Bayview Ave)* takes its names from the initials of its three renowned Toronto chef-

owners. Reservations for dinner are only taken exactly one week in advance. The forethought is worth it when fine French send-offs like grilled scallops with lobster and sorrel cost from $15. You'd be even better served by taking the chefs up on their 'Trust Me' four-course dinner ($50) with 'Trust Us' wine pairings ($27).

Finally, and a fitting finish to this chapter, *Auberge du Pommier (☎ 416-222-2220, 4150 Yonge St)* is still the classic French and Mediterranean culinary training ground for many of Toronto's best chefs. The restaurant was constructed out of a 19th century wood-cutters' cottage, oddly placed inside a corporate tower complex. But the elegance inside is effortless, with mains like roast Québec pheasant or filet of Arctic char costing $30 to $40 at dinner (closed Sunday). It's far north of the city center, just past the intersection of Yonge St and York Mills Rd/Wilson Ave, where the York Mills subway station is.

PLACES TO EAT

Entertainment

Montréalers will sneer, but Toronto's nightlife keeps everyone busy long after dark, with plenty of entertainment during the daylight hours, too. In summer there are free outdoor festivals going on all the time (see the Special Events section in the Facts for the Visitor chapter). The city's most complete entertainment guide is provided by the free weekly *Now,* followed up by *Xtra* and *eye,* which stay on top of the club and live-music beats. All three daily newspapers also provide weekly entertainment listings. Check the Thursday *Star,* Friday *Sun* or Saturday *Globe & Mail.*

If the entertainment scene ever seems lacking, blame it on Torontonians not having any caffeine in their Mountain Dew to keep them wired.

Tickets

For a booking fee, Ticketmaster (☎ 416-870-8000) sells tickets for major theater, sports and concert events, both online (www .ticketmaster.ca) and at various city outlets. The one at Tower Records (Map 5), 2 Queen St W, is open 9:30 am to 8:30 pm weekdays, until 5:30 pm Saturday. Beware the added service fee. The classified sections of newspapers also list tickets available for every event in town, from opera to Rolling Stones, hockey to baseball. For a price, any seat is yours.

For half-price and same-day rush tickets, T.O. Tix has a booth on the lower level of Eaton Centre (Map 5), near the Dundas Mall corridor. It's open noon to 7:30 pm Tuesday to Saturday. Tickets are sold in-person on a first-come, first-served basis only, for theater, comedy and dance performances, even those outside the city as far away as Stratford and Niagara-on-the-Lake. You can check what's available first by calling ☎ 416-536-6468. Rush tickets may also be available at theater box offices for any given show.

PUBS & BARS

The Liquor Control Board of Ontario (LCBO) strictly limits where and how beer can be sold. Bar hours are 11 am to 2 am but specially licensed clubs stay open until 3 or 4 am, and who knows how many illegal mercurial boozecans there are where drinks can be had at all hours. Large-scale retail sales are done only through The Beer Store (no, it's not a souvenir shop) and LCBO outlets. The most interesting LCBO (Map 3) is at 1121 Yonge St, at Summerhill Ave beside an overpass. This prominent building with its high clocktower was once North York train station, built in the 1920s by the Canada Pacific Railroad in competition with Union station, and it quickly failed.

In the 1990s Toronto passed strict anti-smoking bylaws that banned lighting up in virtually any indoor public place. When that didn't work, the laws were repealed and most bars and pubs now permit smoking. Thomas Hinds Tobacconist (Map 6; ☎ 416-927-7703, 1-800-637-5750, 8 Cumberland St) is doing quite a business out of its walk-in humidor these days, especially with US citizens who just can't get Cuban cigars back home.

Yanks, get your Cohibas in Canada.

Toronto's martini craze isn't over. The *Library Bar*, at the Royal York Hotel (Map 4), is said to have the best classic ones in town, though wilder combinations pop up everywhere – chocolatini or berry-tini, anyone?

Pubs

Considering its British heritage, it's odd that Toronto has so many out-of-the-box pubs, starting with a generic Duke or Bishop and ending with Newcastle, Firkin or something just as predictable. Pubs are generally open seven days a week from lunch until after midnight.

Toronto's longest running pub (since 1849) is the *Wheat Sheaf Tavern (Map 9; ☎ 416-504-9912, 667 King St W)* where a host of faithful regulars sit around the dartboards and pool tables. North of Yorkville and a bit out of place in rich Rosedale, the merry and rough *Rebel House (☎ 416-927-0704, 1068 Yonge St)* has 16 patriotic Canadian brews on tap and well-trained chefs (yes, chefs) in the kitchen.

At the west end of Greektown, *Dora Keogh (Map 10; ☎ 416-778-1804, 141 Danforth Ave)* is as authentic as stepping into a corner pub in the west country of Ireland. Neighboring *Allen's (Map 10; ☎ 416-463-3086, 143 Danforth Ave)* has exhaustive beer and whiskey lists, over 100 types of each. Both places host live music acts (see Folk & International, later in this chapter) and have earned quite a reputation for their country cooking.

In and near The Annex, you'll find plenty of pubs provide procrastination venues for UT students. *The Madison (Map 6; ☎ 416-927-1722, 14 Madison Ave)* is a sprawling establishment built from three Victorian houses with old-time lamps lighting the curtained upper floors at night. The green Christmas lights stay on year-round at *James Joyce Traditional Irish Pub (Map 8; ☎ 416-324-9400, 386 Bloor St W)* where live music occasionally makes the whole house sway.

Near Yorkville, a real mix of people chatter over their roast beef sandwiches and ales at the bright and cheery *Duke of York (Map 6; ☎ 416-964-2441, 39 Prince Arthur Ave)*. The hoary *Pilot Tavern (Map 6; ☎ 416-923-5716)* has live jazz on Saturday afternoon and a friendly front patio, despite its foreboding black-on-black decor.

Bars

Almost every bar is open from Thursday to Sunday, though some close a few days per week or don't open before dark.

For a free rooftop view of the city, head to *Panorama (Map 6; ☎ 416-967-1000)* on the 51st floor of the Manulife Centre. It's a bit tricky to find, but it's open daily 5 pm until 2 am. A beer costs $6 or more up here (skip the food). If you stand up, you can see the city over the balcony at the Park Hyatt's *Rooftop Lounge (Map 6; ☎ 416-925-1234)*. At high-priced *Canoe (Map 4; ☎ 416-364-0054, 66 Wellington Street W)*, the bar stools face outward toward awe-inspiring views of Lake Ontario and the Toronto Islands, day or night. Drink prices at all three places rise accordingly with the elevation.

Near the Bay St financial district, the *Courthouse (Map 4; ☎ 416 214-9379)* has a plush downstairs lounge furnished with overstuffed seats and an inviting fireplace. Much farther west, *The Banknote (Map 9; 665 King St W)* has an old-fashioned bank vault behind its pool tables.

West of Spadina Ave, *Left Bank (Map 9; ☎ 416-504-1626, 567 Queen St W)* has gilt mirrors in the bathroom, fireplaces, bohemian atmosphere and a huge dance floor. *Element (Map 9; ☎ 416-359-1919, 553 Queen St W)* is one of those pretty, backlit bars with DJs almost every night. Late night at Azul restaurant (Map 9), *Drincläb (☎ 416-703-9360, 181 Bathurst St)* lounge has the best sake cocktails in town, plus drag queen bingo on Tuesday and soothing weekend DJs. Much grungier, *Velvet Underground (Map 9; ☎ 416-504-6688, 508 Queen St W)* looks like industrial scrap metal from the outside and the crowd could all be extras from *Bladerunner*. It's a popular Sunday night wind-down spot. (Most of the other Queen St bars are listed under Live Music later.)

ENTERTAINMENT

Swank see-and-be-seen places come and go along Little Italy's College St. *Ciao Eddie (Map 8;* ☎ *416-927-7774, 489 College St)* has been throwing its attitude around for a while, though why no one has yet thrown the lava lamps is a mystery. Laid-back foozball and billiards are played right next door at casual *ClearSpot (Map 8;* ☎ *416-921-7998).*

Closer to Kensington Market, *Cobalt (Map 8;* ☎ *416-923-4456, 426 College St)* has church-like alcoves and ambient DJs. On Sunday night the owners (and DJs) offer a chef's tasting menu ($40) supper club – reserve in advance.

Near the UT campus you'll find barebones student haunts like *Ein-stein Cafe & Pub (Map 6;* ☎ *416-597-8346, 229 College St)* notable for its board games. However, the classic dive remains *Sneaky Dee's*, at College and Bathurst Sts (see the boxed text 'Late-Night, All Night' in the Places to Eat chapter). Those from Down Under can drop in at *TRANZAC (Toronto Australia New Zealand Club; Map 8;* ☎ *416-923-8137, 292 Brunswick Ave)* where there is a bar open to all.

Even if you don't stop by, phone the *Bedford Ballroom (Map 6;* ☎ *416-966-4450, 232 Bloor St W)* after hours just to hear its answering machine message. The staff smile when they ask you which one of the many Ontario beers you

want, the grub is decent and a pool table is usually up for grabs.

Next to the film studios, *Waterside Sports Club (Map 10;* ☎ *416-203-0470, 225 Queen's Quay E)* has a groovy bar mixed with stars taking a break, young Torontonians in the know and middle-aged cruise groupies. The views of the lake are unspoiled.

Farther east, The Beach neighborhood is filled with places for unwinding after the sun sets. If it's just drinks and not frat boys you're after, try *Lion on the Beach (Map 11;* ☎ *416-690-1984, 1958 Queen St E).*

Smoky, macho espresso sports bars line the streets (like a gauntlet) in Corso Italia and Little Portugal.

It's still a man's world at hoary *Tivoli Billiards (Map 9; 268 Augusta Ave)*, in Kensington Market; there's nary a woman within spitting distance. For more mannered ladies and gents, there's *Rivoli Pool Hall (Map 5;* ☎ *416-596-1501, 334 Queen St W)* or the *Billiards Academy (Map 10;* ☎ *416-466-9696, 485 Danforth Ave)*. *The Charlotte Room (Map 4;* ☎ *416-598-2882, 19 Charlotte St)* charges higher than average prices ($12 per hour) but has live jazz on Saturday night (closed Sunday).

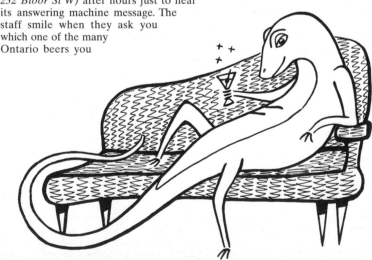

Look out for that lascivious-lookin' lounge lizard....

Ale Trail of Tears

Anyone who sits down for a beer and tastes the fizzy carbonation of Ontario's usual brews will think: Is this real ale, or Canada Dry?! And how do these Canucks drink this *!&% stuff?

You can't blame it entirely on beer-drinkers in Ontario, though, since they don't enjoy the right to choose. The Beer Store (no, it's not for beer souvenirs) is one of only two places where beer can be legally bought. It's a private monopoly owned almost exclusively by the major breweries, Labatt and Molson, who strictly limit the number of microbrews that can be sold. LCBO outlets, the only alternative, sell even fewer brands. It's enough to make even a liberal stand up and shout 'I am a free marketeer! For the sake of beer!'

With the market so tied up, smaller breweries have few options. One is to tempt the drinking public to on-site stores and brewpubs. Toronto's first microbrewery was **Amsterdam Brewing Co** (Map 9; ☎ 416-504-1040, 600 King St W), which stays open until 11 pm daily (6 pm on Sunday). Their Nut Brown Ale uses four different Canadian and international malts, including a chocolate variety from Belgium. Just downhill from the SkyDome and CN Tower, **Steamwhistle Brewing** (Map 4; ☎ 416-362-2337, 255 Bremner Rd), actually blows its whistle when you tour the premises (open noon to at least 6 pm daily). **Denison's Brewing Co** (Map 4; ☎ 416-360-5877, 75 Victoria St) dispenses Bavarian-style brews from large copper vats at its small brewpub (closed Sunday) and the Granite Brewery serves award-winning 'Peculiar Strong Ale' at **Beer Street** (Map 10, ☎ 416-405-8100, 729 Danforth Ave). Last but not least, an in-house brewmaster at **C'est What** (see the Specialty Bars section) creates a velvety Coffee Porter and smooth Hemp Ale that are heavenly.

If you're getting the idea that you have to really know where to look for good beer in Ontario, you're right. Modeled after Niagara's successful Wine Route drive, the emerging Ale Trail (☎ 1-800-334-4519, www.aletrail.on.ca) spotlights outlying provincial breweries that are mostly still missable. You're better off settling yourself into a chair at **Allen's** (see Pubs) or the **Esplanade Bier-Market** (see Specialty Bars), where you can order local brews that may truly satisfy. Recommended are Conners Best Bitter, Kawartha Lakes raspberry wheat or Ste André Vienna Lager, the only type made at the Ste André brewery in Guelph and personally delivered around town in a vintage Citroen. Also look out for daredevil brews by Niagara Falls Brewing Co (see the Excursions chapter), the first in North America to make Eisbock, an ambitious, sweet, malty ice beer with a potency of 10% or more, resulting from freezing off the extra water and thereby increasing the concentration of alcohol.

When the Toronto Festival of Beer rolls around at Fort York in August, know that your $20 admission ticket goes for a good cause. By turning out to sample the products of over 30 local microbreweries, you're helping to make Ontario less of an Ale Trail of Tears.

Specialty Bars

Wine aficionados peruse the serious lists at **Vines Wine Bar** (Map 4; ☎ 416-861-9920, 38 Wellington St E) or dally in new Ontario wines on tasting nights.

While the **Esplanade BierMarkt** (Map 4; ☎ 416-862-7575, 58 The Esplanade) may not have all the right glasses, they do have Belgian and German beers on tap. Be careful to avoid those that are actually brewed in Ontario, losing flavor and smoothness in their trans-Atlantic translation. The beer menu covers Trinidad to South Africa, needing its own table of contents.

C'est What (Map 4; ☎ 416-867-9499, 67 Front St E) has 30 whiskeys and over two dozen Canadian microbrews, including Coffee Porter and Hemp Ale by an in-house brewmaster. You can drink your way across the nation as you listen to eclectic music, live nightly.

For a real gas, inhale the atmosphere of Canada's first **O2 Spa Bar** (Map 3; ☎ 416-322-7733, 2044 Yonge St). Modeled after the

O₂: Come for the atmosphere, pay for the air.

I-need-a-boost stations of Japan, patrons are hooked up to a pure oxygen hose for 20 minutes ($16, half-price on Wednesday). Private lounges with mood lighting and reclining leather seats are perfect for dates.

CLUBS

Mainstream dance clubs crowd the entertainment district, nicknamed 'Clubland,' between Queen and King Sts W, mostly along the smaller streets of Duncan, John and Peter. The whole area is jammed on weekends; just take a wander and check out the people queuing to find one to your taste. *Whiskey Saigon* (*Map 4; ☎ 416-593-4646, 250 Richmond St W*), *Joker* (*Map 4; ☎ 416-598-1313, 318 Richmond St W*) and *Limelight* (*Map 4; ☎ 416-593-6216, 250 Adelaide St*) are all major players. Of the same type, but closer to the waterfront, the enormous *Guvernment* (*Map 4; ☎ 416-869-0045, 132 Queen's Quay E*) complex is full of out-of-towners. It's dependable, but things can get a bit out of line – a bouncer was recently killed there.

Cover charges of $5 to $12 apply on weekends, though early birds and women on 'ladies nights' may get in free. Hats, sportswear and ripped jeans are not usually allowed. If you visit www.groovesociety .com, you can put yourself on several VIP lists (no waiting, no cover) for free.

In Clubland, take a break among the velvet curtains at the backlit bar of the low-key *Living Room* (*Map 4; ☎ 416-979-3168, 330 Adelaide St W*), which also hosts annual pajama parties and DJs.

For more alternative venues where the emphasis is on the music, not looks, the closing of landmark Industry has left a hole. *Hooch* (*Map 9; ☎ 416-703-5069, 815 Queen St W*), upstairs from Gypsy Co-op, heats up on Tuesday and Thursday with no cover and DJs spinning soul, jazz, garage and house. The unfortunately named *Bovine Sex Club* (*Map 9; ☎ 416-504-4239, 542 Queen St W*) also has DJs – look for the Christmas lights and garage chic.

A bit past its prime, *Phoenix* (*Map 10; ☎ 416-323-1251, 410 Sherbourne St*) across town is reviving these days with Q107 broadcasting live on Friday, Edge 102 on Saturday and Energy 108 Sunday. Whoah.

Upstairs from Lee's Palace, 'exclusively alternative' *Dance Cave* (*Map 8; ☎ 416-532-1598, 529 Bloor St W*) has retro '80s grooves for club kids with no cover except on weekends ($4).

A modish Little Italy crowd often heads for *Lava Lounge* (*Map 8; ☎ 416-966-5282, 507 College St*). The singles here look a little desperate, but the dance floor on retro nights is well attended. Better-heeled party-goers go to Yorkville, especially *Sassafraz* (see the Places to Eat chapter).

West of the W Queen St W area, there's after-hours madness on the huge dance floor of *The Matador* (☎ 416-533-9311, 466 Dovercourt Rd). It's only open 1:30 to 5:30 am on Friday and Saturday. Live bands play honky-tonk and classic rock, though the owner once wrangled Leonard Cohen into a surprise show.

Toronto's rave scene is pretty well out in the open, although edgy city officials have just started cracking down. Look for rave flyers at record shops on Queen St and on the 'Underground Tip' page of *Now*.

For Latin, *El Convento Rico* (*Map 8; ☎ 416-588-7800, 750 College St*) sees more straight than gay clientele these days, though drag shows still go on. Beginners who can't swing their hips are welcome to free salsa lessons – call to check time. Next to Sneaky Dee's, *Plaza Flamingo* (*Map 8; ☎ 416-603-8884, 423 College St*) is an empty barn on weeknights, but the queue on Friday and Saturday is enormous. There are live flamenco shows 'direct from Spain' on most nights and free salsa lessons (closed Monday).

Spacious and very island-like, *Cutty's Hideaway* (*Map 10; ☎ 416-463-5380, 538 Danforth Ave*) plays Caribbean music with live performances on weekends (covers around $10).

And swing is still big in Toronto. Beginners take their first Lindy Hops with the **Toronto Swing Dance Society** (☎ 416-638-8737) on Friday night at various locations around town ($7).
Web site: www.dancing.org/tsds

LESBIGAY VENUES

Cruising Church St and hanging out in front of Second Cup is enough for some, but for others, the best source for what's in and what's not is the free weekly *Xtra*. Special events listings include one-off performances by Toronto's Drag Kings.

Eternally popular **Woody's** *(Map 6;* ☎ *416-972-0887, 467 Church St)* actually sells more beer than any other bar in Canada. Inside there are a few separate bars, including the less cruisy *Sailor's*. Leather men go to **Black Eagle** (☎ *416-413-1219, 457 Church St)*, where strict dress codes are in full effect.

The most popular place for women is **Tango** *(Map 6;* ☎ *416-972-1662, 510 Church St)* next door to men's **Crews** (nice pun) with drag shows on weekends. The tiny elevated front patio is perfect for people-watching. **Pope Joan** *(Map 10;* ☎ *416-925-6662, 547 Parliament St)* is another steady favorite for women, though it's farther east in Cabbagetown and only open Thursday to Saturday.

The bright **Slack Alice** *(Map 6;* ☎ *416-969-8742, 562 Church St)* bridges the gap between the sexes with a glitzy backlit bar open to all. For dancing, jam-packed **Talullah's Cabaret** *(Map 6;* ☎ *416-975-8555, 12 Alexander St)* at Buddies in Bad Times Theatre is entirely mixed and charges a miniscule cover ($3). The **Red Spot** *(Map 6;* ☎ *416-967-7768, 459 Church St)* also pulls in all kinds of folk.

The **Pegasus Billiard Lounge** *(Map 6;* ☎ *416-927-8832, 491 Church St)* above the *Xtra* offices is open seven days a week for shooting racks or worshipping at the Miss Piggy shrine.

Allen's (see Pubs, earlier) has gay-friendly vibes, as does the **Cameron House** on W Queen St W.

LIVE MUSIC

Anyone who doubts that Toronto's live music scene measures up must attend the North by Northeast (NXNE) independent music festival, the northern sister of South by Southwest in Austin, Texas. An $18 wristband gets you in free to any of 400 new music shows at over two dozen clubs, all squeezed into one long weekend in June.

Mega-tour concerts by everyone from Sting to BB King and Phish to Céline Dion all stop in Toronto for power performances at the SkyDome, Air Canada Centre, and Molson Amphitheatre at Ontario Place. Tickets and listings are available through Ticketmaster (see Tickets, earlier).

Rock, Reggae & Alternative

The hottest venues in Toronto are on Queen St and around the edges of Kensington Market. Expect to pay anywhere from nothing to a few dollars on weeknights and up to $20 for breakthrough weekend acts.

At the **The Comfort Zone** *(Map 8;* ☎ *416-975-0909, 480 Spadina Ave)*, an eclectic mix of live reggae, hip-hop and trance DJs net people for under $10. Farther south **El Mocambo** *(Map 9;* ☎ *416-968-2001, 464 Spadina Ave)* has a palm tree nightclub sign that suggests Miami, but it's all North American grit inside. Local acts play here on the same stage Mick Jagger and the Rolling Stones once writhed on (while the former prime minister's wife stood on the tabletops). Across the street, **Grossman's** *(Map 5;* ☎ *416-977-7000, 379 Spadina Ave)* is grubby but one of the cheapest places in town, but it's very hit-and-miss.

Dan Aykroyd first worked on his Blues Brothers routine here.

In the market, **Graffiti's** (Map 9; ☎ 416-506-6699, 170 Baldwin St) has credible acoustic acts and 'cabarets' that could (and almost certainly will) contain anything.

Past its 50th birthday, the legendary **Horseshoe Tavern** (Map 5; ☎ 416-598-4753, 370 Queen St W) is still showcasing 'roots, rock and alt nu music.' Its long bar has a country & western feel. The Police played here to an almost empty house on their first North American tour, when Sting did an encore in his underwear.

Local bands get their first gigs nearby at **The 360** (Map 5; ☎ 416-593-0840, 326 Queen St W). **Bamboo** (Map 5; ☎ 416-593-5771, 312 Queen St W) is very popular, with lots of African and reggae sounds. There's a rooftop patio to catch your breath and a kitchen serving tasty, spicy Caribbean fare.

West of Spadina Ave, **Cameron House** (Map 9; ☎ 416-703-0811, 408 Queen St W) gets down with soul, R&B, acid jazz and other alternative live music. Mad Bastard Cabaret ('accordion singing about love, lust and Spain') and live swing nights are packed. Above the Big Bop, **Holy Joe's** (Map 9; ☎ 416-504-6699/0744, 651 Queen St W) is a groovy little room with acoustic shows and **Reverb** hosts serious indie shows. There's always a bellicose crowd of pseudo-punk toughs with their bad-ass hounds just outside.

In 'Clubland,' restaurant **Fez Batik** (Map 4; ☎ 416-204-9660, 129 Peter St) mixes up live music and DJs, sometimes scoring a winner. For more experimental music, there's the avant-garde **Music Gallery** (Map 4; ☎ 416-204-1080, 179 Richmond St W) between Simcoe and Duncan.

Historic **Lee's Palace** (Map 8; ☎ 416-532-1598, 529 Bloor St W) once set the stage for Dinosaur Jr, Buffalo Tom and The Cure. It's still a viable concert venue, but you'll see more goth kids here than anything else. Kurt Cobain started an infamous bottle-throwing incident when Nirvana played here in 1990.

Down by the Esplanade, **C'est What** has a new act nearly every night (see Specialty Bars, earlier).

Over the river, the **Opera House** (Map 10; ☎ 416-466-0313, 735 Queen St E) regularly books new rock, funk and soul acts that are as varied as its vaudeville past.

Jazz, Swing & Blues

Top-of-the-line local and international jazz cats appear in front of the petite table lamps at **Montreal Bistro** (Map 10; ☎ 416-363-0179, 65 Sherbourne St). Another fine jazz standard is **Top O' the Senator** (Map 5; ☎ 416-364-7517, 249 Victoria St), a cozy upper-story club filling the most exacting of tall orders every night except Monday. Cover charges at either place are between $12 and $20 for big-name weekend acts. The **Victory 3B Lounge** above the Senator lets you hear what's going on below for free while you swirl your swizzle stick.

Rising up out of its down-at-heel past, **The Rex** (Map 5; ☎ 416-598-2475, 194 Queen St W) has 12 different experimental, Dixieland and other local jazz acts every week. Drinks are cheap and covers $6 maximum.

New Orleans-like **Southern Po' Boys** (Map 9; ☎ 416-593-1111, 159 Augusta Ave) has jazz combos in the upstairs bar and pianists downstairs in the restaurant. Low cover charges, good stiff drinks and potent Mardi Gras house cocktails make this joint worthy of a far greater following.

The intimate supper club at **Reservoir Lounge** (Map 4; ☎ 416-955-0887, 52 Wellington St E) is so jumpin' with swing and boogie-woogie that reservations are a must (closed Sunday). If this stuff doesn't get your feet tapping, you're probably dead.

True blues reign at **The Silver Dollar** (Map 8; ☎ 416-975-0909, 486 Spadina Ave), where big-name acts from down south (Chicago, that is) kick the ticket prices above $30 on weekends. Mid-week blues jams are free. No cover is ever charged at **Chicago's** (Map 5; ☎ 416-598-3301, 335 Queen St W) or **St Louis** (Map 3; ☎ 416-480-0202, 2050 Yonge St), uptown.

Folk & International

Allen's restaurant has live Celtic and East Coast music on Tuesday and Saturday nights. Next door, **Dora Keogh** has Celtic jam sessions on Thursday night and Sunday afternoon (see Pubs, earlier).

For live acoustic folk music, try *Free Times Café* (☎ 416-967-1078, 320 College St) at Bella's Bistro (see the boxed text 'Brunch Hunt' in the Places to Eat chapter).

COMEDY CLUBS

Attached to Tim Sims Playhouse, *Second City* (Map 4; ☎ 416-343-0011, 56 Blue Jays Way) is legendary – just look at the wall of star photos as you climb up the stairs. Many *Saturday Night Live* stars got started here, among them Gilda Radner, Dan Aykroyd and Mike Myers. Pro mainstage shows cost $19 to $25, less for students. Every night after the last show ends (variable) 30-minute improv sessions are absolutely free, as are Second City comedy school improv performances.

You could also squeeze inside *The Laugh Resort* (Map 4; ☎ 416-364-5233, 26 Lombard St), where Paula Poundstone and Adam Sandler once cracked jokes. Tickets start at $5.

Costing from $7, *Comedywood Downtown* (Map 6; ☎ 416-761-0543, 194 Bloor St W) has rotating acts every night except Monday.

Yuk Yuk's Superclub (Map 3; ☎ 416-967-6425, 2335 Yonge St) has huge live acts that are sometimes funny, sometimes gross, sometimes a joke – just like Jim Carrey, the Toronto native who was first seen here. Expect to pay at least $15 on weekend nights.

The very cool Pirate Video Cabaret happens Sunday night at *Clinton's* (Map 8; ☎ 416-535-9541, 693 Bloor St W); cover $5. ALT.COMedy Lounge at *The Rivoli* (Map 5; ☎ 416-596-1908, 332 Queen St W) livens up Monday nights and, as an added bonus, is PWYC (Pay What You Can). If it's Tuesday, head to *Ein-stein* (see Bars, earlier) for free Steamin' Heap O' Comedy nights.

SPOKEN WORD

For over 25 years, Canadian and international literary giants have been headlining the renowned *Harbourfront Reading Series* (Map 4; ☎ 416-973-4760) at various locations on the Harbourfront. Tickets for Wednesday night readings cost $8, more during special

Gilda Radner

events and the International Festival of Authors in October. For details contact the Harbourfront box office (☎ 416-973-4000) inside York Quay Centre.

Insomniac Press (☎ 416-504-9313) publishes *Word: Toronto's Literary Calendar,* available online at www.insomniacpress .com/word/index.htm, which lists all of the city's regular reading series and one-off events. Another alternative is *Clit Lit*, a monthly performance space at the Red Spot (see Lesbigay Venues, earlier) for queer and straight local women authors. During summer it's on hiatus.

THEATER

There is plenty of first-rate theater in Toronto; only London and New York sell more tickets. Productions range from Broadway-type spectacles to radical new Canadian dramas. The season runs from September to June, though musicals run throughout summer. For high-flying theater festivals at Stratford and Niagara-on-the-Lake, see the Excursions chapter.

Toronto's Fringe Theatre Festival takes place in early July at miscellaneous venues – the best advice says the sexier the title, the worse the play will be. During the summer, don't miss the World Stage Festival at the Harbourfront.

The city's longest-running play is Agatha Christie's *The Mousetrap*, which has played at the just North of Yorkville *Toronto Truck Theatre* (☎ 416-922-0084, 94 Belmont St) since 1976! A ticket costs $20. Death is on the menu at *Mysteriously Yours* (☎ 416-486-7469, 2026 Yonge St) interactive murder-mystery dinner theater ($60 to $70).

Big-time musicals like *Mamma, Mia!* and *The Lion King* have their tryouts, indefinite runs and encore engagements on the Theatre Block on King St. Full-price seats start at $25 and go over $100. One of the more impressive theaters is the traditional *Royal Alexandra Theatre (Map 4; ☎ 416-872-1212, 260 King St W)*, known as just the 'Royal Alex.' A block away is the lavish *Princess of Wales Theatre (Map 4; ☎ 416-872-1212, 300 King St W)*, both owned by Honest Ed Mirvish. Near Eaton Centre, the restored historic double-decker *Elgin & Winter Garden Theatre Centre (Map 5; ☎ 416-872-5555, 189 Yonge St)* presents high-profile productions. For an inside look at all three theaters, see the Things to See & Do chapter.

The Dream in High Park (Map 13; ☎ 416-367-1652 x500) is a wonderful mid-summer presentation of Shakespeare during July and August. A donation of $10 is requested and shows begin almost nightly at 8 pm. Go early (and take a blanket) or you'll be turned away. For reservations up to one week in advance, call the *Canadian Stage Company (Map 10; ☎ 416-368-3110, 26 Berkeley St)* at its downtown theater. The company produces top-rate new plays by the likes of David Mamet and Tony Kushner, both there and at the St Lawrence Centre.

Many smaller non-profit Toronto theaters stage at least one PWYC (Pay What You Can) performance per week, usually a Sunday matinee. Suggested donations are around $5. For 'Theater Beyond Walls,' try *Theatre Passe Muraille (Map 9; ☎ 416-504-7529, 16 Ryerson Ave)*, interestingly housed in the old Nasmith's Bakery & Stables dating from 1902. Truly alternative *Factory Theatre (Map 9; ☎ 416-504-9971, 125 Bathurst St)* stages premiere performances of new Canadian plays year-round in its roomy Victorian house. Modern drama also lives with the Royal Alex's impoverished cousin, *Poor Alex Theatre (Map 8; ☎ 416-324-9863, 296 Brunswick Ave)*.

Buddies in Bad Times Theatre (Map 6; ☎ 416-975-8555, 12 Alexander St) has been an innovative venue for lesbigay and Canadian plays since 1979. It's tiny – only 300 seats for the main stage, and even fewer in the Tallulah's Cabaret performance space for comedians, writers and singers.

CINEMAS

At any time of year there's always a film festival going on, whether it's a week-long ethnic-community celebration or the famous Toronto International Film Festival, when all of Hollywood comes north (see the boxed text 'Hollywood o' the North' in the Facts for the Visitor chapter). Also not to be missed is the Inside/Out Lesbian + Gay film festival in May.

In the spirit of it all, Toronto's second-run and repertory film houses have banded together as the *Festival Cinemas* (☎ 416-690-2600). They include founding member *Bloor Cinema (Map 8; 506 Bloor St W)*, *The Royal (Map 8; 608 College St)* in Little Italy, *The Fox (Map 11; 2236 Queen St E)* at The Beach and *The Music Hall (Map 10; 147 Danforth Ave)* – you may recognize the last from *Studio 54* or as the place where James Brown got down when he came to T.O. Daily-changing movies, anything from classic European to new Hong Kong, cost $7.50, but only $4 for members who pay a $6 annual fee.

Cinematheque Ontario (Map 5; ☎ 416-968-3456), at the Art Gallery of Ontario, screens non-commercial world films and mounts retrospectives of classic directors, sometimes introduced by famous critics and Canadian authors. Non-members can purchase tickets ($8) at the box office 30 minutes before the first screening (usually 6:30 pm, but get there early since they usually sell out).

For first-run movies, the UT-Yorkville area is full of movie theaters, including the *Cineplex Odeon Varsity (Map 6; ☎ 416-961-*

6303) and *Alliance Atlantic Cumberland 4 (Map 6;* ☎ *416-699-5971, 159 Cumberland St).*

Downtown, the *Cineplex Odeon Carlton (Map 5;* ☎ *416-598-2309, 20 Carlton St)* screens non-mainstream new releases. The *Eaton Centre Cinemas (Map 5;* ☎ *416-593-4535)* show second-run new movies for only $3, ($1.50 on Tuesday).

Famous Players Paramount (Map 4; ☎ *416-368-5600),* on the corner of Richmond St W and John St, features new releases and the latest in IMAX (☎ 416-368-6089) technology, including 3D. You can catch other IMAX movies at Ontario Place's *Cinesphere* (☎ *416-314-9900)* and double features at the *Ontario Science Centre Omnimax* (☎ *416-696-1000),* too.

The old Art Deco *Eglinton* (☎ *416-487-4721, 400 Eglinton Ave W),* west of Avenue Rd, has a big screen, spacious seating and good sound.

Toronto personality Reg Hartt has been showing the same classic movies in his living room for years. You'll see his ads wrapped around telephone poles advertising the *Cineforum* (☎ *416-603-6643).* Animation retrospectives are his specialty, as are rare Salvador Dali prints. Bring your own food and drink and come prepared for educational lectures, sometimes right during the movies.

There's no better nostalgia trip than the *Mustang Drive-in* (☎ *519-824-5431)* about a two-hour drive west of Toronto via Hwy 401 – take the Hwy 6 exit north into downtown Guelph, then go east on Hwy 7 to Jones Baseline and turn right. The drive-in is 1km farther down on your right. Admission is $9 for adults, children under 12 free; call for schedules.

CLASSICAL MUSIC, OPERA & DANCE

The dance, symphony and opera seasons start in September and run straight through until spring.

The Toronto Symphony Orchestra plays at *Roy Thompson Hall (Map 4;* ☎ *416-872-4255, 60 Simcoe St),* not far from the CN Tower. A range of other classical concerts as well as performances of music from around the world are presented here. You can also catch the TSO on the city's oldest concert stage, *Massey Hall (Map 5;* ☎ *416-872-4255, 178 Victoria St),* which has excellent acoustics.

The *Canadian Opera Company* (☎ 416-363-8231) has plans to liven up the corner of Queen St and University Ave with a grand new opera house, but so far government bodies haven't been forthcoming with funds. The opera company performs at the *Hummingbird Centre (Map 4;* ☎ *416-393-7469, 1 Front St E)* for now. Advance tickets are sold through Ticketmaster, although a few dozen go on sale at the box office one week before each opera starts. The center is also home to the *National Ballet of Canada* (☎ *416-345-9595).*

The marvelous George Weston Recital Hall at the *Ford Centre for the Performing Arts (Subway: North York Centre,* ☎ *416-870-8000, 5040 Yonge St)* presents classical concerts by the world's top musicians and vocalists. It's a long drive (or subway ride) north of the city center.

Excellent medieval, early music and European folk performances take place during summer on Music Mondays at noon in the *Church of the Holy Trinity (Map 5;* ☎ *416-598-4521),* at Eaton Square; donations requested. The world-renowned Tafelmusik orchestra performs baroque and classical music on period instruments in the atmospheric *Trinity-St Paul's Centre (Map 8;* ☎ *416-964-6337, 427 Bloor St W),* as does the *Toronto Consort* for early music.

In the downtown CBC complex, noontime classical music concerts at the *Glenn Gould Studio (Map 4;* ☎ *416-205-5555),* where the soundtrack for *Schindler's List* was recorded, are often free.

For dance, look into what's happening at the Harbourfront's *Premiere Dance Theatre (Map 4;* ☎ *416-973-4000, 207 Queen's Quay W),* on the 3rd floor of Queen's Quay Terminal. The Toronto Dance Theatre company performs here and at the *Winchester Street Theatre* (Map 10; ☎ 416-967-1365, 80 Winchester St), a restored church in Cabbagetown. The *DuMaurier Theatre Centre (Map 4;* ☎ *416-954-5199, 231 Queen's Quay W)* also hosts touring dance companies. The

Fringe Dance Festival in August happens at Buddies in Bad Times Theatre (see Theater earlier).

SPECTATOR SPORTS

The Toronto Blue Jays (☎ 416-341-1234) of Major League Baseball's American League play at the SkyDome (Map 4). The Jays won the World Series in 1992 and 1993 – the only times that baseball's top prize has been won by a non-US team. The season runs from April to the end of September.

For a fee, tickets can be bought with a credit card by phone (☎ 1-888-654-6529), online at www.bluejays.com or through Ticketmaster (see Tickets, at the beginning of the chapter). You can buy tickets for cash at the SkyDome box office, Gate 9, open daily except on select Sundays. The cheap tickets are a mere $7 but are a long way above the field. Recommended are the $23 seats at the 500 level behind home plate. Family four-packs will save you 25% and seniors and children receive discounts on tickets for any games with a 12:35 pm start and all games on Saturday.

The Toronto Argonauts of the professional Canadian Football League (CFL) also play in the SkyDome between July and November. Ticket prices range from $10.50 to $35, less for students and seniors, and are available through Ticketmaster. At the SkyDome food and drink, especially beer, is expensive. However, bottles or cans cannot be taken into the stadium. Bring a jacket as things cool off at night when the roof is open.

In winter, the National Hockey League Maple Leafs play at the Air Canada Centre (Map 4; ☎ 416-815-5500). Every game is pretty well sold out, but a limited number of single game tickets go on sale through Ticketmaster at 10 am on the last Saturday of every month during hockey season (October to April). Hockey tickets are costly, with the 'cheap' seats around $30, even though the Maple Leafs haven't won the Stanley Cup since '67. Tickets can be bought without difficulty at prices that will give you an additional chill from scalpers outside the door just before the game.

During the same season, the Toronto Raptors of the National Basketball Association (NBA) also play at the Air Canada Centre. Single game tickets are sold through Ticketmaster for $10.50 and up.

During summer you can catch amateur indoor hockey games at arenas scattered around the Greater Toronto Area, especially in Etobicoke. An ice-resurfacing machine, called a Zamboni, makes an appearance between every game.

Secretariat's last race was run at Woodbine Racetrack (Map 1; ☎ 416-675-7223, 1-888-675-7223). The racetrack features thoroughbred and standardbreds (harness racing). Millions have been spent to turn it into a flashy entertainment complex à la Niagara. Free 'Backstretch Tours' are given at 9:30 am on Saturday and Sunday from early May to late September. Look for the bronze statue of Canada's famous Northern Dancer.

The racetrack is northwest of downtown at 555 Rexdale Blvd near Hwy 27. Admission and parking are free; binocular rental costs $2. By public transportation, take the subway to Islington, then a Mississauga Transit Bus to Westwood Mall and catch the direct express 'Race' bus that runs every 30 minutes – call for schedules and directions.

Shopping

WHERE TO SHOP

In Toronto, the only question is where not to shop. Each ethnic neighborhood and major thoroughfare has its own grab-bag assortment of shops, satisfying the quirkiest and most conventional of shoppers. The city is not a bargain paradise, especially once high taxes are added in, but refunds on taxes are possible (see the Facts for the Visitor chapter), and hey, Canadian 'dollar discount stores' are really '70¢ stores,' in American terms.

It all started in 1868, when historic Eaton's department store was established on Yonge St by enterprising Timothy Eaton. His dry-goods business succeeded due to 'revolutionary' sales policies of fixed prices, cash only and refunds for dissatisfied customers. The chain went bankrupt in 1999, but not before spawning the immense **Eaton Centre** (Map 5; ☎ 416-598-8700 ext 4455), 220 Yonge St, between Dundas and Queen Sts. This everyday-people's mall has hundreds of shops, fast-food outlets and ATMs. Business hours are 10 am to 9 pm weekdays, 9:30 am to 7 pm Saturday and noon to 6 pm Sunday.

Eaton's major competitor during the Victorian era was Robert Simpson, whose successful department store was bought by the Hudson's Bay Company in 1991. Now known simply as **The Bay** (Map 4; ☎ 416-861-9111), 176 Yonge St, it still sells fur – just like in colonial times. Notice the broad yellow stripe across the entrance doors that echoes the blue stripes used to measure animal pelts on the original Hudson's Bay traders' blankets.

The mazelike **PATH underground shopping mall** (Map 7) extends as far north as the other Bay branch on Bloor St and south almost to the CN tower. Most underground PATH shops are true bargain basements for discount clothing and everyday goods and services. Over 10 kilometers of haphazardly connected tunnels ensure Torontonians never need see the grim light of a winter's day while shopping downtown. When you become lost (as you almost certainly will), look up for cardinal directions on ceilings or wall maps. With luck, you will eventually surface at City Hall, Union Station, Eaton Centre or First Canadian Place, an upscale shopping mall attached to the Toronto Stock Exchange. Then again, you may end up in some anonymous, obscure downtown office building by mistake and never be heard from again.

Toronto shops are generally open 10 am to 6 pm Monday to Saturday, though prime shopping areas may stay open until 9 pm or later, especially from Thursday onward. As a rule many shops are closed Sunday, a holdover from the days of Toronto the Good, when Eaton's drew its curtains to discourage 'sinful' window-shopping. The rest keep shorter hours (usually noon to 5 pm). All of the following shops are open daily, unless otherwise stated.

Shopping Districts

Toronto's most vibrant and varied shopping street is **Queen St W** (Maps 5 and 9), where eclectic shops rub shoulders with predictable giants like HMV and the Gap. The street itself is schizophrenic. The stretch east of Spadina Ave is dominated by yuppie clothing boutiques and outdoor cafés, perfect for watching earnest fashion-hunters waltz by. West of the Spadina divide, the street gets funkier the farther you go.

Often called the 'longest road in the world,' **Yonge St** (Maps 4, 5 and 6) actually seems to be the start of the world's longest, most unrelenting strip of porn theaters, exotic-dance venues and XXX lingerie boutiques. Tucked in between are record warehouses and name-brand shoe and clothes shops, plus the occasional Canadiana souvenir store vending maple-leaf T-shirts for $3.99.

The chichi shops of **Bloor St** (Maps 6 and 8) begin east of the Royal Ontario Museum. International stars like Chanel, Tiffany's and MAC are all here. The grandiose Club

Monaco (Map 6; ☎ 416-591-8837), 157 Bloor St W, was once the UT Department of Household Sciences, which explains the giggle-inducing Ionic columns over the entryway.

Compactly situated north of Bloor St, **Yorkville** (Map 6) is Toronto's most exclusive shopping district. Believe it or not, this power-shopping and day-spa mecca was once flower-power central for hippies during the 1960s. Nothing is free here nowadays, least of all love from the haughty sales clerks.

West of the University of Toronto (UT), students and more affluent locals frequent **The Annex** (Map 8) for its specialized bookstores, used-music shops, clothing boutiques and hodgepodge of 'ethnic' shops. At the intersection of Bloor and Bathurst Sts is landmark Honest Ed's (Map 8; ☎ 416-537-1574), 581 Bloor St W, a discount bonanza for clothes, household and outdoor-activity goods, strangely reminiscent of a three-ring circus. Call Ed's answering machine to check opening hours.

One block farther west on Markham St is the unique **Mirvish (Markham) Village** (Map 8), a hidden treasure chest of artists' workshops and galleries, underground print and video shops and African stores.

Like its counterparts around the world, Toronto's gigantic **Chinatown** (Map 5) offers rock-bottom prices on clothes, everyday goods, groceries and Asian imports. The main thoroughfare is Spadina Ave.

Gerrard St E in **Little India** (Map 10) is studded with subcontinental food vendors, gorgeous sari emporia and blaring Hindi video-music shops. **Corso Italia** (Map 2), on St Clair Ave W, and **Little Italy** (Map 8), on College St, are where traditional grocers hawk their produce as sleek young *belle* seek out the latest imported Italian fashions.

West of Chinatown, **Kensington Market** (Map 9) is worth a look even if you're not hungry. This is where Toronto's young bohemians buy their flower-child, Rastafarian and retro clothing, along with beads or superhero lunchboxes. If you tire of being a

consumer, drop by Anarchist Free Space (Map 9; ☎ 416-203-0191), 254 Augusta Ave, a sort of Christian Science reading room for the political left. Or turn off your brain entirely at Roach-o-Rama (Map 9; ☎ 416-203-6990), 66½ Nassau St, a head shop that has been proudly 'serving potheads since, ah, I forget.'

Discount Stores

Honest Ed's (see Shopping Districts, earlier) is your first stop for bargain shopping, albeit with an overdose of kitsch. Competing discount stores are scattered around the intersection of Bloor and Bathurst Sts.

Goodwill (Map 10; ☎ 416-362-4710), 234 Adelaide St E, sells clothing by the pound and cheap jackets for travelers who come unprepared for the Great White North. The men's section has Toronto festival T-shirts from years past for a buck or two each.

Value Village, a major thrift-shop chain, has branches at 1319 Bloor St W (☎ 416-539-0585), two blocks west of Lansdowne subway stop at St Helen's St, and 924 Queen St E (Map 10; ☎ 416-778-4818), at Logan St on the 501 Queen streetcar line.

WHAT TO BUY
Art & Crafts

Museum shops around town all stock arty reproductions, prints, jewelry, clothes and other not-too-expensive miscellany. If you've got serious cash to spend on authentic art and photography, wander the city's evolving art-gallery scene (see the 'Gallery Hopping' boxed text, in the Things to See & Do chapter).

Buying Inuit, First Nations and contemporary Canadian works can be pricey, but you're paying for quality and authenticity. Inside Queen's Quay Terminal (Map 4), 207 Queen's Quay W, Proud Canadian Design (☎ 416-603-7413) blends national pride with tongue-in-cheek humor (a rarity in Canada). Purchasing Inukshuk figurines or polar footwear next door at Arctic Canada (☎ 416-203-7889) will benefit Nunavut Development Corporation, hailing from Canada's newest Native-run territory. A short walk west, York Quay Centre (Map 4), 235 Queen's

Quay W, turns up a Bounty (☎ 416-973-4993) of contemporary Canadian crafts. Resident artisans in the adjacent Craft Studio are busy blowing glass, molding clay and teaching (see Activities, in the Things to See & Do chapter).

The Ontario Crafts Council runs Guild Gallery shops in Yorkville (Map 6; ☎ 416-921-1721), 118 Cumberland St, and downtown at the Richmond-Adelaide Centre (Map 4; ☎ 416-367-0349); open weekdays. Ceramics, jewelry and glassworks by Ontario artisans make up the bulk of displays, though the staff are knowledgeable about Native art.

The atmospheric Bay of Spirits Gallery (Map 4; ☎ 416-971-5190), 156 Front St W, specializes in Native carvings and prints, as well as unique embroidered items and handcrafted jewelry. For cheaper prints, go to Armen Art Gallery (Map 6; ☎ 416-924-5375), 16 Wellesley St W; for carvings, browse at The Arctic Bear (Map 6; ☎ 416-967-7885), 125 Yorkville Ave. All three shops are closed Sunday.

The Annex's Harbord St has eclectic arts-and-crafts shops. Clay Design (Map 8; ☎ 416-964-3330), 170 Brunswick Ave, even has an on-site potters' workshop.

Mirvish Village is just as full of workshops and galleries, some of which are attached to (or even inside of) artists' houses. Most are closed Monday. Firsthand Canadian Crafts (Map 8; ☎ 416-516-3641), 589 Markham St, has Canadian license plate bound journals and whimsical soaps. Wood masks, dolls, textiles and prints hang on the walls of Ashanti Room (Map 8; ☎ 416-588-3934), 28 Lennox St.

Antiques & Furnishings

Harbourfront Antique Market (Map 4; ☎ 416-260-2626), 390 Queens Quay W, may be as overrated as it is well known. Except for some old Canadian prints, there aren't many attention-grabbing deals here (closed Monday).

Year-round on Sundays, the St Lawrence Antiques & Collectibles Market (Map 4; ☎ 416-410-1310), 92 Front St E, in the North Market, is overrun by salt-of-the-earth dealers with mixed bags of treasures and flea-market kitsch. The casual, bantering atmosphere guarantees real prices for real people.

More exclusive fine-antique dealers have set up shop in Yorkville and in Rosedale, north of Bloor St on Yonge St. The beauty of the pieces – and their accompanying price tags – will make you gasp.

Queen St W also has some antique shops, most selling only ordinary pieces at ludicrous prices. Red Indian Art Deco (Map 9; ☎ 416-504-7706), 536 Queen St W, is an exception, with wonderful pieces seemingly pulled off an Agatha Christie BBC special set. At Quasi-Modo (Map 9; ☎ 416-703-8300), 789 Queen St W, you may be stumped by the exact function of the sleek, ultramodern furnishings, but the designs are unbeatable (closed Monday).

Ride the No 501 Queen streetcar east of Don River to Leslieville's good-value antique and secondhand shops along Queen St E. Machine Age Modern (Map 10; ☎ 416-461-3588), 1000 Queen St E, is an Art Deco haven.

For contemporary Canadian interior design with an industrial twist, try cheerful pea-green Space (Map 10; ☎ 416-955-4559), 479 Queen St E, on the other (west) side of Don River (closed Monday and Tuesday). A few blocks south, serious international design shops line King St W between Sherbourne and Berkeley Sts, known as the Design Strip.

Books

Torontonians seem to be an awfully literate bunch, considering the variety of exceptional independent bookstores.

Of course, the megachains are here, too, with attached cafés and comfy chairs for browsing (and even drowsing). Huge four-story Chapters (Map 6; ☎ 416-920-9299), 110 Bloor St W, has self-serve Internet terminals and two Starbucks coffee shops; it's open 9 am to midnight daily. The Chaters Web site (www.chapters.ca) spotlights emerging Canadian authors. Indigo (Map 5; ☎ 416-591-3622), at Eaton Centre, is just as monolithic. See www.indigo.ca

for scheduled author events and musical performances.

Many of Toronto's first-rate independent bookstores belong to the Book Specialists Association (www.thebookspecialists.com). Toronto Women's Bookstore (Map 8; ☎ 416-922-8744), 73 Harbord St, has hard-to-find books authored by women of all backgrounds, including First Nations, African and Caribbean. Omega Centre Bookstore (Map 6; ☎ 416-975-9086), 29 Yorkville Ave, is a serene mecca for those interested in alternative religion and philosophies; ambient Hari Krishna music drifts past reading couches placed underneath dreamcatchers. You can even have your tarot cards read here by a local radio personality.

If you're wondering what Canadian cuisine might actually be, check out The Cookbook Store (Map 6; ☎ 416-920-2665), 850 Yonge St. Its Web site (www.cook-book .com) has famous recipes for moose stew and other northern treats. TheatreBooks (Map 6; ☎ 416-922-7175), 11 St Thomas St, carries scripts and music, film and drama-theory books for fans and professionals. Finally, The Sleuth of Baker Street (Map 3; ☎ 416-483-3111), 1600 Bayview Ave, has mystery books of all kinds, including out-of-print and first editions. It specializes in Sherlockiana – look for back editions of the *Canadian Holmes* 'zine.

Not to be missed, Open Air (Map 4; ☎ 416-363-0719), 25 Toronto St, has travel guidebooks, literature, histories and maps brilliantly shelved by geographic region, not genre. It also has books on nature, camping and other outdoor activities. Look for the downstairs entrance on the south side of Adelaide St E, two blocks east of Yonge St (closed Sunday).

Pages (Map 5; ☎ 416-598-1447), 256 Queen St W, has a selection of new literature and nonfiction titles. Small press, chapbook and free journals cover the weird outer limits of Toronto's art, music and rave scenes. For original 'zines and art, visit The Beguiling (Map 8; ☎ 416-533-9168), 601 Markham St, in Mirvish Village.

Librarie Champlain (Map 10; ☎ 416-364-4345), 468 Queen St E, is an enormous

Only in Toronto

Stuffed to the gills with maple-leaf memorabilia (get your cute stuffed moose here)? Then leave behind the touristy traps for T.O.'s one-of-a-kind shops, where you can buy souvenirs that will make the folks back home very jealous (or very grateful).

Arcade Coin & Stamp Co (Map 4; ☎ 416-368-6656), 137 Yonge St; closed Sunday. Antique coins and Royal Canadian Mint bank notes.

Beatlemania (Map 4; ☎ 416-977-2782), 120 Peter St. Vintage T-shirts, tasteful memorabilia from Abbey Rd to Sgt Pepper's and the friendliest ownership in town.

Down East Gallery and General Store (Map 8; ☎ 416-925-1642), 508 Bathurst St; closed Monday. 'Awful good stuff from Atlantic Canada,' including folk arts-and-crafts, Sussex Golden ginger ale, maple barbecue sauce, PEI Seaman's pop, Newfy (that's Newfoundland to you) and Nova Scotia quiz books.

Fastball Sportscards (Map 6; ☎ 416-323-0403), 624 Yonge St. Autographed hockey pucks starting at $35.

Lush (Map 6; ☎ 416-960-5874), 116 Cumberland St; (Map 5; ☎ 416-599-5874), 312 Queen St W; (Map 6; ☎ 416-924-5874), 663 Yonge St. An organic body, bath and beauty store that has a huge Internet business (www.lushcanada.com), but you can get special products for half the price in person, like More than Mortal body scrub, Fizzy O' Therapy and Feel Good in the Southern Hemisphere bath bombs or Pleasure Dough bubble-bath bars. Just inhale the scents…ahhhh.

Mackenzie House (Map 5; ☎ 416-392-6915), 82 Bond St; closed Monday. Handmade printing-press items, such as 'Mackenzie: Rebel with a Cause' T-shirts, and reproductions of the Ye Olde variety.

Ontario Specialty Co (Map 5; ☎ 416-306-9327), 133 Church St; closed Sunday. Zany stuff, like 2000 millennial fake eyeglasses and assorted gag gifts. It's just like in the movie *Good Will Hunting,* which was filmed here (look for autographed movie stills under the glass counter).

Wayne Gretzky's Restaurant (Map 4; ☎ 416-348-0099), 99 Blue Jays Way. Don't leave town without your 'Property of Wayne Gretzky' T-shirts.

Toronto's burgeoning immigrant scene means you can find items here that you'd otherwise have to cross the globe to get. A quick browse through the ethnic neighborhoods will uncover many more, but here are our picks:

Delek (Map 6; ☎ 416-513-0980), 69 Yorkville Ave; closed Sunday. Rising above simple trends, the smiling staff sell real Tibetan Buddhist statues, religious texts, prayer wheels and flags

Islamic Books & Souvenirs (Map 10; ☎ 416-778-8461), 1395 Gerrard St E. Arabic calligraphy mugs, prayer mats, 'I love Islam!' bumper stickers, mosque-shaped clocks and multilingual versions of the Koran.

The Japanese Paper Place (Map 9; ☎ 416-703-0089), 887 Queen St W. Strikingly beautiful imported paper goods, but you could probably buy a plane ticket to Japan with the money required to buy more than a few sheets.

Maharani Emporium (Map 10; ☎ 416-466-4486), 1417 Gerrard St E. Little India's resource for *tanpura* drums, Ganeshas, garlands, tapes, books and *puja* items.

Things Japanese (Map 8; ☎ 416-967-9797), 159 Harbord St; closed Monday. Rice-paper stationery, tea ceramics, lanterns and large *tansu* (chests of drawers).

North of downtown at the intersection of Yonge St and Eglinton Ave, nicknamed 'young and eligible,' some very specialized shops serve the whims of the affluent. Secondhand riding gear? Belly-dancing jewelry? It's all here, but the best fun is at Spytech (Map 3; ☎ 416-482-8588), 2028 Yonge St. The staff can set you up with private-eye surveillance and security equipment that would make Q proud. It's closed Sunday.

French bookstore that also carries magazines, videos, language-learning texts and Montreal Jazz Festival recordings (closed Sunday).

This Ain't the Rosedale Library (Map 6; ☎ 416-929-9912), 483 Church St, is a lesbigay community institution. Then there's Glad Day (Map 6; ☎ 416-961-4161), 598A Yonge St, which has been fighting Canadian customs for the right to import politically (and erotically) hot lesbigay material since the early 1970s. Directly below – and it's certainly a strange juxtaposition – is Bakka Science Fiction Bookstore (☎ 416-963-9993).

Other cheap used-book shops on Yonge St sell surprisingly classic titles, despite many having over-18-only pornography sections curtained off at the back. ABC Books (Map 6; ☎ 416-967-7654), 662 Yonge St, has back issues of *National Geographic* magazine.

The Annex neighborhood is also well stuffed with used bookstores, along Bloor and Harbord Sts. Open until midnight, Seekers Books (Map 8; ☎ 416-925-1982), 509 Bloor St W, stocks both academic and popular titles covering everything Asian, Indian, alternative, mystical and eastern. A Different Book List (Map 8; ☎ 416-538-0889), 746 Bathurst, specializes in 'live literature from the 'third world'' (closed Sunday).

For discount new and best-selling titles, World's Biggest Bookstore (Map 5; ☎ 416-977-7009), 20 Edward St, one block north of the Eaton Centre, is a browser's delight. It's open 9 am to 10 pm daily, closing Sunday at 8 pm.

Periodicals & Foreign Press

Maison de la Presse Internationale (Map 6; ☎ 416-928-2328), 124 Yorkville Ave, sells an impressive array of world newspapers alongside French-language guidebooks and cigars. There are smaller Presse Internationale shops in The Annex and Little Italy.

The Great Canadian News Co chain carries a few international papers and a healthy number of periodicals at 561 Yonge St (Map 6) and 368 Queen St W (Map 5).

Fashion, Shoes & Vintage Clothes

Look out for Roots, a maple leaf–emblazoned version of The Gap. The main stores are at Eaton Centre (Map 5) and 95A Bloor St W (Map 6; ☎ 416-323-3289). It may not be hip, but it's unmistakably Canadian.

Montreal-based chains like Le Château, also called Chateâuworks (Map 5; ☎ 416-971-9314), 336 Queen St W, and Bedo (Map 5; ☎ 416-506-1580), 318 Queen St W, have lime-green snakeskin-print cocktail dresses and tight men's suits that average-sized people may expire trying to fit into.

Canadian-born shoes with attitude are made by John Fluevog (Map 5; ☎ 416-581-1420), 242 Queen St W. They've been in business for 30 years, and the one-of-a-kind shoes come as chunky or Victorian (pointy-style) as you like – there's even an 'Absolut Fluevog' silver high heel made with a recycled vodka bottle in the Bata Shoe Museum (see the Things to See & Do chapter). The designer claims as his influences '50s furniture design and anything vintage. The Web site (www.fluevog.com) has previews of his latest whimsies, costing $160 to $370 a pair. Although pretty to look at, some say the footwear won't take much wear-and-tear.

Black Market (Map 5; ☎ 416-591-7945), 319 Queen St W, has '70s and '80s retro icon T-shirts, like Reese's and ET. Basement-level Black Market Warehouse (Map 5), 256A Queen St W, across the street, has thrift store–worthy deals on Levi's, jackets and western shirts.

So Hip It Hurts (Map 5; ☎ 416-971-6901), 323 Queen St W, has skate- and snowboard knockoff wear – just watch for rock stars making their way past graffiti up to the 2nd-floor entrance. For cutting-edge Japanese and UK shoes that make Doc Martens look positively plain, stray inside Get Out Side (Map 5; ☎ 416-593-5598), 437 Queen St W.

Even more radical clothes shops are found on Queen St W west of Spadina Ave; many are operated by vintage-clothes collectors or the designers themselves. Siren: A Goth Emporium (Map 9; ☎ 416-504-9288), 463 Queen St W, seems to stock everything in purple, black or blood-red; medical supplies are shelved ominously next to wilder choices. Peach Berserk (Map 9; ☎ 416-504-1711), 507 Queen St W, strikes a happy-go-lucky note with its silk-screened girlie creations; bring in your own print pattern for custom-made items.

Cabaret Nostalgia (Map 9; ☎ 416-504-7126), 672 Queen St W, has everything that swings: big-band gowns, old-time suits and gloves. Local designer Annie Thompson has her own shop at 674 Queen St W (Map 9; ☎ 416-703-3843) with creations that model a comfy, urban modish look for both sexes (closed Sunday and Monday).

Nowhere else is there better vintage clothing than at Kensington Market. Some places have been here for decades, like Courage My Love (Map 9; ☎ 416-979-1992), 14 Kensington Ave, where secondhand slip dresses and retro pants line the walls next to bead, leather and silver counters (closed Sunday). More outrageously glam Exile (Map 9; ☎ 416-596-0827) has bright-colored wigs and over-the-top fashions you thought had disappeared for good.

The colorful original knitwear at Fresh Baked Goods (Map 9, ☎ 416-966-0123), 274 Augusta Ave, is as lighthearted as it is one-of-a-kind.

Music & Movies
Toronto has fantastic used-music stores, with CDs averaging $5 to $10 in most neighborhoods.

Queen St W has the lion's share of shops, many holding vinyl recordings you'll be hard pressed to find anywhere else. CD Cat (Map 9; ☎ 416-703-4797), 539 Queen St W, is mainstream, while Rotate This (Map 9; ☎ 416-504-8447), 620 Queen St W, is perfect for those who always know the next cutting-edge band months before anyone else does. Other used-vinyl shops specialize, like Cosmos (Map 9; ☎ 416-603-0254), 607A Queen St W, offering jazz, Latin, African and soul beats (closed Monday).

DJ specialists, look to Metropolis (Map 9; ☎ 416-364-0230), 162A Spadina Ave, a CD 'bar' that supplies vinyl in categories few truly comprehend.

Corporate giants like Tower (Map 5; ☎ 416-593-2500), 2 Queen St W, with its trademark selection of pop books and magazines, and HMV (☎ 416-596-0333), 333 Yonge St, are found near Eaton Centre. The gargantuan Canadian chain Sam the Record Man (Map 5; ☎ 416-977-4650), 347 Yonge St, looks less glitzy but has extensive imports and Canadian music from east-coast traditional to rock.

Classical, jazz and new-world music aficionados must visit L'Atelier Grigorian (Map 6; ☎ 416-922-6477), 70 Yorkville Ave, which has listening stations in-house.

The renowned Suspect Video has two locations, 605 Markham (Map 8; ☎ 416-588-6674) and 619 Queen St W (Map 9; ☎ 416-504-7135). These renowned, truly alternative shops stock hundreds of videos spanning all genres, from '70s kung-fu to international art flicks; it's open daily noon until midnight.

Outdoor Gear
Canadians are serious about outdoor sports, period. Mountain Equipment Co-op (Map 4; ☎ 416-340-2667), 400 King St W, sells quality gear, including an affordable in-house line of backpacks. Lifetime membership costs $5. Across the street, Europe Bound Outfitters (Map 4; ☎ 416-205-9992), 383 King St W, carries more comprehensive (and expensive) name-brand gear, such as The North Face and Columbia. There's another Europe Bound Outfitters on Front St E, just down from Trailhead (Map 4; ☎ 416-862-0881), 61 Front St E, a top-notch store that rents and sells outdoor equipment. Don't overlook the Canada Map shop in the basement.

Tilley Endurables is a Canadian company that turns out some of the finest, toughest, low-maintenance threads imaginable (they are geeky, but they do last). Tilley signature hats have been worn by everyone from explorers to royalty. Visit the outlet in Queen's Quay terminal at Harbourfront (Map 4).

Discount army-navy surplus stores can be found along Yonge St, Spadina Ave or Queen St W. Honest Ed's, in The Annex, and Canadian Tire outlets also sell cheap sleeping bags, tents and camping gear. Environmentally friendly shampoos, toiletries and cotton wear can be picked up at Grassroots (Map 8; ☎ 416-944-1993), 408 Bloor St W.

Toys, Comics & Candy

Kidding Awound (Map 6; ☎ 416-926-8996), 91 Cumberland St, sells yo-yos, wind-ups and witty gifts in joyful heaps; don't overlook the collectible toys displayed behind glass. On the concourse level of Holt Renfrew Centre, Science City (Map 6; ☎ 416-968-2627), 50 Bloor St W, has games and puzzles for science fans young and old.

Silver Snail Comic Shop (Map 5; ☎ 416-593-0889), 367 Queen St W, sells new and hard-to-find limited edition comics, plus plenty of vintage and sci-fi action figures and memorabilia. In Mirvish Village, Yesterday's Heroes (Map 8; ☎ 416-533-9800), 742 Bathurst, has even more.

Hip candy stores have burst onto the Toronto scene, some staying open as late as 3 am for club kids and stoners. Most candy stores now sell more than just sweets, like the nostalgia T-shirts on offer at Sugar Mountain (Map 9; ☎ 416-861-1405), 571 Queen St W. F/X (Map 9; ☎ 416-504-0888), 515 Queen St W, has kitsch collectibles, vintage clothes and ice cream, not to mention an enormous outdoor plastic-flower collage. Almost equally amazing is the PEZ collection at Sucker's (Map 8; ☎ 416-926-0979), 402 Bloor St W.

Erotica

The city may once have been called Toronto the Good, but the innumerable sex shops on Yonge St flirt with every conceivable fetish nowadays.

Unshakably cool customers no longer opt for the discreet back door at family-owned Northbound Leather (Map 6; ☎ 416-972-1037), 586 Yonge St. Times have changed, but the quality of custom-crafted fetish gear has not. (The proprietors have 20-plus years of experience, and absolutely nothing fazes them.)

Low-key and cozy, Good for Her (Map 8; ☎ 416-588-0900), 175 Harbord St, is woman-owned, -operated and -patronized (men are welcome, too). Its discriminating selection of art, how-to books and videos is rounded out by lesbian-friendly paraphernalia and Japanese-manufactured toys. Check out schedules of sex-positive workshops at the Web site (www.goodforher.com). The store is open daily; women-only shopping hours are Thursday 11 am to 2 pm and Sunday noon to 5 pm.

Catering equally to both sexes and all orientations, Come As You Are (Map 9; ☎ 416-504-7934), at 701 Queen St W, was Canada's first co-op sex shop (closed Tuesday). The selection of erotic literature and photography books may induce you to go upstairs to join in the workshops. You can visit the Web site at www.comeasyouare.com.

Excursions

The name 'Ontario' is derived from an Iroquois word meaning 'rocks standing high near the water,' probably referring to Niagara Falls. While Niagara surely deserves its millions of visitors each year, there is more to be uncovered inside Ontario's 1 million sq km than its famous falls.

Quick escapes from the city – including anything from high-speed theme parks or stargazing to Canadian art masterpieces and falconry – will entertain and educate anyone of any age. The Stratford and Shaw summer theater festivals draw residents and travelers alike out into the countryside. Digging even deeper into southwestern Ontario will reveal wellsprings of Native and German-Mennonite culture, as well as the beautiful vineyards of the Niagara escarpment.

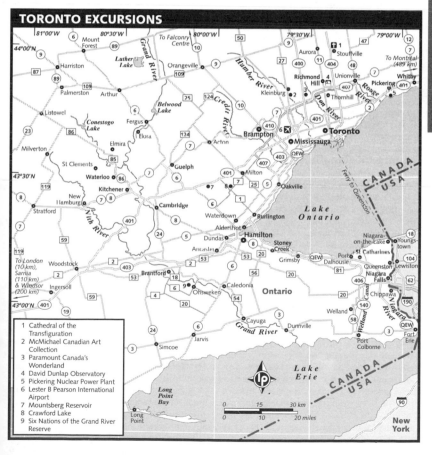

TORONTO EXCURSIONS

1 Cathedral of the Transfiguration
2 McMichael Canadian Art Collection
3 Paramount Canada's Wonderland
4 David Dunlap Observatory
5 Pickering Nuclear Power Plant
6 Lester B Pearson International Airport
7 Mountsberg Reservoir
8 Crawford Lake
9 Six Nations of the Grand River Reserve

NORTH OF TORONTO
David Dunlap Observatory

Just north of the Toronto city limits, the David Dunlap Observatory (☎ 905-884-2112) offers brief introductory talks on modern astronomy, followed by a bit of stargazing through Canada's biggest telescope (1.9m) if skies are clear. Tickets cost $5/3 for adults/children and are sold on a first-come, first-served basis. The talks are given on Friday and Saturday nights most months of the year, but call ahead to check current schedules.

To reach the observatory, drive for about 40 minutes up Bayview Ave past 16th Ave to Hillsview Ave, turn left onto Hillsview and drive 1km west until you see the white dome on your left. If you reach Major Mackenzie Dr, you've gone too far. Alternatively, GO Transit Bayview buses from the York regional terminal near Finch subway station, the northern terminus of the Yonge-University line, stop at Hillsview Dr, from where it's a 20-minute walk to the observatory.

Paramount Canada's Wonderland

Wonderland (☎ 905-832-7000) is a state-of-the-art amusement park with over 50 rides, including some killer roller coasters and the Cliffhanger super-swing, which slams through walls of water allows riders to experience zero gravity. Wonderland also has an exploding 'volcano,' a 5-hectare water park (bring a bathing suit) and Hanna Barbera kiddie land. Lines for rides can be lengthy, except on overcast days, and most rides operate rain or shine. On-site food is expensive; bring a picnic or patronize the food vendors who set up outside in the parking lots.

A one-day pass, good for most attractions and rides, is $43 plus tax, less for seniors and children under age 6. There are also discounted grounds-admission tickets good for some rides. Internet coupons are available at www.canadas-wonderland.com. Parking is another $6.50. The park is open daily late May to early September, and on weekends only roughly a month before and after these dates. Hours are 10 am to 10 pm in peak season.

Wonderland is about an hour's drive northwest of downtown Toronto on Hwy 400, at the Rutherford Rd exit, 10 minutes north of Hwy 401. From Yorkdale or York Mills subway station, catch GO Transit 'Wonderland Express' buses ($3.75).

Kleinburg

The **McMichael Collection** (☎ 905-893-1121, 1-888-213-1121) is an excellent art gallery just north of the city, in the village of Kleinburg. The rustic handmade wood buildings that house the gallery are set among walking trails that crisscross conservation-area wetlands.

The gallery advertises itself as '100% Canadian' and is well known for its extensive collections of Canada's best-known landscape painters, the Group of Seven, much of whose work was created in northern Ontario (see Arts, in the Facts about Toronto chapter). First-time visitors are equally drawn to the Inuit and British Columbian Native prints, photography and carvings, which are not easily found in museums downtown. The tasteful gallery shop sells art history books and high-quality crafts.

Admission is $9, less for children, seniors and families. The gallery is open 10 am to 4 pm weekdays, 11 am weekends, and is closed Monday from November to April. Be forewarned the museum is overrun with gaggles of boisterous schoolchildren on weekday mornings.
Web site: www.mcmichael.on.ca

In the town of Kleinburg, a rather pricey retreat from Toronto, there are numerous antique shops, small galleries and places for a nosh, all squeezed into a few blocks of the main street. If you're hungry, hop on over to **Mr McGregor's House**, just north of Kellam St. The homemade quiche and soups are very budget-friendly, and the self-serve afternoon tea table out back is near the flower garden, where, naturally, rabbits occasionally scamper.

From downtown Toronto, take Queen Elizabeth Way (QEW) to Hwy 427, then drive north on Hwy 7, which turns into Hwy 27. Turn right onto Major Mackenzie Dr, then left onto Islington Ave, and go north; after about 10 minutes, the gallery gates appear on your right. Allow almost an hour for the trip. Parking is $5, but fees help maintain the gallery's 40 hectares of conservation land. You can park in the town of Kleinburg and walk down through the gates to the gallery buildings in about 25 minutes.

Public transport is of little use. Take TTC bus No 37 north from the Islington subway station to Steeles Ave ($2, 35 minutes), then transfer to Vaughan Transit bus No 3 ($2), which runs *only* during weekday rush hours, to Nashville Rd and Islington Ave, a short walk north of Kleinburg town. Call Vaughan Transit (905-832-8527) to check schedules in both directions before setting out.

The Falconry Centre
Hidden in Ontario farm country, about 45 minutes north of Toronto, this unique center (☎ 905-936-1033, 1-888-782-5667) breeds and trains birds in the millennia-old art of falconry. Some of the birds of prey are used for species conservation, while others are privately sold to the likes of Saudi Arabian sheikhs and European royalty. Inside the faux medieval castle walls you come nose-to-beak with over 200 bald eagles, peregrine falcons, snowy owls etc, sitting on traditional bow-shaped perches. The passionate falconers explain the history and biology of their art and winged charges during 'Raptors in Flight' demonstrations, taking place at least once a day at 2 pm. There's also a self-guided audio tour around the bird enclosures.

The center is open 10 am to 5 pm Thursday to Monday mid-May to mid-October. Admission is $9 for adults, less for seniors and children. Visit www.falconrycentre.com for a discount coupon, virtual tour and falconry-course information, if you'd like to literally try your own hand at it.

From Toronto, take Hwy 400 north past Canada's Wonderland to Hwy 9, then drive west to Hwy 10, which runs north toward Tottenham. Turn right onto Hwy 10 and after about 1km turn left at 2nd Line Rd.

Peregrine falcon

The center is 10 minutes farther down on the right. Allow at least 1¼ hours for the trip.

Toronto Metro Zoo (Map 1)
This 283-hectare zoo (☎ 416-392-5900) has over 5000 animals, some in natural-setting pens the size of football fields. Each of the areas covers a major world geographical zone: 'The African Savanna' recreates an African game reserve complete with an elephant highway, while jaguars prowl the Mayan temple 'ruins' underneath the South American waterfall. Simulated indoor climates feature a black-light pavilion for observing nocturnal animals and an underwater viewing area home to beavers, polar bears and seals. Pony and camel rides are given daily in summer ($3.50). There is a small Zoomobile train ($3) that operates around the site Easter to Thanksgiving. Don't forget to bring a picnic lunch unless you want fast food courtesy of *Mr Sub* or *Harvey's*.

The zoo is open daily 9 am to 7:30 pm in summer, until 4:30 pm in winter; admission is $13/8 per adult/child. Parking costs $6.

The complex is at the eastern edge of the city on Meadowvale Rd in Scarborough, approximately 2km north of Hwy 401. From

Kennedy station on the Bloor-Danforth subway line, take the No 86A Scarborough bus. It's quite a trip – allow at least an hour, plus waiting time.

Pickering Nuclear Plant

About 40km east of Toronto on the Lake Ontario shoreline is this nuclear power station, which has portions open to the public. The visitors center (☎ 905-837-7272), 1675 Montgomery Park Rd, is open 9 am to 4 pm weekdays. Whether you're for or against nuclear plants, the interactive educational exhibits and free films are riveting (even for kids). Public walking tours of site operations (for adults only) are popular enough that spots must be reserved two to three weeks in advance.

Apparently, the nuclear plant has been the subject of intense UFO scrutiny since 1975 (see the full Mufon report on the Web at members.home.net/tlemire/pickering.html). If your kids are born glowing in the dark, don't blame Lonely Planet.

SIX NATIONS OF THE GRAND RIVER RESERVE

To the southeast of Brantford, and larger than the city itself, is Ohsweken, the Six Nations of the Grand River Reserve. Established in the late 18th century, it is now one of the largest and most politically active Native communities in the country.

Begin at the gathering place, **Odrohekta** (☎ 519-758-5444), 2498 Chiefswood Rd, near the junction with Hwy 54. The information center here has some educational cultural displays. Nearby, **Chiefswood Mansion**, the home of poet E Pauline Johnson, can be visited. Through the week (and on weekends by appointment), tours are given of the reserve and its Band Council House, the seat of decision-making.

Various gatherings are held through the year, including the Six Nations Pageant, a summer theater program established in 1948, and an annual handicraft bazaar in November. The **Grand River Pow Wow**, held for two days in late July at the Chiefswood Tent & Trailer Park, is a major event with hundreds of colorful dancers, traditional drumming and singing, as well as Native foods and craft sales. Another fall powwow is held at the Six Nations Fairgrounds in late August. (Nominal entry fees are charged.)

Nearby, about 3km southeast of the city of Brantford on Mohawk St, are three more sites: the **Woodland Cultural Centre Museum**; **Her Majesty's Chapel of the Mohawks**, the oldest Protestant church in Ontario and the world's only Royal Indian Chapel; and **Kanata**, an authentic handmade replica of an Iroquois longhouse village.

NIAGARA PENINSULA WINE COUNTRY

If it seems strange to find wine-making here in the Great White North, remember that the Niagara peninsula sits on the 43rd parallel, at the same latitude as Northern California and south of Burgundy, France. The moderate microclimate created by Lake Ontario and the Niagara escarpment and the mineral-rich soil have contributed significantly to the area's viticultural success. Since the 1980s, the small cottage industry has grown up and international award-winning vintners are now capably turning out international-caliber vintages.

Ongoing experimentation with different grape varieties results in erratic quality, but the predominant Riesling, Chardonnay and Gewürztraminer are steadily improving; reds like Cabernet and Shiraz (Syrah) are so far, with very few exceptions, missable. It's the expensive late-harvest and ice wines (sweet and fruity) that have garnered the region a sterling international reputation, regularly beating French varieties in blind taste tests. An ever-increasing number of wineries – there are now over 30 – use the Vintner's Quality Alliance (VQA) designation. By the time you get here, at least half a dozen new wineries will have appeared, so be adventurous (tastings are almost always *gratis*).

Wine Country Drive

Many wineries are open daily year-round and offer tours. Before setting out, pick up a *Wine Regions of Ontario* map from any Ontario Tourism office. The brochure has extensive lists of wineries, opening hours, tours and special events like the Niagara Grape & Wine Festival (☎ 905-688-0212; www.grapeandwine.com), which takes place for 10 days starting the third Friday in September, and summer events like the Hillebrand jazz festival and Henry of Pellham's 'Shuck 'em, Suck 'em, Eat 'em Raw!' oyster festival. The map outlines the 'Wine Route,' which is posted with blue signs and a grape symbol at exits off the QEW and along backcountry roads. The following suggested drive hits the highlights, for both quality and style, of area wineries and farm stands along the way.

Coming from Toronto, get off the QEW at Exit 78/Fifty Rd and follow signs to **Pud-**dicombe Farms** (☎ 905-643-1015). In season, you can pick your own cherries or raspberries (July), peaches (August) or apples (September/October). The country store is open daily May to October.

Loop back toward the QEW to **Kittling Ridge Estates Winery & Spirits** (☎ 905-945-9225), 297 South Service Rd, which looks rather factory-like. Just one taste of the award-winning ice and late harvest wines ($3) will win you over.

Continue east on what eventually becomes rambling Hwy 81. Before reaching Beamsville, look out for the photogenic **Peninsula Ridge Estates Winery**. The new wines taste unfinished, but the log-cabin interior and hilltop setting are beautiful.

Liquid Gold

Niagara's regional wineries burst onto the scene at Vinexpo 1991 in Bordeaux, France. In a blind taste test, judges awarded one of the coveted gold medals to an Ontario ice wine, and international attendees' mouths fell open. These specialty vintages, with their arduous harvesting and sweet taste, continue to draw aficionados and the curious to the Niagara wine country.

For ice wine, a certain percentage of grapes are left on the vines after the regular harvest season is finished. The vines are then covered with netting to protect them from birds. If storms and mold do not destroy them, the grapes grow ever more sugary and concentrated until three days of consistent, low winter temperatures of -8°C or below freeze them entirely in December or January. When this happens, rapid harvesting must be done by hand (so as not to explode the grapes) in the pre-dawn darkness (so that the sun doesn't melt the ice inside and dilute the resulting grape juice). The icy grapes are subsequently pressed and aged in barrels for several months, up to a year. After decanting, the resulting smooth vintage tastes intensely of apples or perhaps even more exotic fruits and has quite an alcoholic kick.

Why are ice wines so expensive? First, it takes 10 times the usual number of grapes to make just one bottle of ice wine. This, combined with labor-intensive production methods and the risk of crop failure, drives the price above $30 per 375mL bottle. Late-harvest wines picked earlier in the year are less costly (and less sweet), but just as full flavored and aromatic.

Many Niagara regional wineries put on ice-wine harvesting events (usually $180 per person) in January during which you can help pick grapes for Ontario's 'liquid gold,' but be warned that it's *really* cold out there. A warmer alternative is the Hillebrand Estates Winery ice-wine festival, which holds its pressings and tastings indoors.

Farther east is Vineland, the original source of viticulture in the Niagara region. Like an elder statesman, **Vinelands Estates Winery** (☎ 905-562-7088, 1-888-846-3526), 3620 Moyer Rd, impresses everyone with its gray stone buildings (one is a tiny B&B and the other a restored 1857 carriage house). Almost all the wines here are excellent, especially the Pinot Gris (tastings free). The attached gourmet restaurant has unbeatable views of the vineyards and an impressive dessert list – too bad the main courses are blah.

Web site: www.vineland.com

If you're hungry, detour 15 minutes north to *The Olde-Fashioned Lunch Box*, at the intersection of 1st Ave and Hwy 24. Signs warn customers that this isn't fast food; homemade sandwiches and burgers this tasty take time to make (and they're cheap, at under $5). Besides, there's a wall of Canadian cartoons to read while you wait.

Hwy 81 meanders east past **Stoney Ridge Cellars** (☎ 905-562-1324), 3201 King St, where surprisingly good cranberry wines are produced, and through the rolling countryside to Jordan. Farther on, turning right on 5th St, is **Henry of Pelham Family Estate**

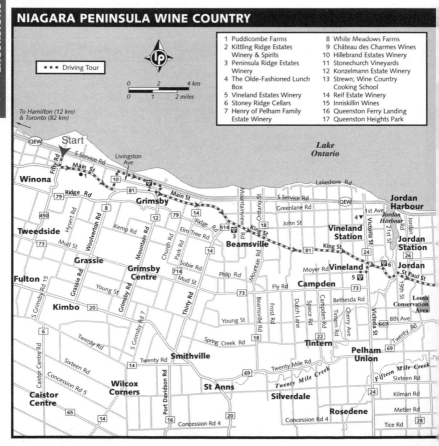

NIAGARA PENINSULA WINE COUNTRY

1 Puddicombe Farms
2 Kittling Ridge Estates Winery & Spirits
3 Peninsula Ridge Estates Winery
4 The Olde-Fashioned Lunch Box
5 Vineland Estates Winery
6 Stoney Ridge Cellars
7 Henry of Pelham Family Estate Winery
8 White Meadows Farms
9 Château des Charmes Wines
10 Hillebrand Estates Winery
11 Stonechurch Vineyards
12 Konzelmann Estate Winery
13 Strewn; Wine Country Cooking School
14 Reif Estate Winery
15 Inniskillin Wines
16 Queenston Ferry Landing
17 Queenston Heights Park

Winery. Here, detour down Effingham St to **White Meadows Farm** for its small store, which sells maple sugar, candy and syrup, all family-made.

In another 20 minutes, you'll enter the Niagara-on-the-Lake region. No one could miss the grandiose **Château des Charmes** (☎ 905-262-5202), 1025 York Rd. Built to look like a French country manor, it features skylit tasting rooms opening onto a canopy-covered terrace facing the vineyards. The vintages aren't nearly so delightful.

On Niagara Stone Rd (Hwy 55), the wines of **Hillebrand Estates Winery** (☎ 905-

468-1723, 1-800-572-8412) are for mass consumption, not connoisseurs. For those who've never visited a winery before, their introductory tours run every hour, on the hour. Call first to ask about specialty ice-wine and bicycle vineyard tours.

Farther north, near Lake Ontario, **Stone-church Vineyards** has a self-guided walking tour of its vineyards. **Konzelmann Estate Winery** (☎ 905-935-2866) is one of the oldest around and the only one to take full advantage of the lakeside microclimate. The late-harvest Vidal (samples $2) tastes of golden apples, and the ice wines, helped

EXCURSIONS

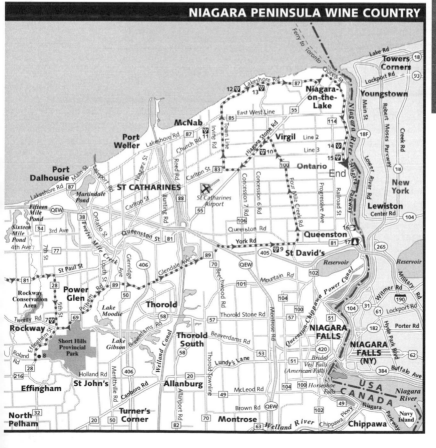

NIAGARA PENINSULA WINE COUNTRY

along by freezing winter winds off the lake, are superb.

Next on the right is the four-year-old **Strewn** (☎ 905-468-1229), 1139 Lake Shore Rd, already producing medal-winning vintages and home to the popular Wine Country Cooking school (www.winecountrycooking.com). Two-hour, weekend and week-long classes are pure indulgence.

The Wine Route passes through Niagara-on-the-Lake and down the Niagara Parkway toward **Reif Estate Winery** (☎ 905-468-7738), 15608 Niagara Parkway. Situated between Line 2 and Line 3 Rds, this well-established winery has tours at 1:30 pm from May to September and tastings every day of the year. Last on our drive, but one of the first Niagara-on-the-Lake wineries, **Inniskillin Wines** (☎ 905-468-3554, 1-888-466-4754) has been a leading award winner in the region since 1975. Self-guided displays outline the history of wine-making in Niagara.

Organized Tours If you're lacking transport (or, more critically, a designated driver), there are a few other options. Niagara Airbus (☎ 905-374-8111, in Toronto ☎ 905-677-8083) operates hop-on, hop-off tours that hit the big wineries (but miss the hidden gems). Tours operate weekends and holidays May to October, daily July to Labour Day, starting in Niagara-on-the-Lake ($29), Niagara Falls ($49) or Toronto ($101).

Steve Bauer Bike Tours (☎ 905-562-0788) organizes half- ($65) and full-day ($125) rides around Vineland or the Niagara-on-the-Lake wine region, most starting at the aptly named Yellow Jersey bicycle shop in Niagara-on-the-Lake (see the following section). Niagara Wine Tours (☎ 905-468-1300) offers daily summer bicycle tours of the area ($74), which take in wine tastings and visits to five local wineries, as well as a private vineyard lunch.

NIAGARA-ON-THE-LAKE

Originally a Native Indian site, this small town 20km downstream (north) from Niagara Falls was settled by Loyalists from New York State after the American Revolution. In the 1790s it became the first capital of Ontario. Today it's considered one of the best-preserved 19th-century towns in North America, but stampedes of tour buses barreling down the small streets completely ruin the effect. If it weren't for the acclaimed Shaw theater festival, it wouldn't be worth more than the briefest of stops.

Information
The friendly tourist office (☎ 905-468-4263) is on the corner of King and Prideaux Sts, two blocks northwest of Simcoe Park. The office is open 9:30 am to 5 pm daily, closed Sunday during January and February.

Shaw Festival
The only festival in the world devoted to producing the plays of George Bernard Shaw and his Victorian contemporaries takes place April to October at three theaters around town – the Court House Theatre, the Festival Theatre and the Royal George, a one-time vaudeville house and cinema. There are specialized seminars and informal Q&A conversations with cast members throughout the season.

Tickets range from $25 up to $75 for the best seats in the house on weekends. Students and seniors may attend specially discounted matinees. Cheaper rush seats go on sale at 9 am on the day of the performance at the Festival Theatre box office (☎ 905-468-2172, 1-800-511-7429). If you're planning to visit, call before tickets go on sale in January and request a complete Shaw Festival guidebook, also available over the Internet at the festival Web site (www.shawfest.sympatico.ca).

Things to See & Do
The town's main street, **Queen St**, has many shops of the Ye Olde variety selling antiques, Scottish souvenirs, fudge and baked goodies; the people at **Greaves**, No 55 Queen St, are fourth-generation jammakers. Farther east is the charming 1866 **Niagara Apothecary**, now a museum fitted with great old cabinets, remedies and jars (admission free).

South of Simcoe Park, the **Historical Museum**, 43 Castlereagh St, opened in 1907 and has a vast collection relating to the town's past, ranging from First Nations artifacts to Loyalist and War of 1812 collectibles ($3; open daily during summer).

One of the **Underground Railroad** routes bringing black slaves from the US across the border to freedom in Canada ran from Buffalo across to Fort Erie, then north along the Niagara River to Niagara-on-the-Lake. Pick up the *Niagara's Freedom Trail* guide to local historical sites at the tourist office.

The only Niagara Falls–like attractions in town, the Whirlpool Jet (☎ 905-468-4800, 1-888-438-4444), 61 Melville St, takes passengers on an hour-long trip through the rapids of the lower Niagara River. Reservations are required and tickets cost – brace yourself – $52.

Places to Stay & Eat

Accommodations are expensive and often booked out to boot. The tourist office runs a free accommodations reservation service for most of the town's lovely B&Bs. The *Bunny Hutch (☎ 905-468-3377, 305 Centre St)* has rooms with shared bath at just $60/65 with a full breakfast.

Queen St is loaded with places for a bite, all serving the tourist trade. The pub-style *Buttery (19 Queen St)* puts on a thoroughly kitschy Henry VIII–style feast on weekends. *Fans Court (135 Queen St)* provides some excellent Cantonese and pan-Asian diversion in this most Anglo of towns. Across from Simcoe Park, the *Prince of Wales Hotel (6 Picton St)* has a dining room for finer, more costly eating or an afternoon cream tea.

Getting There & Around

There are no direct buses between Toronto and Niagara-on-the-Lake. From Toronto you must go to Niagara Falls and then transfer to a shuttle bus (☎ 905-357-4000, 1-800-667-0256), running three times daily May to October ($10/16 one-way/roundtrip). During winter, taxis are the only reliable option, costing around $25 each way.

For information on the high-speed hydrofoil between Toronto and Queenston, south

of Niagara-on-the-Lake, see the Getting There & Away chapter.

If you're driving from Toronto take the QEW west to Exit 38B/Niagara Stone Rd (Hwy 55), which becomes Mississauga St and intersects Queen St downtown. With tour buses and Sunday drivers crowding the roads, count on it taking two hours.

Between April and October, Yellow Jersey (☎ 905-262-9898), 77 Queenston St S, rents bicycles by the half-day ($15) or full day ($25), including a helmet, lock and map.

NIAGARA PARKWAY

The slow, pleasant two-lane **Niagara Parkway** runs for 56km almost the length of the Niagara River, from Niagara-on-the-Lake past the falls to Fort Erie. Along the way are parks, picnic areas, viewpoints and campgrounds, all part of the Niagara Parks Commission system. A paved recreational trail for cycling, in-line skating or walking parallels the parkway and is marked with historic and natural points of interest. In season, fresh-fruit stands with cold cherry ciders pop up beside the trail.

In the small village of Queenston, just before the Lewiston Bridge to the USA, is the **Samuel E Weir Collection** of Canadian art, which includes early landscapes of Niagara Falls and works by the Group of Seven (open Wednesday to Sunday; free). Farther south, the **Laura Secord Homestead** belonged to one of Canada's best-known heroines. During the War of 1812, she hiked nearly 30km to warn the British soldiers of impending attack by the USA (interestingly, she was a US citizen by birth). Nearby is the historic **Mackenzie House Printery**, where William Lyon Mackenzie once edited the hell-raising *Colonial Advocate*. Both historical sites charge $2 and are open daily May to October.

A little farther along the parkway is **Queenston Heights Park** (see the Niagara Peninsula Wine Country map), known for its towering monument of Major General Sir Isaac Brock, 'Saviour of Upper Canada.' The winding stairwell inside takes you up 60m to a fabulous view. Self-guided walking tours of the hillside recount the 1812 Battle of Queenston Heights, a significant British victory that helped Canada resist becoming part of the USA.

Past the hideous **floral clock** is the exceptionally well maintained **Niagara Glen Nature Preserve**, the only place where you can gain a sense of what the area was like before the arrival of Europeans. There are seven different walking trails winding down the gorge, past huge boulders, icy cold caves, wildflowers and woods where the falls were situated 8000 years ago. The Niagara Parks Commission (☎ 905-356-2241, 1-877-642-7275) offers guided nature walks four times daily during summer ($3). Take something to drink, as the Niagara is one river from which you do not want to drink – this region is one of the industrial centers of North America.

Almost opposite are the **Botanical Gardens**, with 40 hectares for browsing, free of charge, year-round. For $8 you can step inside the **Butterfly Conservatory** (☎ 905-358-0025), where over 50 species make their way out of chrysalides and flutter about the flowers.

Attractions along the parkway between Queenston and Niagara Falls can all be reached on the Niagara Falls People Mover buses during peak summer season (see Getting Around, in the next section).

NIAGARA FALLS

Napoleon's brother once rode from New Orleans in a stagecoach with his new bride to view the falls, and they (the falls) have been a honeymoon attraction ever since. Spanning the Niagara River between Ontario and upper New York, they are one of Canada's top tourist destinations, drawing over 12 million people annually. In terms of sheer volume, the equivalent of over 1 million bathtubs full of water goes over the falls every second. Even in winter, when the flow is partially hidden and the edges frozen solid – like a freeze-framed film – it's quite a spectacle. Very occasionally ice jams stop the falls altogether. The first recorded instance of this occurred Easter Sunday 1848, and it caused some to speculate that the end of the world was nigh and others to scavenge the river bed beneath the falls.

Even more surprisingly, a good proportion of people who have gone over the falls, suicides aside, do live to tell about it. A schoolteacher named Annie Taylor first devised the padded-barrel method (successfully) in 1901. The first stuntman of the 1990s, witnessed and photographed by startled visitors, went over the edge in a kayak. He's now paddling the great white water in the sky. In 1995 the US citizen who tried to jet-ski over the falls might have made it – if his parachute had opened. **Ride Niagara**, located under Rainbow Bridge, allows everyone to try the plunge via electronic simulation.

Orientation

The town of Niagara Falls is split into two main sections. The 'normal' part of town, where locals go about their business, is called 'old downtown.' The area around Bridge St, near the corner of Erie Ave, has both the train and bus stations. Generally, however, there is little to see or do in this part of town.

About 3km south along River Rd (the Niagara Parkway) are the majestic falls and all the tourist trappings – a casino, hotels, artificial attractions and flashing lights – producing a sort of Canadian Las Vegas. The main streets are the busy Clifton Hill, Falls Ave, Centre St, Victoria Ave and Ferry St.

Information

The most central places for tourist information are at Table Rock Centre, right next to the Horseshoe Falls, and at Maid of the Mist Plaza. They are usually open 9 am to 6 pm daily (until 11 pm in summer). The Niagara Parks Commission (☎ 905-371-0254, 1-877-642-7275) runs good but busy desks at both places.

Web site: www.niagaraparks.com

The Ontario Tourism Travel Centre (☎ 905-358-3221), 5355 Stanley Ave, is well equipped but outside town, west on Hwy 420 from the Rainbow Bridge toward the QEW. It's open daily, until 8 pm in summer.

Many of the free tourist booklets around town contain maps, discount coupons for attractions, rides etc. If you don't see any, ask at other attractions, hotels and motels.

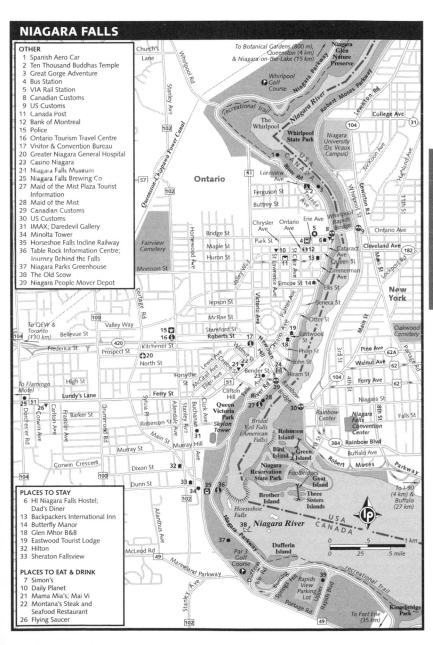

NIAGARA FALLS

OTHER
1 Spanish Aero Car
2 Ten Thousand Buddhas Temple
3 Great Gorge Adventure
4 Bus Station
5 VIA Rail Station
8 Canadian Customs
9 US Customs
11 Canada Post
12 Bank of Montreal
15 Police
16 Ontario Tourism Travel Centre
17 Visitor & Convention Bureau
20 Greater Niagara General Hospital
23 Casino Niagara
24 Niagara Falls Museum
25 Niagara Falls Brewing Co
27 Maid of the Mist Plaza Tourist
     Information
28 Maid of the Mist
29 Canadian Customs
30 US Customs
31 IMAX; Daredevil Gallery
34 Minolta Tower
35 Horseshoe Falls Incline Railway
36 Table Rock Information Centre;
     Journey Behind the Falls
37 Niagara Parks Greenhouse
38 The Old Scow
39 Niagara People Mover Depot

PLACES TO STAY
6 HI Niagara Falls Hostel;
     Dad's Diner
13 Backpackers International Inn
14 Butterfly Manor
18 Glen Mhor B&B
19 Eastwood Tourist Lodge
32 Hilton
33 Sheraton Fallsview

PLACES TO EAT & DRINK
7 Simon's
10 Daily Planet
21 Mama Mia's; Mai Vi
22 Montana's Steak and
     Seafood Restaurant
26 Flying Saucer

EXCURSIONS

There is metered parking around town and various paid lots ($5 to $10 per day). The huge Rapids View Parking Lot, 3.2km south of the falls, is off River Rd where the Niagara People Mover depot is located.

The Greater Niagara General Hospital (☎ 905-358-0171) is at 5546 Portage Rd, and the Niagara Falls After-Hours Clinic (☎ 905-374-3344), 6453 Morrison St, is west of the old downtown area.

The Falls

On the US side, the pretty Bridal Veil Falls (often referred to as the American Falls) crash down onto mammoth rocks that have fallen due to erosion. The grander, more powerful Horseshoe Falls on the Canadian side plunge down into the Maid of the Mist pool, which is indeed misty and clouds views of the falls from afar.

Maid of the Mist boats take passengers right up for a view from the bottom – it's loud and wet and costs $10.65 for adults (cash only). Boats leave across the street from the bottom of Clifton Hill. Everyone heads for the upper deck, but the views from either end of the lower deck are OK, too. Boats sail May to October, until as late as 7:45 pm in peak season.

From near Table Rock Information Centre, you can pay $6.50 at **Journey Behind the Falls**, don a plastic poncho and walk down through rock-cut tunnels halfway down the cliffside – as close as you can get to the falls without getting in a barrel (or going over to the American side). It's open year-round 9 am to 8:30 pm in peak season, but be prepared to wait in line for your brief turn in the spray.

About 6km north of Horseshoe Falls on the Niagara River, past the Great Gorge Adventure (don't bother), is the **Spanish Aero Car**, named for Leonardo Torres Quevedo, the engineer who started its operation in 1916. Open the same hours as the Journey, here a gondola stretched 550m between two outcrops takes you above a deadly whirlpool, created by the falls, so you can peer at logs, tires and other debris spinning in the eddies below ($5.50).

Children, seniors and students are entitled to discounts at these attractions. A Discovery Pass, available at Table Rock Information Centre and various attractions, includes Journey and the Aero Car, as well as the Butterfly Conservatory and Queenston historical sites (see the Niagara Parkway section earlier). Passes cost $26.95/13.50 for adults/children and include the Niagara People Mover.

Other Views

The **Minolta Tower** (☎ 905-356-1501, 1-800-461-2492) is close to the falls and virtually overlooks the lip. The trip up is $7, or $9 for a dual day/night ticket (two trips). It has indoor/outdoor observation galleries and a revolving buffet-style restaurant ($25 minimum) with spectacular views as far as Toronto and Buffalo, NY, on clear days. The similar **Skylon Tower** (☎ 905-356-2651), 5200 Robinson St, is the one with yellow elevators running up the outside. It's slightly more expensive than the Minolta, but the early-bird dinner special (4:30 to 5 pm) at the revolving restaurant saves some money.

Other Attractions

Established in 1827, the **Niagara Falls Museum**, 5651 River Rd, is the first of the many 'daredevil museums' showing history and artifacts of the falls. It was closed for renovation in 2000.

There's another fascinating daredevil museum, called Daredevil Gallery, attached to the **IMAX Theatre** (☎ 905-374-4629), 6170 Buchanan Ave, adjacent to the Skylon Tower. Somewhat outdated 45-minute shows about the history of the falls run nearly continuously, alternating with French versions (8 and 9 am) and other current IMAX features. Tickets cost $9.40/7.65 for adults/children, plus $1 extra for the museum.

Clifton Hill is a street name but generally refers to a slope near the falls given over to sense-bombarding artificial attractions in Disney-like concentration. You name it – Ripley's Believe It or Not, Madame Tussaud's Wax Museum, Criminal's Hall of Fame (you get the drift) – they're all here.

In most cases, paying the entrance fee will leave you feeling like a sucker.

The immensely successful **Casino Niagara**, 5705 Falls Ave, never closes. Free shuttle buses run to its door from hotels and attractions all over town.

Out on the motel strip, **Niagara Falls Brewing Co** (☎ 905-356-2739, 1-800-267-3392), 6863 Lundy's Lane, gives cottage-brewery tours that let you sample its famous Eisbock (German for 'ice ram') beer. Call to check tour times.

Less than 1km south of the Horseshoe falls, the **Niagara Parks** greenhouse and conservatory provide year-round floral displays (free). A bonus is the tropical birds. Across the street, rusting away in the river, the *Old Scow* is a steel barge that has been lodged on rocks and waiting to be washed over the falls since 1918.

Organized Tours

From May to October, Double Deck (☎ 905-374-7423) offers good-value double-decker bus tours ($36.50/20.50 for adults/children) that include Maid of the Mist, Journey Behind the Falls and the Spanish Aero Car. You can take one or two days to complete the hop-on, hop-off loop, which goes as far south as the Old Scow and north to Niagara Glen Preserve.

For budget travelers, Moose Travel and Further Still (see the Getting There & Away chapter) offer affordable day trips ($37) from Toronto May to October. The Further Still itinerary lasts eight hours. It stops at wineries and for a guided escarpment hike, plus an outdoor meal.

JoJo Tours (☎ 416-201-6465) has good one-day small-group trips to Niagara Falls that include a stop at a winery and Niagara-on-the-Lake ($50). Tours operate all year with a price drop in the off-season. All of the above tours can be booked through many Toronto hostels, which are also the pick-up points.

Special Events

Illuminating the falls has been a tradition since 1860, when the tightrope walker Blondin first carried flares and shot off fire-

The tried-and-true 'barrel method'

works. Every night of the year, colored spotlights are turned on the falls, and on Friday nights in summer there are fireworks. The annual Winter Festival of Lights is a season of concerts, fireworks and nighttime parades from the end of November to mid-January.

Places to Stay

Accommodations are plentiful and, overall, prices aren't too bad, what with all the competition on both sides of the border. In summer, on weekends and for holidays (Canadian *and* American), prices spike sharply.

There are excellent *campgrounds* all around town; ask at Table Rock Information Centre for a list. Three are on Lundy's Lane at the west end of the main motel strip, accessible by shuttle bus.

Both hostels in Niagara Falls are open all year and are regularly full during summer. The HI *Niagara Falls International Hostel* (☎ 905-357-0770, 1-888-749-0058, 4549 Cataract Ave) is in the old downtown close to the train and bus stations. The hostel has 70

EXCURSIONS

beds costing $17.50 each for members. In a most impressive house (mansion?) dating from 1896, **Backpackers International Inn** (☎ 905-357-4266, 1-800-891-7022, 4711 Zimmerman Ave) has four-bed dorms for $18 and five rooms for couples at $50, including taxes, morning coffee and muffin. The upstairs rooms, like those in a small European hotel, are particularly charming.

B&Bs offer the best mid-range accommodations values, starting at $45 to $75 per room (ask first if the breakfast is continental or full). Many are along River Rd midway between the falls area and the old downtown. If you didn't make a reservation, just look for 'Vacancy' signs. **Glen Mhor B&B** (☎ 905-354-2600, 5381 River Rd) offers bicycles and pick-up from the bus or train station. Japanese is spoken. Pricier **Eastwood Tourist Lodge** (☎ 905-354-8686, 5359 River Rd) is a fine old home with balconies overlooking the river; German and Spanish are spoken. Beautiful **Butterfly Manor** (☎ 905-358-8988, 4917 River Rd) is a little farther away from the falls.

Many cheaper motels offer enticements such as waterbeds, saunas, and heart-shaped Jacuzzis. There are seemingly millions of them along Lundy's Lane, which leads west out from the falls and later becomes Hwy 20. Prices vary quite a bit, starting at $40/80 in low/high season. As long as you're here, go all-out at the **Flamingo Motel** (☎ 905-356-4646, 1-800-738-7701, 7701 Lundy's Lane).

Hotels tend to be new and expensive – $100 and up for views of the falls at the **Sheraton Fallsview** (☎ 905-374-1077, 1-800-267-8439, 6755 Oakes Dr) or **Hilton** (☎ 905-354-7887, 1-888-370-0700, 6361 Buchanan Dr).

Places to Eat
Finding food in Niagara Falls is no problem, and while the dining isn't great, it isn't all bad either.

Around Clifton Hill or along Victoria and Stanley Aves, there are scads of restaurants, including Japanese, Chinese, German and ever-popular Italian eateries. **Mama Mia's** (5719 Victoria Ave) has been serving standard Italian fare at reasonable prices ($8 to $14) for many years. A few doors down, **Mai Vi** (5713 Victoria Ave) is a neat little place with Vietnamese dishes well under $10. For something a little more stylish (and expensive), try **Montana's Steak & Seafood Restaurant** (☎ 905-356-4410, 5657 Victoria Ave).

For 'out of this world' fast food at any time of day, you can't miss **Flying Saucer** (6768 Lundy's Lane). Famous breakfast specials cost 99½¢ and all other earthling delights are served 6 am to 3 am daily.

In the slow part of town (old downtown), **Daily Planet** (4573 Queen St) is a good place to grab a brew at non-tourist prices. Down near the hostels by the corner of River Rd is **Dad's Diner**, offering cheap basics, and **Simon's** (4116 Bridge St), the oldest restaurant in Niagara Falls (and looking it).

Getting There & Away
Niagara Falls is about a two-hour drive from Toronto via the QEW, past St Catharines. Two bridges run over the Niagara River to New York State: the Whirlpool Rapids Bridge and, closer to the falls, the Rainbow Bridge, which celebrates its 60th year in 2001. You can walk or drive across to explore the falls from the USA side, but both pedestrians and drivers have to pay a bridge toll.

The bus station (☎ 905-357-2133), 4445 Erie Ave, is in the old downtown away from the falls area. Buses to Toronto leave daily about once every two hours from early morning (around 8 am) until 11:30 pm ($24, 1½ to 2 hours). A few Greyhound buses also depart for Buffalo, NY, between 10 am and 1 am. Adult tickets cost $5.40/10.80 one-way/roundtrip and the trip takes approximately one hour. Ask about discounted same-day roundtrip tickets and two-for-one fares.

For now, the cheapskate way to the falls is the Casino Shuttle (☎ 1-877-361-2888) from Toronto. Passengers must be over 19 (ID required), and roundtrip tickets cost $15. You must return on the same day on the return bus from the casino station and show the Casino Players Advantage Club Card (available free inside the casino; no gambling necessary). Upon arrival you are given $15 worth of gambling chips, so there's nothing to stop you (yet) from entering the casino and cashing in your chips, essentially scoring a free ride. Call for schedules (daily runs) and pick-up information.

The VIA Rail station is across the street from the bus station. There are two runs a day to Toronto, at 6:45 am and 5:15 pm; on Saturday and Sunday, the first train leaves at 7:40 am. The trip takes about two hours and the lowest one-way advance-purchase fare is $27.50. See the Getting There & Away chapter for details of Amtrak routes to/from the USA.

Getting Around

Driving in and around the center is nothing but a headache. Follow the signs to one of the several parking districts and stash the car for the day.

Walking is best; most things to see are concentrated in a small area. The Incline Railway runs from near the base of the Minolta tower down the hillside to the falls area. It operates April to mid-October, 9 am to midnight during peak season ($1).

For getting farther afield, the economical and efficient Niagara Parks People Mover bus system operates year-round, weather permitting. In summer, buses run 9 am to 11 pm daily, but after 9 pm they go no farther north than the Aero Car attraction. They run in a straight line from Rapids View parking lot 3.2km south of the falls off River Rd, up past the greenhouse and Horseshoe Falls, along River Rd past the Rainbow and Whirlpool bridges and north to the Aero Car (or, during peak summer season, to Queenston). From there, it turns around and follows the same path 9km back. A day pass costs a bargain $5/2.50 for adults/children and can be purchased at most stops. Parking at Rapids View costs $13 for the day, including one People Mover pass.

Niagara Transit (☎ 905-356-1179) operates three similar shuttle services between May and November. One route, the Red Line Shuttle, goes around the bus and train stations, then downtown and up Lundy's Lane to the motels and campgrounds. The other, the Blue Line Shuttle, runs from the Rapids View depot along Portage Rd to the bottom of Clifton Hill. The Green Line goes from the bus terminal to the Spanish Aero Car, then back down River Rd past the B&Bs to Clifton Hill. Operating hours vary seasonally, but shuttles run every half-hour 9 am to 2 am in summer. One-way is $2.75 and a day pass costs $5 per adult (two accompanying children under 12 ride free).

Out of season, the regular city buses must be used.

MENNONITE COUNTRY

The Mennonites originated in Switzerland in the early 1500s as a Protestant sect. Forced from country to country due to their religious disagreements with the state, they took up William Penn's promise of religious freedom and began arriving in North America around 1640. In the early 1800s, lured by cheaper undeveloped land in southern Ontario, some Mennonites moved northward. Despite their day-to-day differences, most of the dozen different Mennonite sects in Ontario agree on a number of fundamentals, which include the freedom of conscience, separation of church and state, refusal to take oaths and practical piety. Science is rejected by many, and automobiles, much machinery and other trappings of modern life are shunned.

Old Order Mennonites are the strictest in their adherence to tradition. Women wear bonnets and long, plain dresses; men tend to wear black and grow beards. The Amish are a group that split from the main body of Mennonites, believing them to be too worldly. Mennonite and Amish communities are largely self-sufficient, and they do not proselytize.

It's not uncommon to see Mennonite carriages rolling along local roads or, on Sunday, parked by their churches in the countryside surrounding Kitchener-Waterloo. Many local stores sell Mennonite quilts and simple, well-made furniture. Their organic produce and meat, as well as baked goods and delicious jams, are inexpensive and readily available, except when farmers piously hang up signs reading 'No Sale Sunday.'

EXCURSIONS

Kitchener-Waterloo

The twin cities of Kitchener and Waterloo are about a 1½-hour drive west of Toronto on Hwy 401, in the heart of rural southern Ontario. 'Downtown' refers to the southern portion of Kitchener, which is nearly three times the size of Waterloo. King St is the main street and runs roughly north-south (even though it's called King St W and E), crossing Queen St.

Kitchener-Waterloo Tourism (☎ 519-745-3536, 1-800-265-6959), 80 Queen St N, is open 9 am to 5 pm weekdays, closing earlier in winter.

Web site: www.kw-visitor.on.ca

Things to See & Do Since 1839, the central **Farmers' Market** (☎ 519-741-2287) has featured Mennonite products – breads, jams, many cheeses and sausages, and handicrafts such as quilts – but there are also many equally skilled bakers, craftspeople and farmers who aren't, in fact, Mennonite.

It's open 6 am to 2 pm Saturday year-round, and Wednesday from July to September. The indoor/outdoor complex is at the corner of Frederick and Duke Sts, one block northeast of King St. On Benton St, west of the market, a 23-bell **carillon** plays a musical tribute to the Grimm Brothers at noon and 5 pm.

Farther southwest is the **Joseph Schneider Haus** (☎ 519-742-7752), 466 Queen St S, the restored Georgian-style residence of a prosperous German Mennonite from Pennsylvania. It's a living museum of mid-1850s country life with collections of German-Canadian folk art ($2.25; open 10 am to 5 pm daily July and August, closed certain days at other times of year).

Organized Tours For getting around to some of the area events and attractions like St Jacob's or Elora, consider the half-(around $20) and full-day ($30) van trips offered by Town & Country Tours (☎ 519-894-4831).

Special Events About 55% of the city's 215,000 inhabitants are of German origin (which probably explains why Kitchener

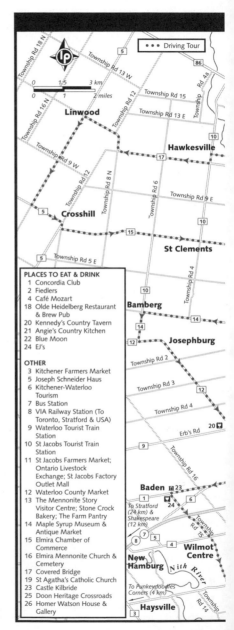

PLACES TO EAT & DRINK
1   Concordia Club
2   Fiedlers
4   Café Mozart
18 Olde Heidelberg Restaurant & Brew Pub
20 Kennedy's Country Tavern
21 Angie's Country Kitchen
22 Blue Moon
24 EJ's

OTHER
3   Kitchener Farmers Market
5   Joseph Schneider Haus
6   Kitchener-Waterloo Tourism
7   Bus Station
8   VIA Railway Station (To Toronto, Stratford & USA)
9   Waterloo Tourist Train Station
10 St Jacobs Tourist Train Station
11 St Jacobs Farmers Market; Ontario Livestock Exchange; St Jacobs Factory Outlet Mall
12 Waterloo County Market
13 The Mennonite Story Visitor Centre; Stone Crock Bakery; The Farm Pantry
14 Maple Syrup Museum & Antique Market
15 Elmira Chamber of Commerce
16 Elmira Mennonite Church & Cemetery
17 Covered Bridge
19 St Agatha's Catholic Church
23 Castle Kilbride
25 Doon Heritage Crossroads
26 Homer Watson House & Gallery

MENNONITE COUNTRY

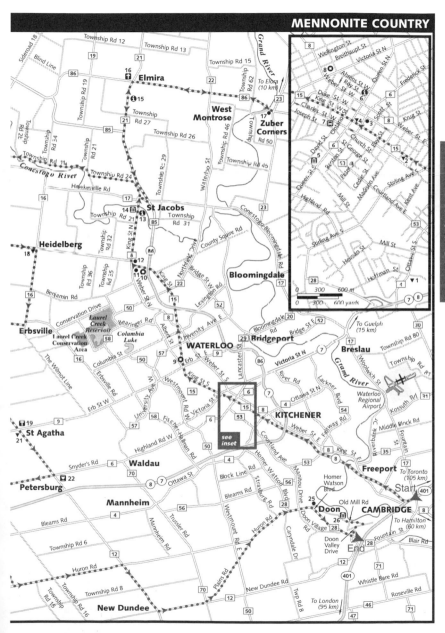

was originally named Berlin). The event of the year is **Oktoberfest** (☎ 519-570-4267), said to be the largest outside Germany. The nine-day festival attracts 500,000 people and starts with the ceremonial Tapping of the Keg in early October, extending to over 20 beer halls for German music and food. Visit one of the reception areas for tickets and instructions on how to tie on your stein so you don't lose it.

Web site: www.oktoberfest.ca.

Places to Eat There are quite a few European delis and bakeries like old-fashioned *Café Mozart (45 Queen St S)* in Kitchener. *Fiedlers (197 King St E)* is stacked full of cheeses, rye breads, sausages and salamis.

For solid German fare, head south of town to the *Concordia Club* (☎ 519-745-5617, 429 Ottawa St S), a popular site during Oktoberfest. It offers live entertainment most weekends.

Getting There & Away The Kitchener bus station (☎ 519-585-7555), 15 Charles St W, is one block northwest of Queen St. There are frequent services to Toronto ($19, 1½ to two hours). Same-day roundtrip tickets cost $21.50. Greyhound buses depart for Stratford ($6.50, one hour) around noon and 6 pm.

There are two VIA Rail trains daily from Toronto ($24, 1½ hours), but they depart at inconvenient times. From Kitchener westbound trains reach Windsor across from Detroit, USA, in three hours ($58). The station is on the corner of Victoria and Weber Sts, a quick walk north of downtown.

St Jacobs

About 15km north of Kitchener-Waterloo (take King St) is St Jacobs, a historic Mennonite village that overflows with daytrippers in the handmade quilt shops, antique stores and bakeries housed in 19th-century buildings on the main street. For hungry road-trippers, a visit to **Stone Crock Bakery** and the neighboring **Farm Pantry** should be seriously considered.

Next door is the **Mennonite Story Visitor Centre** (☎ 519-664-3518), 33 King St, an ex-

cellent interpretive center on the Mennonites and their history. It's open daily (afternoons only on Sunday), closed weekdays from Christmas until April. Admission is by donation and includes a 15-minute video.

Opposite and slightly uphill is an antique market holding the **Maple Syrup Museum** (☎ 519-644-1243), 8 Spring St, which will tell you everything about the production of this Canadian specialty (open daily; free).

Two kilometers south of town is the gigantic **St Jacobs Farmers' Market** (☎ 1-800-265-3353), with horse-and-buggy sheds still in place. The maple fudge, fresh Ontario peaches and sour cherry jams are amazing. It's open 7 am to 3:30 pm Thursday and Saturday year-round, and Tuesday during summer. Near the market quilt shop, Country Livery Service (☎ 519-888-0302, 1-877-647-4337) organizes horse-drawn trolley tours of local farms ($11, market days only) and sleigh rides in winter. Cattle are auctioned next door at the Ontario Livestock Exchange, and the more authentic (and cheaper) **Waterloo County Market** is on the opposite side of the highway (King St).

All of this good country charm clashes with the hulking **St Jacobs Factory Outlet Mall** across the way. Get your super-modern Levis and Reeboks here (open daily).

Getting There & Away From downtown Kitchener, take Grand River Transit bus No 7 to Conestoga Mall, then transfer to the No 21 bus for St Jacobs market and village. The No 21 runs every half-hour 7:30 am to 3 pm on Thursday and Saturday only during summer.

The Waterloo–St Jacobs Railway (☎ 519-746-1950), a 1950s-style tourist train that operates between the St Jacobs market and uptown Waterloo, should be back in operation in 2001.

Mennonite Country Drive

Some 8km north of St Jacobs up Hwy 86 is **Elmira**. It's less touristy than St Jacobs and is a real, working country-Mennonite town. The simple **Elmira Mennonite Church** on Church St has an old Mennonite cemetery set in the middle of fields. The first week in

April sees the province's biggest and best **Maple Syrup Festival** (☎ 519-669-2605), attracting thousands of visitors with its pancake breakfasts, quilt shows and countryside tours.

About 7km east in **West Montrose** is the only covered bridge remaining in Ontario. Built in 1889, it's known as the **Kissing Bridge**. You can drive or walk across it, but look out for horse droppings and don't smoke.

At this point, you could detour to **Elora**, known for its scenic old mill set beside the powerful Grand River falls. Mennonites and other Ontarian day-trippers come to walk the old-fashioned main streets, linger at riverbank restaurants and rent tire tubes for a trip through the limestone canyon of **Elora Gorge Conservation Area** (☎ 519-846-9742). In late July and early August, the **Elora Music Festival** (☎ 519-846-0331) of classical, choral and folk music holds some of its outdoor performances on an illuminated stage floating in the quarry.

Otherwise, backtrack through Elmira almost to St Jacobs, turning off on Township Rd 24, a gravel road with fine riverside scenery, and drive west to Hawkesville, where there is a blacksmith's shop. Continue to Linwood and St Clements – both are Mennonite towns with country general stores.

Farther east, at the junction of Hwys 15 and 16, is the touristy *Olde Heidelberg Restaurant & Brew Pub* (☎ *519-699-4413*). Built in 1838, it sells German country-style meals with Bavarian beer brewed on-site (closed Sunday).

Meander through the countryside down to St Agatha, with its landmark church steeple and old fogies' *Kennedy's Country Tavern* (☎ *519-747-1313*). It has a bit of an Irish slant (shamrocks *go bragh!*), although much of the food shows a German influence. Across the street, *Angie's Country Kitchen* is highly recommended.

Farther south, in Petersburg, *Blue Moon* (☎ *519-634-5421, 1677 Snyder's Rd*) is a Georgian-style inn dating from 1848 (closed Sunday), but you can give it a miss and head straight west to *EJ's* (☎ *514-634-5711, 39 Snyder's Rd W*) in Baden. It's the best historic country tavern of the lot, with some intriguing original decor including hand-painted ceiling tiles. Beer from around the world is on tap. It's closed Sunday and Monday.

Along the way, you'll pass Exit 51, the turnoff to **Castle Kilbride** (☎ 519-634-8444), 60 Snyder's Rd W, an Italianate Victorian villa with lavish interior furnishings and unique 3D and *trompe l'oeil* artwork (open 1 to 4 pm Tuesday to Sunday; $5). It was built for Scottish immigrant James Livingston, 'the flax and oil king of Canada.'

From Baden, go south to New Dundee and slowly loop back to Hwy 401. If you have time, stop at the **Homer Watson House & Gallery** (☎ 519-748-4377), 1754 Old Mill Rd, which commemorates one of Canada's most notable landscape painters. Nearby on Homer Watson Blvd, **Doon Heritage Crossroads** (☎ 519-748-1914) is a re-creation of a 1914 pioneer settlement and a Russian Mennonite Village ($6 for adults). Opening hours vary seasonally at both places, but they are open daily in summer.

STRATFORD

Stratford is a fairly typical slow-paced, rural Ontario town – except that it's consciously prettier than most and home to the world-famous Shakespearean Festival.

The Avon River flows peacefully beside the town and adds to its charm. Almost everything is close to Ontario St, which runs roughly east-west. Queen's Park and the Festival Theatre are at the east end of town, just north of Ontario St. From the park, Lakeshore Dr runs along the river back into town and meets York and Ontario Sts near the Perth County Courthouse, one of the town's most distinctive landmarks. A few blocks southeast along Downie St is the old-fashioned City Hall, at the corner of Wellington St.

The summer tourist office (☎ 519-273-3352, 1-800-561-7926) is beside the river off York St. Stop in to peruse photos of guesthouses and get a free-parking sign for your car. You can purchase hiking and biking maps of the surrounding countryside here. Bike rental is available for $7.50 per hour or

$25 per day (with a $200 refundable credit-card deposit) from the Stone Maiden Inn (☎ 519-271-7129), 123 Church St.

During the off-season (November to May), Tourism Stratford (☎ 519-271-5140), 88 Wellington St, offers visitor information.

Shakespearean Festival

Sir Alec Guinness played Richard III on opening night of the Stratford Theatre Festival, which in 1953 began humbly in a huge tent at Queen's Park beside the Avon River. The festival has achieved international acclaim and the productions are first-rate, as are the costumes, and respected actors are always on stage. Aside from the plays, there are a number of other interesting programs to consider, some of which are free; for others a small admission is charged. Among them are postperformance discussions with the actors, Sunday-morning backstage tours, warehouse tours for a look at costumes and readings by famous authors.

There are three theaters – all in town – that stage contemporary and modern drama and music, operas and, of course, works by the Bard. Main productions take place at the Festival Theatre, with its round, protruding stage. The Avon Theatre, seating 1100 people, is the secondary venue and the Tom Patterson Theatre is the smallest.

The season runs May to October, and tickets cost $23 to $75. Tickets go on sale in early January through the Festival Theatre box office (☎ 519-273-1600, 1-800-567-1600), and by show time nearly every performance is sold out. Spring previews and fall end-of-season shows are discounted 30% to 50%; students and seniors also receive discounts at selected shows. In Toronto the Roy Thompson Hall box office handles ticket sales. A limited number of rush seats are available at T.O. Tix (see the Entertainment chapter) or after 9 am in person (by telephone after 9:30 am) from the Festival Theatre box office.

Call or write to the Festival Theatre box office, PO Box 520, Stratford, Ontario N5A 6V2, for the *Stratford Festival Visitors' Guide,* which gives all the details on the year's performances and ticket order forms.

Also in the booklet is an accommodations request form, so you can organize everything at once.

Web site: www.stratford-festival.on.ca.

Things to See & Do

Even though the play's the thing, pretty Stratford lures visitors with other pleasant ways to pass the time. Just north of the courthouse are the **Shakespearean Gardens**, on the site of an old wool mill run along the waterfront. Near the bridge is a bust of Shakespeare.

On fine days, heritage walks depart from the tourist office at 9:30 am Saturday (daily except Sunday during July and August). With the descriptive map put out by the Local Architectural Conservation Advisory Committee, you could instead do your own walking tour of history and architecture around downtown.

Queen's Park has good footpaths leading from the Festival Theatre and following the river past Orr Dam and a stone bridge, dating from 1885, to the formal **English flower garden**. Beside the theater, the **Stratford-Perth Museum** (☎ 519-271-5311), 270 Water St, has collections of early-20th-century Canadiana and special annual exhibitions. It's open 10 am to 4 pm daily, closed Monday from December to May ($2).

The Gallery/Stratford (☎ 519-271-5271), 54 Romeo St N, is in a renovated 1880s Victorian pump house near Confederation Park. Featured inside are rotating international shows of contemporary art, emphasizing Canadian works and festival themes. It's open 9 am to 6 pm daily, closed Monday from September to June ($5).

If you'd like to do some dressing up yourself, there's **Victoria Costumiére**, 24 Ontario St, for Victorian, Edwardian, Napoleonic threads – it's all here.

Some 12km east of Stratford along Hwy 8, the town of **Shakespeare** has a touristy main street chockablock full of antique, furniture and craft shops. If you're hungry, there's *The Best Little Pork Shoppe (☎ 519-625-8194),* with meats, cheeses and baked goods, or *Harry Ten Shilling Tea Room (☎ 519-625-8333).*

Organized Tours

Small tour boats depart from behind the tourist office. The 35-minute trip costs $6 for adults and glides by swans, parks and grand houses with even grander gardens. Canoes and paddleboats can also be rented ($15 per hour).

Places to Stay

Lodging is, thankfully, abundant. To find an economical bed, book through the Stratford Festival Visitor Accommodation Bureau (☎ 519-273-1600, 1 800 567 1600). By far the majority of rooms are in B&Bs and the homes of residents with a spare room or two. They cost as little as $38.50/43 single/double, plus $7 for private bath. For a couple more dollars, breakfast can be included. Payment must be made in full when booking.

Campers head for **Stratford Fairgrounds** (☎ 519-271-5130, 20 Glastonbury Drive). Farmers' markets and bingo take place on the grounds, which are quite central, only seven blocks from the tourist office on the north side of the river.

William St parallels the river, north of the downtown core. After a 15-minute walk, you'll come to the Queen Anne–style **Burnside Guest Home** (☎ 519-271-7076, 139 William St). Immaculate singles cost $50 and doubles $70. There is also a cheaper but good hostel-style room downstairs for $30 per person. All rates include breakfast.

The **Stratford Knight's B&B** (☎ 519-273-6089, 66 Britannia St, stratfordknights@hotmail.com), off Mornington St, is a fine old Victorian house with a sizable, in-ground heated pool. Doubles cost $100 including full breakfast.

In addition, there are several well-appointed traditional inns in refurbished, century-old hotels. The historic **Queen's Inn** (☎ 519-271-1400, 1-800-461-6450, 161 Ontario St), near Waterloo St, is the oldest hotel in town and charges $130/140 single/double during festival season.

Places to Eat

Even the famous Stratford Chef's School can't turn out enough graduates to feed the annual influx of festival visitors. From November to February, they train at the **Old Prune** (☎ 519-271-5052, 151 Albert St), which serves fresh innovative contemporary food year-round with just a hint of Québecois. The prix fixe dinner costs $60 and is served overlooking a tranquil garden. One-day ($40) and four-day ($120) cooking classes for the general public reveal some of the chef's secrets.

Another grande dame of Stratford's restaurant scene is the atmospheric **Church Restaurant** (☎ 519-273-3424, 70 Brunswick St), at the corner of Waterloo St. It's inside the old Christ Church (1874), with organ and altar still intact. Prix fixe dinners cost upward of $65 and require reservations. Lunch or late-night meals at the attached **Belfry Grill** are cheaper.

With whiffs of Parisian cafés and gilt mirrors, **Down the Street Bar & Cafe** (☎ 519-273-5886, 30 Ontario St) is yet very neighborly and stays open until 1 am daily. At dinner, main courses like grilled salmon with citrus salsa cost $15. The long, distinguished bar is impressive.

Nearer the tourist office, **York St Kitchen** (41 York St) turns out excellent sandwiches ($5) and picnic plates that might include a bit of smoked salmon or corn on the cob. There is a take-out window, and the riverside park is right across the street. It's open daily 8 am to 8 pm.

For making your own picnic, visit **Franz Kissling Delicatessen** (26 Wellington St) and pick up a butter tart at **Ragueneau Bakery** (50 Wellington St). The bakery is next door to its sister restaurant **Tapuz**, where meticulous 'meals for your senses' start at $15. Also near the Avon Theatre is **Trattoria Fabrizio** (☎ 519-272-2091, 71 Wellington St), which is good for Italian sandwiches and pastas under $7, and for fine espresso as well.

As befits an English-style town, there are quite a few pubs about like **Stratford's Olde English Parlour** (101 Wellington St), serving a ploughman's lunch. The pub and attached grill at **Bentley's Inn** (99 Ontario St) serve warm wood-oven pizzas and deliciously hearty grub.

Getting There & Away

Several small bus lines operate out of the VIA Rail station, which is quite central at 101 Shakespeare St, off Downie St about eight blocks from Ontario St. Cha-Co Trails (☎ 519-271-7870, 1-800-265-6037) buses connect Stratford with Kitchener-Waterloo ($6.50, one hour, 9:20 am and 4:25 pm), for continuing service to Toronto on Greyhound ($25.63, three hours total). In the reverse direction, Greyhound buses depart Toronto at 10 am and 3:30 pm and connect through Kitchener.

For selected weekend matinees in July and August, direct buses from Toronto depart at 10 am from Yorkdale Mall, a short walk from the Yorkdale subway station, returning from Stratford at 7 pm ($30 round-trip). Call the Festival Theatre box office for advance reservations (required).

There are two daily trains to Toronto ($30, two hours) via Kitchener ($13, 40 minutes) from the VIA Rail station. If you can't get the best possible fares quoted above, take the bus instead. Amtrak trains between Chicago and Toronto stop in Stratford (see the Getting There & Away chapter).

If you're driving, it'll take just over two hours from Toronto. On Hwy 401 from Toronto, take Exit 278 at Kitchener, then follow the signs for Hwys 7/8 west to Stratford.

LONELY PLANET

You already know that Lonely Planet produces more than this one guidebook, but you might not be aware of the other products we have on this region. Here is a selection of titles which you may want to check out as well:

Canada
ISBN 0 86442 752 2
US$24.95 • UK£14.99

Great Lakes
ISBN 1 86450 139 1
US$19.99 • UK£13.99

Montréal
ISBN 1 86450 254 1
US$15.99 • UK£9.99

New England
ISBN 0 86442 570 8
US$19.95 • UK£12.99

New York City
ISBN 1 86450 180 4
US$16.99 • UK£10.99

USA
ISBN 0 86442 513 9
US$24.95 • UK£14.99

Available wherever books are sold.

Index

Text

Bold indicates maps.

Places to Stay

Places to Eat

Bold indicates maps.

Boxed Text

MAP 1 GREATER TORONTO AREA

Rouge Park
Toronto Zoo
To Glen Rouge Park
To Montreal
Rouge River
Neilson Rd
Finch Ave E
Morningside Ave
Morningside Park
Galloway Rd
Guildwood Pkwy
Guildwood Park
Highland Creek
Markham Rd
Scarborough Golf & Country Club
Scarborough Bluffs Park
McCowen Rd
Ellesmere Rd
Highland Creek
Kingston Rd
Sheppard Ave E
Macdonald-Cartier Freeway
Midland Ave
Kennedy Rd
Scarborough
Thomson Memorial Park
Danforth Rd
Pine Hills Cemetery
Lake Ontario
Birchmount Rd
Warden Ave
Lawrence Ave E
Eglinton Ave E
Warden Woods
Toronto Hunt Club Golf Course
Steeles Ave E
Charles Sauriol Conservation Reserve
O'Connor Drive
St Clair Ave E
Taylor Creek Park
Taylor Creek
Kingston Rd
Queen St E
Ashbridge's Bay Park
Victoria Park Ave
Don Mills Rd
Don Valley Parkway
Woodbine Ave
German Mills Creek
East Don Parkland
Sheppard Ave E
Moatfield Farm Park
York Mills Rd
Windfields Park
Wilket Creek Park
Ernest Thompson Seton Park
Coxwell Ave
Danforth Ave
Tommy Thompson Park
E Don River
Finch Ave E
Bayview Ave
Sunnybrook Park
Pape Ave
Broadview Ave
North Shore Park
Yonge St
W Don River
Don Valley Golf Course
Mt Pleasant Cemetery
Gerrard St E
Lake Shore Blvd E
Toronto Outer Harbour
Wilket Creek
York Cemetery
Parliament St
Don Valley Brick Works Park
Jarvis St
Mt Pleasant Rd
Yonge St
Toronto Inner Harbour
Toronto Islands
Earl Bales Park
Avenue Rd
University Ave
Bathurst St
West Don Parkland
Upper Canada College
University of Toronto
Spadina Ave
Toronto City Centre Airport
North York
WR Allen Rd
Bathurst St
Dupont St
Bloor St W
Queen St W
G Ross Lord Park
Keele St
York University
Lawrence Ave W
Dufferin St
College St
Gardiner Expressway
Ontario Place
Downsview Dells Park
Wilson Ave
Prospect Cemetery
St Clair Ave W
Dundas St W
Finch Ave W
Sheppard Ave W
Jane St
Black Creek
Eglinton Flats
Smythe Park
Keele St
High Park
Western Beaches
Humber Bay
Weston Rd
Scarlett Rd
Jane St
S Kingsway
Black Creek Pioneer Village
Lion's Park
Etienne Brûlé Park
Humber Marshes Park
Humber Bay Park
Weston Rd
Rowntree Mills Park
West Humber Parkland
Pine Point Park
Royal York Rd
Colonel Samuel Smith Park
W Humber River
Dixon Rd
Islington Ave
The Queensway
Lake Shore Blvd W
Claireville Conservation Area
To Kleinburg (8.5 km)
Wild Water Kingdom
Claireville Reservoir
Albion Rd
Rexdale Blvd
Etobicoke
Eglinton Ave W
West Deane Park
Kipling Ave
Bloor St W
Etobicoke Valley Park
Marie Curtis Park
Woodbine Racetrack
Mimico Creek
Etobicoke Creek
Humber River
Lester B Pearson International Airport
To Kitchener, Waterloo, Stratford & Windsor
MISSISSAUGA
Hurontario St
To Hamilton & Niagara Falls
QEW

4 km
2 miles
2
1
0
0

27
48
2
11
401
404
11
400
409
407
427
427
401
401

MAP 2 TORONTO

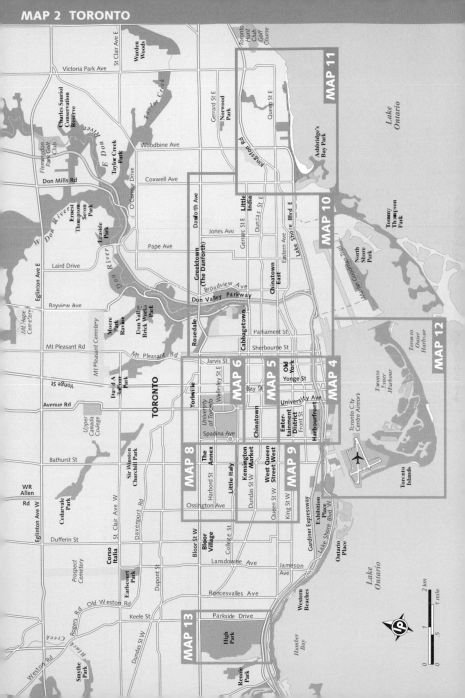

MAP 11

MAP 10

MAP 12

MAP 4

MAP 5

MAP 6

MAP 8

MAP 9

MAP 13

Lake Ontario

Lake Ontario

Toronto Hunt Club Golf Course

Warden Woods

Charles Sauriol Conservation Reserve

Flemington Park Golf Club

E Don River

Taylor Creek

Taylor Creek Park

Ernest Thompson Seton Park

Leaside Park

W Don River

Don River

Mt Hope Cemetery

Mt Pleasant Cemetery

Moore Park Ravine

Don Valley Brick Works Park

David A Balfour Park

Upper Canada College

Sir Winston Churchill Park

Cedarvale Park

Corso Italia

Prospect Cemetery

Earlscourt Park

Smythe Park

Rennie Park

High Park

Roncesvalles Ave

Humber Bay

Western Beaches

Ontario Place

Exhibition Place

Toronto City Centre Airport

Toronto Islands

Toronto Inner Harbour

Toronto Outer Harbour

Tommy Thompson Park

North Shore Park

Ashbridge's Bay Park

Norwood Park

Little India

Chinatown East

Old York

Yorkville

The Annex

Little Italy

Kensington Market

Chinatown

West Queen Street West

Entertainment District

Harbourfront

Rosedale

Cabbagetown

Greektown (The Danforth)

Bloor Village

TORONTO

University of Toronto

Don Valley Parkway

Gardiner Expressway

Martin Goodman Trail

St Clair Ave E

Victoria Park Ave

Warden Ave

Don Mills Rd

Woodbine Ave

Coxwell Ave

Pape Ave

Laird Drive

Rayview Ave

Eglinton Ave E

Mt Pleasant Rd

Mt Pleasant Rd

Mt Pleasant Rd

Yonge St

Avenue Rd

Bathurst St

Davenport Rd

St Clair Ave W

Dupont St

Dufferin St

Eglinton Ave W

WR Allen Rd

Old Weston Rd

Rogers Rd

Weston Rd

Keele St

Dundas St W

Parkside Drive

Lansdowne Ave

College St

Jameson Ave

Bloor St W

Ossington Ave

Harbord St

Dundas St W

Queen St W

King St W

Front St

University Ave

Yonge St

Bay St

Wellesley St E

Jarvis St

Sherbourne St

Parliament St

Spadina Ave

Broadview Ave

Danforth Ave

Jones Ave

Gerrard St E

Dundas St E

Eastern Ave

Lake Shore Blvd E

Queen St E

Gerrard St E

Kingston Rd

O'Connor Drive

Lake Shore Blvd W

Black Creek

0   1   2 km

.5   1 mile

N

MAP 3 TORONTO METRO

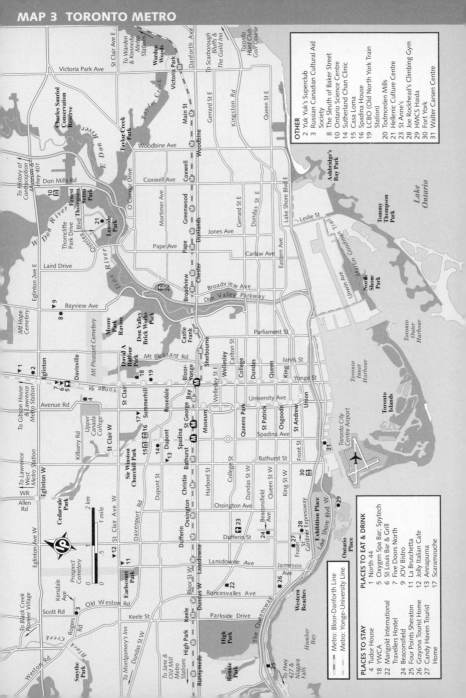

DOWNTOWN TORONTO (SOUTH)

PLACES TO STAY
- 7 Canadiana Guesthouse & Backpackers
- 15 Hilton; Tundra
- 17 Sheraton Centre
- 21 Cambridge Suites Hotel
- 28 Global Village Backpackers
- 37 Holiday Inn on King
- 48 Hotel Victoria
- 50 Le Royal Meridien King Edward; Café Victoria
- 53 Hostelling International (HI) Toronto
- 58 Renaissance Hotel
- 64 Strathcona
- 66 Royal York Hotel; Library Bar; Air Canada; Delta Airlines; Lufthansa; United Airlines; US Airways; Thrifty Car Rentals; American Express; Olde Town Tours
- 72 Novotel Toronto Centre
- 90 Westin Harbour Castle

PLACES TO EAT & DRINK
- 2 Zupa's Deli
- 4 Fez Batik
- 5 The Living Room
- 10 Alice Fazooli's
- 20 Spread
- 25 Denison's Brewing Co
- 27 Sarkis
- 30 Asakusa
- 35 Wayne Gretzky's
- 36 Mercer Street Grill
- 38 N'Awlins
- 40 Peel Pub
- 46 Canoe
- 52 Nami; The Courthouse

- 54 Vines Wine Bar
- 57 Golden Griddle
- 59 Hard Rock Cafe
- 61 Accolade; Crowne Plaza
- 76 Esplanade BierMark
- 77 C'est What

OTHER
- 1 Gallery 44; A Space; V Tape
- 3 Beatlemania
- 6 Sugar Mountain
- 8 Joker Club
- 9 Famous Players Paramount; IMAX
- 11 Limelight
- 12 Whiskey Saloon
- 13 Music Gallery
- 14 Simcoe Gallery
- 16 Guild Gallery; Japan Airlines
- 18 Cloud Forest Conservatory
- 19 The Bay; Thomson Gallery
- 22 Guardian International Foreign Exchange
- 23 Arcade Coin & Stamp Co
- 24 Ontario Black History Society
- 26 The Laugh Resort
- 29 Discount Car Rental
- 31 The Charlotte Room
- 32 Europe Bound Outfitters
- 33 Mountain Equipment Co-op
- 34 Second City; Tim Sims Playhouse
- 39 Princess of Wales Theatre
- 41 Royal Alexandra Theatre
- 42 Swiss Consulate
- 43 Goethe-Institut
- 44 Singapore Airlines
- 45 Toronto Stock Exchange
- 47 Design Exchange
- 49 Thomas Cook

- 51 Open Air
- 55 Reservoir Lounge
- 56 Sunday Antique & Collectibles Market
- 60 Info T.O.62
- 62 Spanish Consulate
- 63 Bay of Spirits Gallery
- 65 Citibank
- 67 National Car Rental
- 68 GPO
- 69 BCE Place; Marche Mövenpick
- 70 Hockey Hall of Fame
- 71 St Lawrence Centre
- 73 Europe Bound Outfitters; TravelCUTS
- 74 Flatiron (Gooderham) Building
- 75 Trailhead; Canada Map Store
- 78 Market Gallery
- 79 Centre Francophone de Toronto
- 80 Harbourfront Antique Market
- 81 Harbourfront Canoe & Kayak School
- 82 Wheel Excitement
- 83 Pier Waterfront Museum
- 84 Harbourfront Centre Information Desk & Box Office
- 85 Harbourfront Centre Concert Stage
- 86 Power Plant Art Gallery
- 87 Tourist Office; Premiere Dance Theatre
- 88 McBride Cycle Rental
- 89 Toronto Harbour Commissioners; York St Slip; Second Cup
- 91 Toronto Island Ferry Terminal
- 92 Shaker Cruise Lines
- 93 Redpath Sugar Museum
- 94 Guvernment

SARA BENSON

Historical mural, *Toronto Sun* building

MAP 4 DOWNTOWN TORONTO (SOUTH)

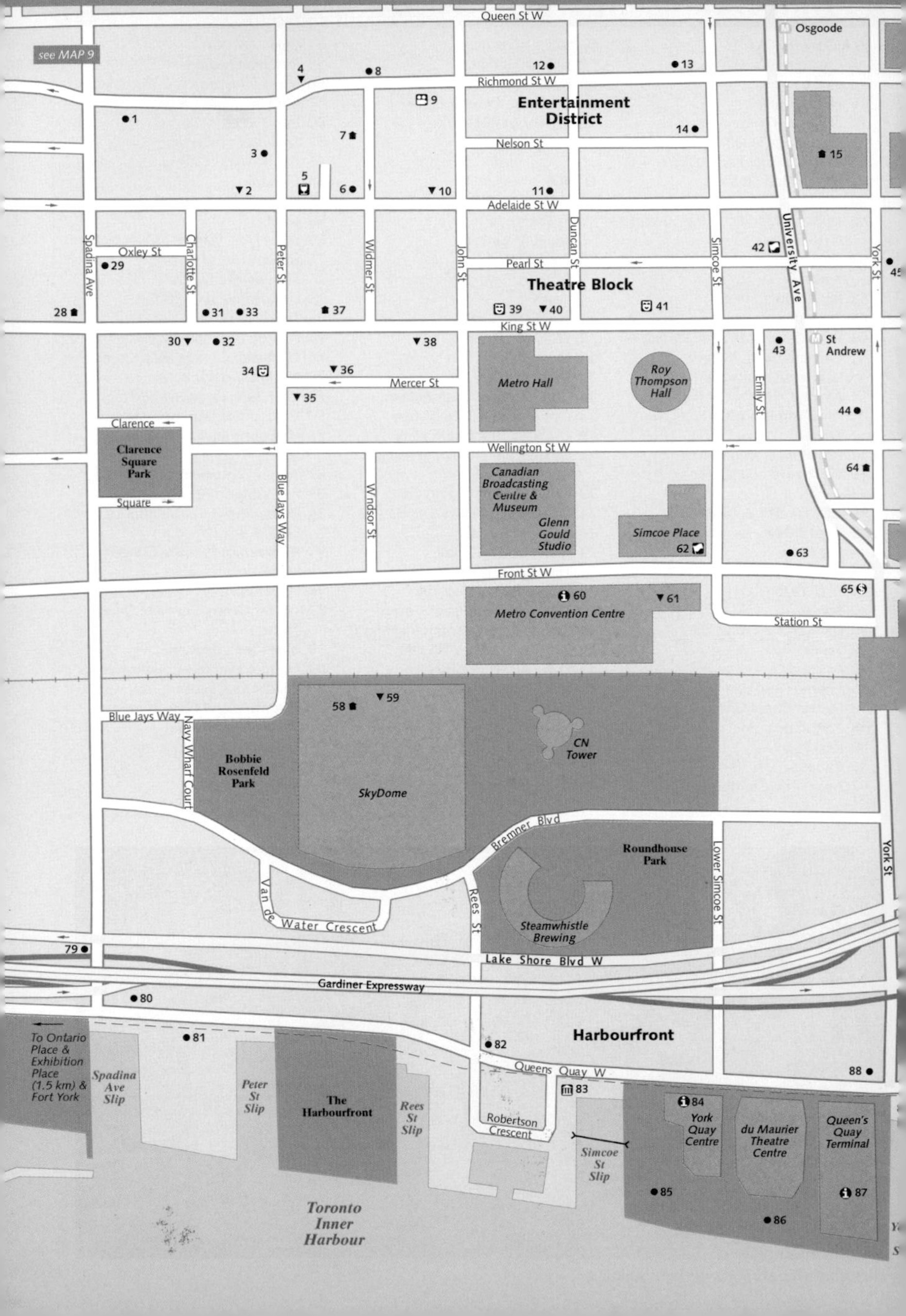

see MAP 9

Queen St W

Osgoode

4
● 8

12 ●
Richmond St W
● 13

9

1

Entertainment District

14 ●

Nelson St

7

3 ●

15

5
▼ 2
6 ●
▼ 10

11 ●
Adelaide St W

Spadina Ave

Oxley St
29

Charlotte St

Peter St

Widmer St

John St

Duncan St

Pearl St

Simcoe St

University Ave

York St

42

45

Theatre Block

28
31 ● 33
37

39 ▼ 40
41

King St W

30 ▼ 32

▼ 38

43

St Andrew

34

▼ 36

Metro Hall

Roy Thompson Hall

44 ●

▼ 35

Mercer St

Emily St

64

Clarence

Clarence Square Park

Square

Blue Jays Way

Windsor St

Wellington St W

Canadian Broadcasting Centre & Museum

Glenn Gould Studio

Simcoe Place

62

● 63

Front St W

65

60

▼ 61

Metro Convention Centre

Station St

Blue Jays Way

Navy Wharf Court

58
▼ 59

CN Tower

Bobbie Rosenfeld Park

SkyDome

Bremner Blvd

Roundhouse Park

Lower Simcoe St

York St

Van de Water Crescent

Rees St

Steamwhistle Brewing

79 ●

Lake Shore Blvd W

Gardiner Expressway

● 80

To Ontario Place & Exhibition Place (1.5 km) & Fort York

● 81

Harbourfront

82

Queens Quay W

88 ●

Spadina Ave Slip

Peter St Slip

The Harbourfront

Rees St Slip

Robertson Crescent

83

84
York Quay Centre

du Maurier Theatre Centre

Queen's Quay Terminal

Simcoe St Slip

● 85

87

● 86

Toronto Inner Harbour

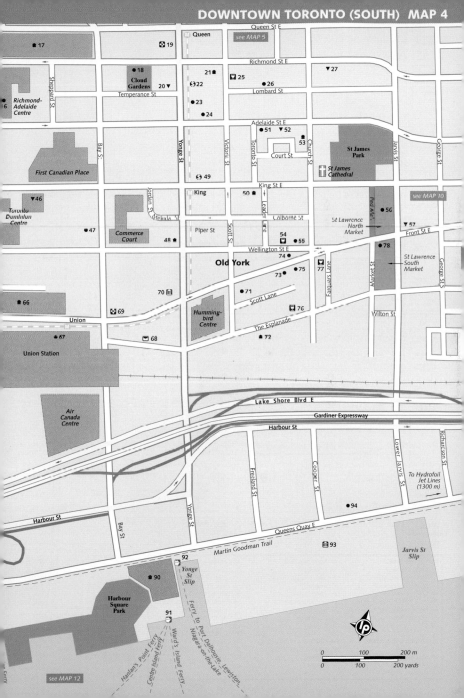

■ 17

☒ 19

□ Queen

Queen St E

see MAP 5

Richmond St E

● 18

Cloud
Gardens

Temperance St

20 ▼

21 ■

❋ 22

● 23

● 24

☒ 25

● 26

Lombard St

▼ 27

Sheppard St

Richmond-
Adelaide
Centre

■ 6

Bay St

Yonge St

Victoria St

Toronto St

Adelaide St E

● 51   ▼ 52

53 ■

Court St

St James
Park

St James
Cathedral

Jarvis St

George St

First Canadian Place

▼ 46

Toronto
Dominion
Centre

● 47

Commerce
Court

48 ■

Jordan St

Melinda St

Yonge St

❋ 49

□ King

King St E

50 ●

Leader Lane

Scott St

Colborne St

Piper St

54
☒

● 55

see MAP 10

Fed Ave

● 56

▼ 57

Front St E

St Lawrence
North
Market

Wellington St E

74 ●

73 ●   ● 75

77
☒

Farquars Lane

Market St

● 78

St Lawrence
South
Market

George St

Old York

● 66

70 🏛

☒ 69

● 71

Scott Lane

76 ☒

Wilton St

Hummingbird
Centre

The Esplanade

Union

□ 68

● 72

● 67

Union Station

Air
Canada
Centre

Lake Shore Blvd E

Gardiner Expressway

Harbour St

Harbour St

Freeland St

Cooper St

Lower Jarvis St

Richardson St

To Hydrofoil
Jet Lines
(1300 m)

● 94

Harbour St

Bay St

Yonge St

Queens Quay E

Jarvis St
Slip

Martin Goodman Trail

🏛 93

92 ☒

Yonge
St
Slip

● 90

Harbour
Square
Park

91 ☒

Ward's Island Ferry

Centre Island Ferry

Hanlan's Point Ferry

Ferry to Port Dalhousie, Lewiston,
Niagara-on-the-Lake

see MAP 12

0   100   200 m
0   100   200 yards

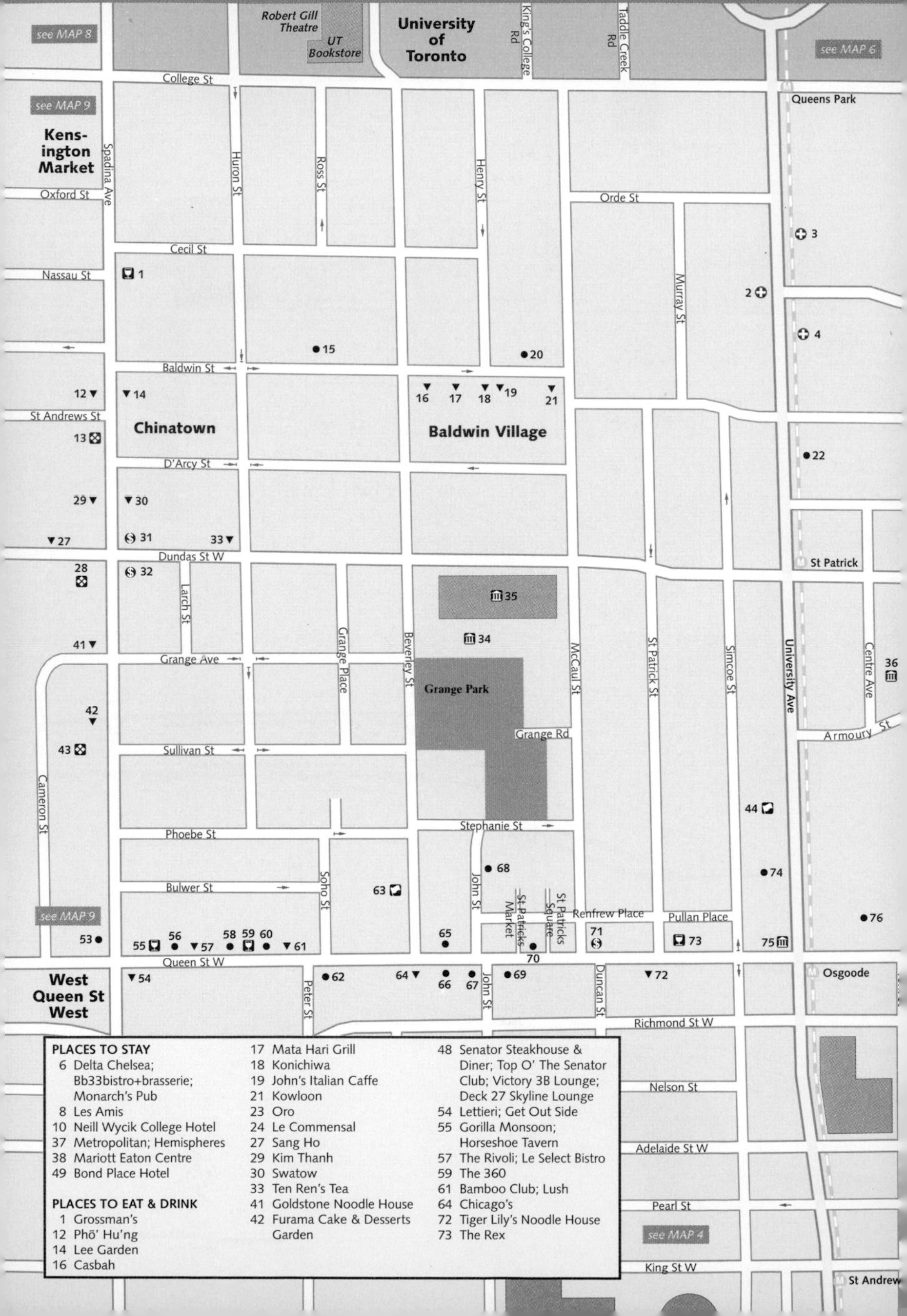

MAP 5 DOWNTOWN TORONTO (NORTH)

see MAP 8

Robert Gill Theatre
UT Bookstore

University of Toronto

see MAP 6

see MAP 9

Kensington Market

College St

Oxford St

Nassau St

Cecil St

Baldwin St

St Andrews St

Chinatown

D'Arcy St

Dundas St W

Grange Ave

Sullivan St

Phoebe St

Bulwer St

see MAP 9

West Queen St West

Queen St W

Spadina Ave

Huron St

Ross St

Larch St

Cameron St

Soho St

Peter St

Henry St

King's College Rd

Taddle Creek Rd

Orde St

Murray St

Grange Place

Beverley St

Grange Park

Grange Rd

Stephanie St

John St

St Patrick's Market

St Patricks Square

Renfrew Place

Duncan St

McCaul St

St Patrick St

Simcoe St

University Ave

Centre Ave

Armoury St

Pullan Place

Queens Park

Orde St

St Patrick

St Patrick St

Osgoode

Richmond St W

Nelson St

Adelaide St W

Pearl St

see MAP 4

King St W

St Andrew

Queens Park

Baldwin Village

1

3

2

4

15

20

12 ▼ ▼14

13

29 ▼   ▼30

31   33

27

28

32

41 ▼

42 ▼

43

16 17 18 19 21

22

34

35

36

Grange Ave

44

53

55 56 57 58 59 60 61

63

65

66 67

68

69

70

71 73 75

72

74

76

54

62

64 ▼

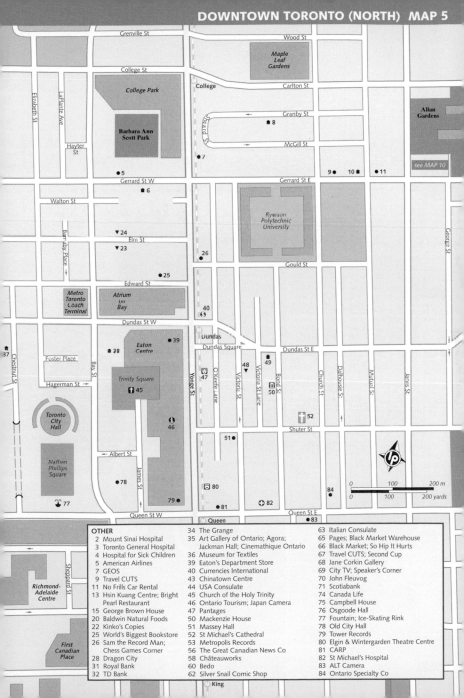

Grenville St

Wood St

Maple Leaf Gardens

College St

College Park

College

Carlton St

Elizabeth St

LaPlante Ave

Barbara Ann Scott Park

Granby St

■ 8

Allan Gardens

Hayter St

McGill St

see MAP 10

● 5

9 ●   10 ■   ● 11

Gerrard St W

Gerrard St E

Walton St

■ 6

Ryerson Polytechnic University

George St

Barnaby Place

▼ 24

Elm St

▼ 23

26
●

● 25

Gould St

Edward St

Metro Toronto Coach Terminal

Atrium on Bay

40
⟨i⟩

Dundas St W

Dundas

Dundas Square

Dundas St E

Foster Place

● 39

Eaton Centre

■ 39

O'Keefe Lane

48 ●
47 ●

49 ●

Bond St

Hagerman St

Bay St

Trinity Square

45

Yonge St

Victoria St

Latre

50 ●

Church St

Dalhousie St

Mutual St

Jarvis St

Toronto City Hall

⟨i⟩
46

Shuter St

✝ 52

51 ●

Nathan Phillips Square

Albert St

James St

📷 80

84 ●

0   100   200 m

0   100   200 yards

♨ 77

79 ●

● 81

✿ 82

● 83

Queen St W

Queen

Queen St E

Chestnut St

37

Richmond-Adelaide Centre

Sheppard St

First Canadian Place

King

OTHER		
2 Mount Sinai Hospital	34 The Grange	63 Italian Consulate
3 Toronto General Hospital	35 Art Gallery of Ontario; Agora;	65 Pages; Black Market Warehouse
4 Hospital for Sick Children	Jackman Hall; Cinemathique Ontario	66 Black Market; So Hip It Hurts
5 American Airlines	36 Museum for Textiles	67 Travel CUTS; Second Cup
7 GEOS	39 Eaton's Department Store	68 Jane Corkin Gallery
9 Travel CUTS	40 Currencies International	69 City TV; Speaker's Corner
11 No Frills Car Rental	43 Chinatown Centre	70 John Fleuvog
13 Hsin Kuang Centre; Bright	44 USA Consulate	71 Scotiabank
Pearl Restaurant	45 Church of the Holy Trinity	74 Canada Life
15 George Brown House	46 Ontario Tourism; Japan Camera	75 Campbell House
20 Baldwin Natural Foods	47 Pantages	76 Osgoode Hall
22 Kinko's Copies	50 Mackenzie House	77 Fountain; Ice-Skating Rink
25 World's Biggest Bookstore	51 Massey Hall	78 Old City Hall
26 Sam the Record Man;	52 St Michael's Cathedral	79 Tower Records
Chess Games Corner	53 Metropolis Records	80 Elgin & Wintergarden Theatre Centre
28 Dragon City	56 The Great Canadian News Co	81 CARP
31 Royal Bank	58 Châteauworks	82 St Michael's Hospital
32 TD Bank	60 Bedo	83 ALT Camera
	62 Silver Snail Comic Shop	84 Ontario Specialty Co

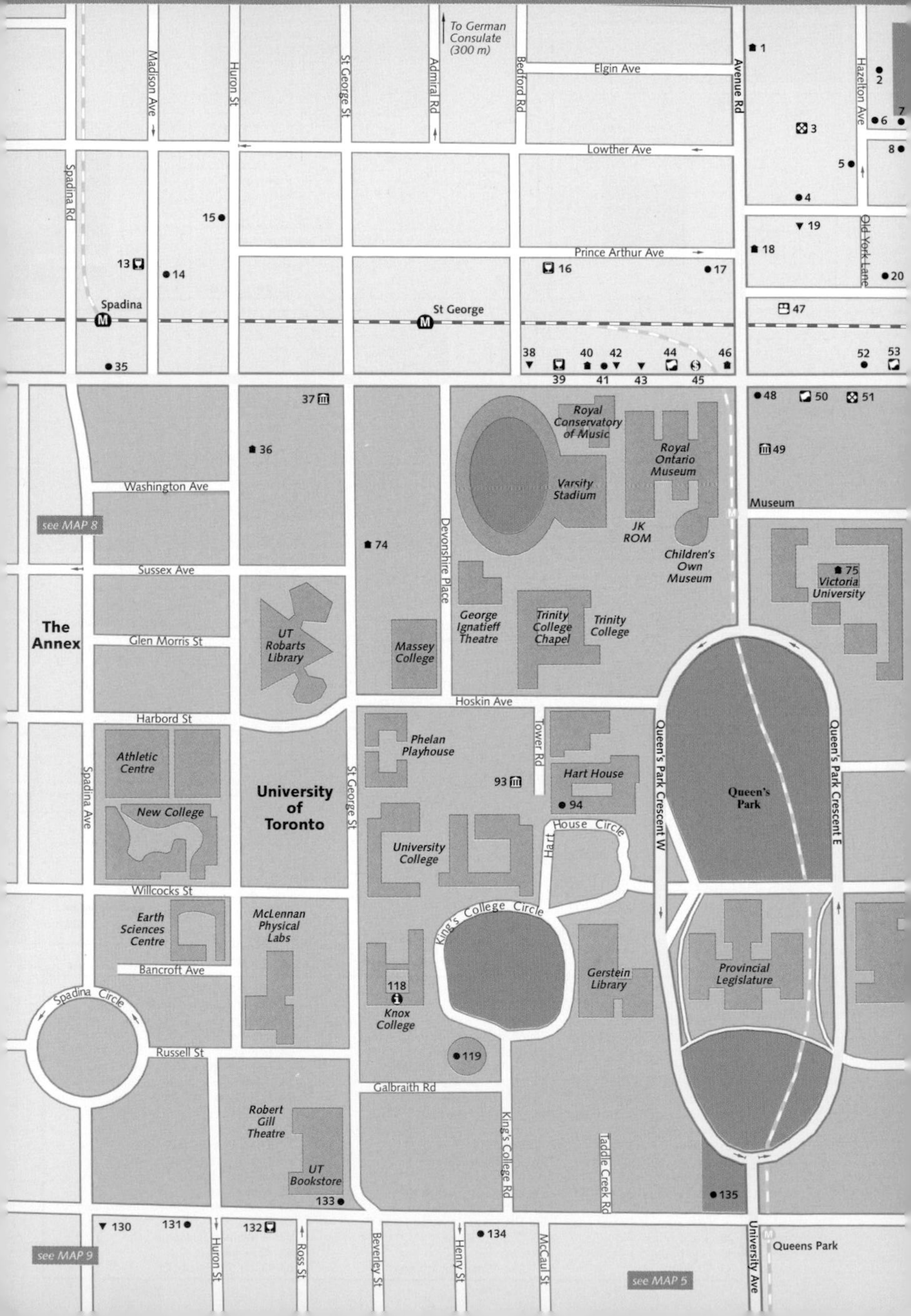

MAP 6 YORKVILLE & UNIVERSITY OF TORONTO

Madison Ave

Huron St

St George St

Admiral Rd

Bedford Rd

To German
Consulate
(300 m)

Elgin Ave

Avenue Rd

Hazelton Ave

■ 1
● 2
● 7
★ 3
● 6
● 8
● 5
● 4

Lowther Ave

Spadina Rd

▼ 19

Old York Lane

15 ●

Prince Arthur Ave

■ 18

● 20

13 ▪

● 14

■ 16

● 17

Spadina
Ⓜ

St George
Ⓜ

47

● 35

38 40 42 44 46
▼ ● ● ▼ ●
39 41 43 45

52 53

37 🏛

● 48 50 ★ 51

■ 36

🏛 49

Museum

Washington Ave

■ 74

Royal
Conservatory
of Music

Royal
Ontario
Museum

■ 75
Victoria
University

see MAP 8

Sussex Ave

Varsity
Stadium

JK
ROM

Children's
Own
Museum

Devonshire Place

The
Annex

Glen Morris St

UT
Robarts
Library

Massey
College

George
Ignatieff
Theatre

Trinity
College
Chapel

Trinity
College

Harbord St

Hoskin Ave

Spadina Ave

Athletic
Centre

University
of
Toronto

St George St

Phelan
Playhouse

Tower Rd

93 🏛

Hart House

Hart House Circle

Queen's Park Crescent W

Queen's
Park

Queen's Park Crescent E

New College

● 94

Willcocks St

University
College

Earth
Sciences
Centre

McLennan
Physical
Labs

King's College Circle

Bancroft Ave

Gerstein
Library

Provincial
Legislature

Spadina Circle

118
Knox
College

Russell St

● 119

Robert
Gill
Theatre

Galbraith Rd

King's College Rd

UT
Bookstore

133

Taddle Creek Rd

● 135

▼ 130   131 ●

132

● 134

University Ave

Queens Park

see MAP 9

Huron St

Ross St

Beverley St

Henry St

McCaul St

see MAP 5

Jesse Ketchum Park

To Toronto Truck Theatre (240 m)

To Rebel Yell, Rosedale & Eglinton Ave

McMurrich St

McMurray St

Davenport Rd

Scollard St

Yorkville

Yorkville Ave

Bellair St

Cumberland St

Bay

Bloor St W

Balmuto St

Sultan St

St Thomas St

Charles St W

a Scala Lane

St Mary St

Inkerman St

Bay St

Irwin Ave

St Nicholas St

St Joseph St

Wellesley St W

Breadalbane St

Ontario Government Ministry Buildings

Grosvenor St

Surrey Place

Grenville St

Elizabeth St

LaPlante Ave

College St

College Park

Aylmer Ave

Rosedale Rd

Pine Hill Rd

Park Rd

Elm Ave

Severn St

Rosedale Valley Rd

Collier St

Church St

Asquith Ave

St Paul's Square

Mt Pleasant Rd

Bloor-Yonge

Bloor St E

Yonge St

Hayden St

Charles St E

Isabella St

Gloucester St

Church St

Jarvis St

Huntley St

Carl St

Monteith St

Cawthra Square Park

Cawthra Square

see MAP 10

Dundonald St

Wellesley

Wellesley St E

Maitland St

Maitland Place

Alexander Place

Mutual St

Alexander St

Wood St

Maple Leaf Gardens

Carlton St

College

▼ 9   ● 10
● 11   ● 12
▼ 21 ▼ 24   ● 25   ● 28   ▼ 30 ▼ 31
▣ 22 ● 23   ● 26 ● 27   ▣ 29   ● 32
● 33
● 34
● 59 ● 60 ●   61   67
M   ▣ 63   64 ▣   71
● 58   ▣ 66   Bloor-Yonge
● 56   57 ●   ▣ 62   65 ●   ▣ 72   73 ●
54 ■   ● 55   ● 68   ● 70
69 ▼   77 ▼
▼ 76   78 ▼   79   85 ■   86 ■
● 84
● 83   91 ■   92
80 ▼   ● 82   90 ■
81 ●   ● 88   ● 89
▼ 87   ● 98   110 ■
97 ●   104 ▼   108 ●
95 ▼   99 ●   103 ■   109 ▲
100 ●   105 ▣   106 ▣   107 ▣
● 96   ● 101   ● 102
111 ▣   112 ●   113 ● ▼ 115
114 ▼   ▼ 116   ● 117
124 ▣   125 ▣   127 ▣   128 ▣
▼ 120   ▣ 122 ▼ 123   126 ●
▼ 121
129 ■
136 ▣   ▼ 137   ● 138   140 ■
▣ 139
141 ▣

0   100   200 m
0   100   200 yards

YORKVILLE & UNIVERSITY OF TORONTO

PLACES TO STAY
1 Howard Johnson Inn
18 Four Seasons; Truffles
36 Campus Co-op
40 Hotel Inter-Continental
46 Park Hyatt; Rooftop Lounge
54 Windsor Arms
71 Mariott Bloor-Yorkville
74 The Innis Residence
75 Victoria University
85 Comfort Hotel Downtown
86 Town Inn
90 Cromwell
91 Daniel's Musical Hideaway
92 The Mulberry Tree
96 Sutton Place Hotel
103 Dundonald House
110 Immaculate Reception
129 Courtyard Mariott
440 Days Inn

PLACES TO EAT & DRINK
9 Le Trou Normand
13 The Madison
16 Duke of York
19 La Pêcherie; Artic Bear
21 Summer's Ice Cream
23 Sassafraz
24 Little Tibet
26 Lettieri
29 Tavern
30 Wanda's Pie in the Sky
38 Mr. Sub; Coffee Time; Harvey's
39 Bedford Ballroom; Swiss Chalet
42 Pizza Hut; Phõ' Hu'ng; Greg's Ice Cream; Comedywood Downtown
43 Wrap 'n Roll
61 Pangaea
69 Spring Rolls
76 Okonomi House
77 Zyng Asian Market & Noodle Café
78 7 West Café
80 Java Lava Juice Lounge
87 Zyweic; Ethiopia House
95 Bistro 990
104 Diablo
105 Slack Alice
114 Zelda's
115 Byzantium
120 Papaya Hut
121 Kathmandu Kathmandu
123 Carman's
124 Wilde Oscar's
125 Tango Crews
127 Woody's; Sailor's
128 The Red Spot; Black Eagle
130 Burger King; Mr Greek; Pizza Nova
132 Ein-stein Cafe & Pub
137 Fran's

OTHER
2 Toronto Heliconian Club
3 Hazelton Lanes
4 Maison de la Presse Internationale
5 Feheley Fine Arts
6 ArtCore
7 Gallery 7 & India Arts Centre
8 Gallery One
10 L'Atelier Grigorian
11 Firehall No 10
12 Toronto Public Library
14 Tengye Ling Tibetan Buddhist Temple
15 Italian Cultural Institute
17 The Isaacs/Inuit Gallery
20 Clinic Ineed
22 Lush; Guild Gallery
25 Delek
27 Berlitz
28 Omega Centre
31 The Cookbook Store
32 Thomas Hinds Tobacconist
33 Metro Toronto Reference Library
34 International Language Academy of Canada
35 Noah's Natural Foods
37 Bata Shoe Museum
41 St George Business & Language School
44 Israel Consulate
45 Calforex Currencies International
47 Alliance Atlantis Cumberland
48 Club Monaco
49 Gardiner Museum of Ceramic Art
50 Danish Consulate
51 The Colonnade; The Japan Foundation
52 Chapters; Nike Toronto
53 French Consulate
55 Theatre Books
56 Roots
57 Varig Brazilian Airlines
58 Olympic Airways
59 Kidding Awound
60 International Travel Agency
62 Manulife Centre; Cafe L'Express; Thomas Cook; Ciniplex Odeon Cinemas; Panorama
63 Holt Renfrew Centre; American Express; Science City
64 Swedish Consulate; Mexicana Airlines
65 Le Château
66 Royal Bank
67 Hudson's Bay Centre; Famous Players Plaza Cinemas
68 Foreign Exchange Centre
70 Spanish Centre
72 Australian Consulate
73 The Black Secretariat
79 Shoppers Drug Mart
81 ABC Books
82 House of Lords
83 Lush
84 Noah's Natural Foods
88 Arabesque Academy
89 Money Mart
93 UT Art Centre
94 Soldiers' Tower
97 Fastball Sportscards
98 "Mail Boxes, Etc"
99 Glad Day Bookshop; Bakka
100 Northbound Leather
101 Armen Art Gallery
102 The Great Canadian News Co
106 Hassle-Free Clinic
107 Rexall Drug Store
108 519 Community Centre
109 AIDS Memorial
111 Gray Region Comics
112 The Laundry Lounge; Captain Andy's Fish & Chips
113 A-Plus Car Rental; Second Cup; TD Bank
116 Pegasus Billiard Lounge
117 This Ain't the Rosedale Library
118 Nona MacDonald Visitors Centre
119 Convocation Hall
122 Buddies in Bad Times Theatre; Talullah's Cabaret
126 Lush
131 Toronto Public Library Lillian H Smith Branch
133 UT Housing Office
134 Travel CUTS
135 UT Greenhouses
136 Metro Toronto Police Museum & Discovery Centre
138 Canadian Automobile Association (CAA)
139 Ciniplex Odeon Carlton Cinemas
141 UK Consulate; Northwest/KLM Airlines

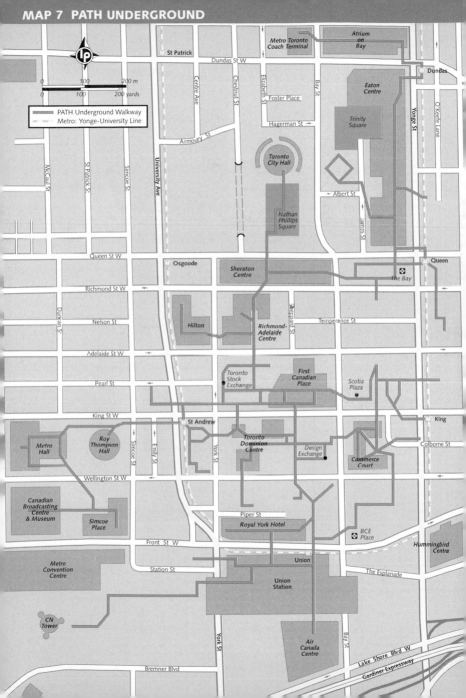

MAP 7 PATH UNDERGROUND

PATH Underground Walkway
Metro: Yonge-University Line

0   100   200 m
0   100   200 yards

St Patrick

Dundas St W

Metro Toronto Coach Terminal

Atrium on Bay

Dundas

Foster Place

Eaton Centre

Yonge St

O'Keefe Lane

Hagerman St

Trinity Square

Armoury St

Centre Ave

Chestnut St

Elizabeth St

Bay St

Toronto City Hall

Albert St

James St

Nathan Phillips Square

McCaul St

St Patrick S

Simcoe St

University Ave

Queen St W

Osgoode

Sheraton Centre

Queen

The Bay

Richmond St W

Duncan S

Nelson St

Hilton

Richmond-Adelaide Centre

Jarvis St

Temperance St

Adelaide St W

Pearl St

Toronto Stock Exchange

First Canadian Place

Scotia Plaza

King St W

St Andrew

Roy Thompson Hall

Simcoe St

Emily St

York St

Toronto Dominion Centre

Design Exchange

King

Commerce Court

Colborne St

Metro Hall

Wellington St W

Canadian Broadcasting Centre & Museum

Simcoe Place

Piper St

Royal York Hotel

BCE Place

Hummingbird Centre

Front St W

Metro Convention Centre

Station St

Union

The Esplanade

Union Station

CN Tower

York St

Air Canada Centre

Bay St

Lake Shore Blvd W

Bremner Blvd

Gardiner Expressway

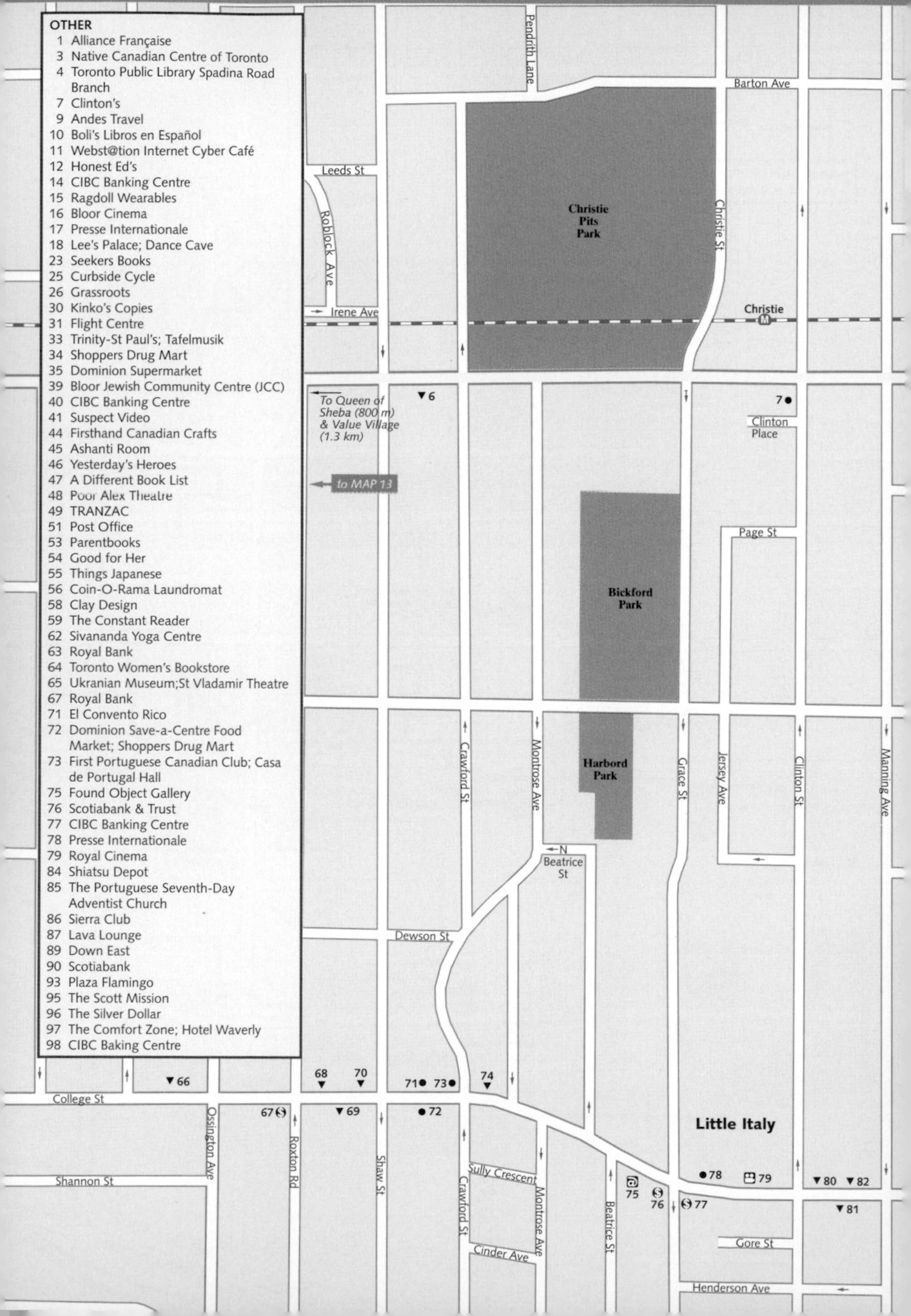

MAP 8 THE ANNEX & LITTLE ITALY

OTHER

1 Alliance Française
3 Native Canadian Centre of Toronto
4 Toronto Public Library Spadina Road Branch
7 Clinton's
9 Andes Travel
10 Boli's Libros en Español
11 Webst@tion Internet Cyber Café
12 Honest Ed's
14 CIBC Banking Centre
15 Ragdoll Wearables
16 Bloor Cinema
17 Presse Internationale
18 Lee's Palace; Dance Cave
23 Seekers Books
25 Curbside Cycle
26 Grassroots
30 Kinko's Copies
31 Flight Centre
33 Trinity-St Paul's; Tafelmusik
34 Shoppers Drug Mart
35 Dominion Supermarket
39 Bloor Jewish Community Centre (JCC)
40 CIBC Banking Centre
41 Suspect Video
44 Firsthand Canadian Crafts
45 Ashanti Room
46 Yesterday's Heroes
47 A Different Book List
48 Poor Alex Theatre
49 TRANZAC
51 Post Office
53 Parentbooks
54 Good for Her
55 Things Japanese
56 Coin-O-Rama Laundromat
58 Clay Design
59 The Constant Reader
62 Sivananda Yoga Centre
63 Royal Bank
64 Toronto Women's Bookstore
65 Ukranian Museum; St Vladamir Theatre
67 Royal Bank
71 El Convento Rico
72 Dominion Save-a-Centre Food Market; Shoppers Drug Mart
73 First Portuguese Canadian Club; Casa de Portugal Hall
75 Found Object Gallery
76 Scotiabank & Trust
77 CIBC Banking Centre
78 Presse Internationale
79 Royal Cinema
84 Shiatsu Depot
85 The Portuguese Seventh-Day Adventist Church
86 Sierra Club
87 Lava Lounge
89 Down East
90 Scotiabank
93 Plaza Flamingo
95 The Scott Mission
96 The Silver Dollar
97 The Comfort Zone; Hotel Waverly
98 CIBC Baking Centre

Barton Ave

Pendrith Lane

Leeds St

Roblock Ave

Christie St

Christie Pits Park

Irene Ave

Christie Ⓜ

To Queen of Sheba (800 m) & Value Village (1.3 km)

▼ 6

Clinton Place

7 ●

to MAP 13

Page St

Bickford Park

Harbord Park

Crawford St

Montrose Ave

Grace St

Jersey Ave

Clinton Ave

Manning Ave

← N
Beatrice St

Dewson St

College St

Ossington Ave

Roxton Rd

Shaw St

Crawford St

Montrose Ave

Beatrice St

Little Italy

Shannon St

Sully Crescent

Cinder Ave

Gore St

Henderson Ave

68 ▼   70 ▼   71 ● 73 ●   74 ▼
67 Ⓖ   ▼ 69   ● 72
● 78   🏠 79
Ⓖ 75   76   Ⓖ 77
▼ 80 ▼ 82
▼ 81
▼ 66

PLACES TO STAY
2 Casa Loma Inn
5 Global Guesthouse

PLACES TO EAT & DRINK
6 Rikishi Japanese Restaurant;
   African Wings Travels & Tours
8 Hodo Kwaja
13 Insomnia
19 Mumbo Jumbo
20 Kensington Natural Bakery
21 Country Style Hungarian
   Restaurant
22 Juice for Life

24 Mel's Montreal Delicatessen
27 By the Way Café; Sucker's
28 Future Bakery & Café
29 James Joyce Traditional Irish Pub
32 Goldfish
36 Real Thailand
37 Basha Sandwich Bar
38 Olympia Fruit Market
42 True Grits; The Beguiling
43 Southern Accent
50 Coffee Time
52 Cora Pizza; Papa Geo's
57 Harbord Fish & Chips
60 Harbord Bakery

61 Latitude
66 Chiado
68 Cafe Societa
69 Ristorante Grappa
70 Supermodel Pizza
74 Sicilian Sidewalk Café
80 Café Diplomaticó
81 John's Italian Pizza
82 Bar Italia
83 Kalendar Koffee House
88 Ciao Eddie; Clear Spot
91 Sneaky Dee's; Royal Bank
92 Mars
94 Cobalt

To Amblecote (200 m)
To Havinn (300 m), Casa Loma & Spadina House (1 km)

Lowther Ave

Walmer Rd

Spadina Rd

To Annapurna & Zen Buddhist!

To Feathers B&B (450 m)

Dalton Rd

Bathurst

Albany Ave

Howland Ave

Spadina

Bloor St W

Koreatown

Mirvish (Markham) Village

Lippincott St

Croft St

The Annex

Lennox St

Sussex Ave

Spadina Ave

Herrick St

Harbord St

Euclid Ave

Palmerston Blvd

Markham St

Bathurst St

Lippincott St

Croft St

Borden St

Brunswick Ave

Major St

Robert St

Sussex Mews

Ulster St

Willcocks St

see MAP 6

Van Koughnet St

Spadina Circle

University of Toronto

89

0   100   200 m
0   100   200 yards

College St

see MAP 9

see MAP 5

Bellevue Ave

Augusta Ave

College Place

Kensington Market

MAP 9 KENSINGTON MARKET & WEST QUEEN STREET WEST

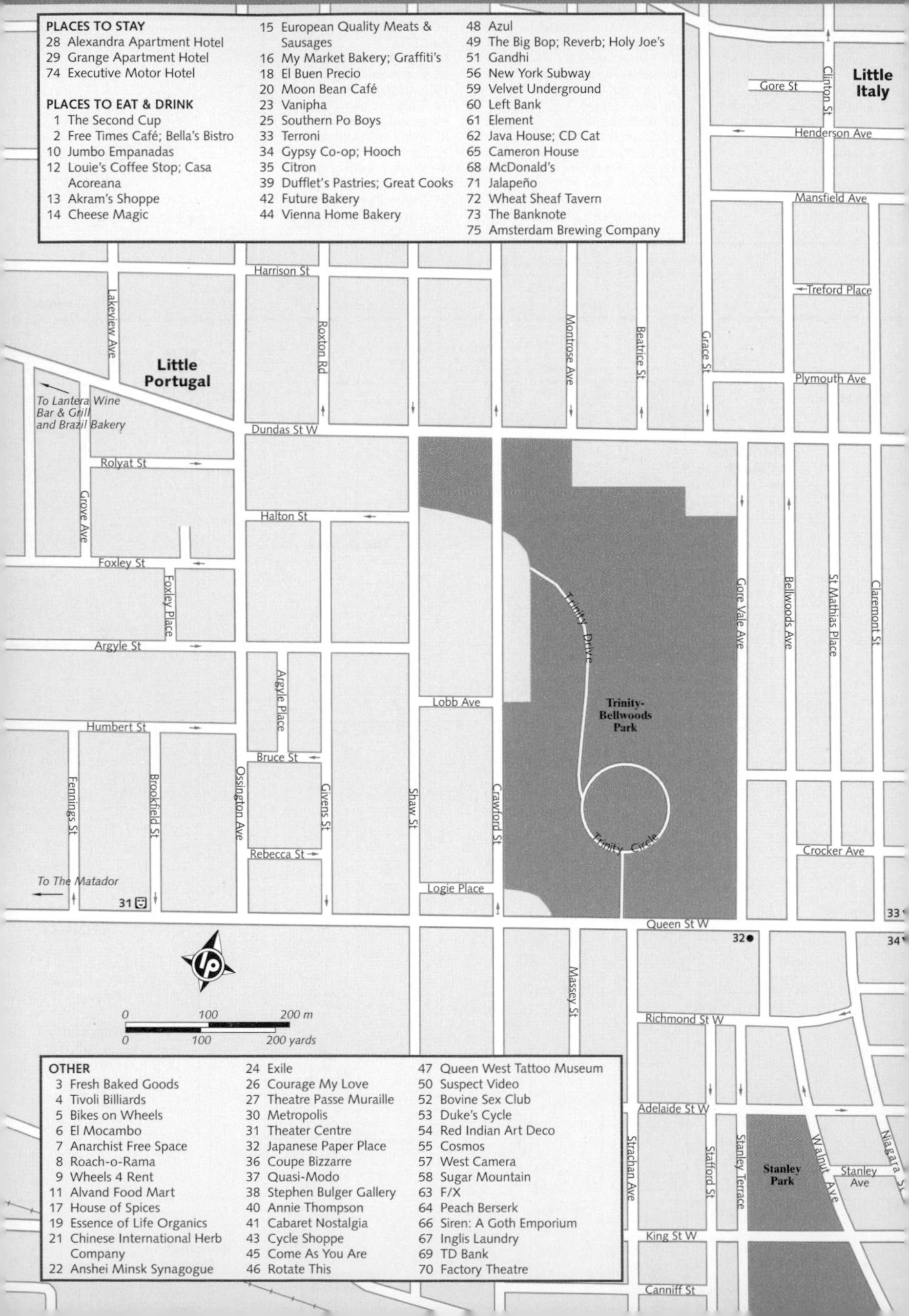

PLACES TO STAY
28 Alexandra Apartment Hotel
29 Grange Apartment Hotel
74 Executive Motor Hotel

PLACES TO EAT & DRINK
1 The Second Cup
2 Free Times Café; Bella's Bistro
10 Jumbo Empanadas
12 Louie's Coffee Stop; Casa Acoreana
13 Akram's Shoppe
14 Cheese Magic

15 European Quality Meats & Sausages
16 My Market Bakery; Graffiti's
18 El Buen Precio
20 Moon Bean Café
23 Vanipha
25 Southern Po Boys
33 Terroni
34 Gypsy Co-op; Hooch
35 Citron
39 Dufflet's Pastries; Great Cooks
42 Future Bakery
44 Vienna Home Bakery

48 Azul
49 The Big Bop; Reverb; Holy Joe's
51 Gandhi
56 New York Subway
59 Velvet Underground
60 Left Bank
61 Element
62 Java House; CD Cat
65 Cameron House
68 McDonald's
71 Jalapeño
72 Wheat Sheaf Tavern
73 The Banknote
75 Amsterdam Brewing Company

Gore St
Clinton St
Little Italy
Henderson Ave
Mansfield Ave
Treford Place
Plymouth Ave

Harrison St
Roxton Rd
Montrose Ave
Beatrice St
Grace St

Lakeview Ave
Little Portugal

To Lantera Wine Bar & Grill and Brazil Bakery

Dundas St W

Rolyat St
Grove Ave
Halton St
Foxley St
Foxley Place
Argyle St
Argyle Place
Humbert St
Fennings St
Brookfield St
Ossington Ave
Bruce St
Givens St
Shaw St
Rebecca St
Crawford St
Logie Place

Lobb Ave

Trinity Drive
Trinity-Bellwoods Park
Trinity Circle

Gore Vale Ave
Bellwoods Ave
St Mathias Place
Claremont St
Crocker Ave

Queen St W
33
32
34

31

0   100   200 m
0   100   200 yards

To The Matador

Massey St
Richmond St W
Adelaide St W
Strachan Ave
Stafford St
Stanley Terrace
Walnut Ave
Niagara St
King St W
Canniff St

Stanley Park
Stanley Ave

OTHER
3 Fresh Baked Goods
4 Tivoli Billiards
5 Bikes on Wheels
6 El Mocambo
7 Anarchist Free Space
8 Roach-o-Rama
9 Wheels 4 Rent
11 Alvand Food Mart
17 House of Spices
19 Essence of Life Organics
21 Chinese International Herb Company
22 Anshei Minsk Synagogue

24 Exile
26 Courage My Love
27 Theatre Passe Muraille
30 Metropolis
31 Theater Centre
32 Japanese Paper Place
36 Coupe Bizzarre
37 Quasi-Modo
38 Stephen Bulger Gallery
40 Annie Thompson
41 Cabaret Nostalgia
43 Cycle Shoppe
45 Come As You Are
46 Rotate This

47 Queen West Tattoo Museum
50 Suspect Video
52 Bovine Sex Club
53 Duke's Cycle
54 Red Indian Art Deco
55 Cosmos
57 West Camera
58 Sugar Mountain
63 F/X
64 Peach Berserk
66 Siren: A Goth Emporium
67 Inglis Laundry
69 TD Bank
70 Factory Theatre

see MAP 6

see MAP 8

College St

1 ▼   ▼ 2

6 ●

3 ●   ● 5
4 ●

Oxford St

Kensington Market

7 ●

Bellevue Ave
Augusta Ave
Lippincott St
Leonard Ave

8 ●

Nassau St

9 ●

▼ 10

11 ●   ▼ 12   14 ▼ 15 ▼ ▼ 16

Baldwin St

13 ▼
17 ●   ▼ 18

20 ▼   22
19 ●   St Andrews St
21

▼ 23
24 ●
26 ●   ▼ 25

Kensington Ave

Wales Ave

Denison Square

Denison Park

Clyde St
Casimir St
Hickory St

Dundas St W

see MAP 5

Chinatown

Alexandra Park

Grange Ave
29 ▪

28 ▪

Bathurst St
Euclid Ave
Palmerston Blvd
Markham St
Way's Lane

Carr St

27 ▣

Denison Ave
Augusta Ave

Wolseley St

Ace Lane

West Queen St West

Willis St

36 ● 38   Euclid Place   43 ● 44 ▼ 46   ▼ 48   52   57
37 ● 39   ● 41   ● 47   51 ▼●● 54   56 ▼ ● ▣ 59
40   42   53 55
▼ 35 ● ▼   45   58 ▼ 60   61 ▣ ▼   ● ● 64   66 ● ●   ◉
                                                                        62   63   67 69

Robinson St

Mann'ng Ave

Venauley St
Cameron St
Spadina Ave

30 ●

65 ▣   68 ▼

▣ 49 ● 50

Richmond St W

Maud St
Morrison St
Brant St

Mitchell Ave

Camden St

see MAP 4

Portugal

▣ 70

Square

Adelaide St W

Tecumseth St
Portland St

▣ 75

King St W

▼ 71   72 ▣   ▣ 73   ▪ 74

Brant Place

MAP 10 EAST CENTRAL TORONTO

To Mt Pleasant Cemetery (2.3 km)

Maple Ave

Rosedale

To Robin's Nest

To Highway 401

Greektown (The Danforth)

2 ▼

Broadview

Hurndale Ave

● 6 ▮

7 ▼

5

8 ▮

Cherry St

Dale Ave

McKenzie Ave

Castle Frank

Rosedale Valley Rd

Prince Edward Viaduct

Glen Rd

Selby St 1 ▮

Sherbourne

Bloor St E

3 ▢ ▮ 4

Dearbourne Ave

Linden St

Fairview Blvd

Howard St

Wolfrey Ave

Isabella St

Bayview Ave

Don River

Hogarth Ave

Earl St

St James Ave

Rosedale Ravine Lands

St James Cemetery

▮ 24

Wellesley Lane

▼ 23

Wellesley St E

25 ⊕ ▼ 27

Cabbagetown

Wellesley Park

Sparkhall Ave

▼ 26

Bain Ave

Riverdale

Rose St

Amelia St

Sumach St

Don Valley Parkway

Withrow Ave

Prospect St

Salisbury Ave

Riverdale Park

Riverdale Ave

▮ 30

34

Bleecker St

⊕ 35

Langley Ave

Winchester St

Parliament St

Bayview Ave

Victor Ave

▮ 31

▼ 33

▼ 36

Aberdeen Ave

▼ 32

Simpson Ave

Carlton St

Necropolis Cemetery

Maitland Place

⊕ 28

29 ▼

Riverdale Farm

Geneva Ave

Riverdale Park

Spruce St

First Ave

Gerrard St E

⊕ 37

Greenhouses

Allan Gardens

Horticultural Ave

River St

Bayview Ave

Munro St

Hamilton St

Broadview Ave

Boulton Ave

Allen Ave

Degrassi St

Mutual St

Jarvis St

George St

Pembroke St

Sherbourne St

Seaton St

Ontario St

Berkeley St

Parliament St

Oak St

see MAP 5

Dundas St E

Chinatown East

47 ●

Milan St

Poulett St

Regent St

Shuter St

Carroll St

Kintyre Ave

Moss Park

Queen St E

Sackville St

Wascana Ave

Thompson St

Britain St 49

● 51

Lombard St

Richmond St E

Ontario St

Berkeley St

Power St

▮ 50

Sumach St

52

54 ▼ 55

● 60

▮▮ 61

▼ 62

King St E

53 ●

Lewis St

Saulter St

St James Park

Adelaide St E

63 ▢

64

Design Strip

Derby St

Eastern Ave

King St E

Eastern Ave

St Lawrence Market

● 65

Front St E

Princess St

66 ●

Overend St

Old York

67 ▢

Mill St

The Esplanade

see MAP 4

Market St

Scadding Ave

Longboat Ave

Lake Shore Blvd E

Gardiner Expressway

Martin Goodman Trail

Keating Channel

Harbour St

To Redpath Sugar Museum (100 m) & The Harbourfront

Queens Quay E

Parliament St Slip

Cherry St

Mill St

Villiers St

Munition St

Basin St

Rolling St

Commissioners St

Jarvis St Slip

▮ 68

69 ▢

To Queenston & Niagara

see MAP 6

Wolverleigh Blvd

22

Strathmore Blvd

Pape • Donlands • Greenwood • Coxwell

Danforth Ave

17 ▼

18 ▼ ⊕ Pape

13 14 15 16

11 ▼ ● 12 ● 19 ▼ 20 ▼ ☐ 21

Hazelwood Ave

Chatham Ave

arnock Ave

Fenwick Ave

Harcourt Ave

Cavell Ave

Mountjoy Ave

Strathcona Ave

Withrow Park

grandview Ave

Wroxeter Ave

East View Park

Frizzell Ave

Felstead Ave

Hanson St

Albemarle Ave

Dingwall Ave

Shudell Ave

Monarch Park

Hunter St

Torbrick Rd

Boultbee Ave

Walpole Ave

Myrtle Ave

Ivy Ave

Fairford Ave

Harriet St

Little India

39

43

38

42 ▼ 44

Gerrard St E

41 ▼ 45

Richard Ave

40

● 46

Endean Ave

Austin Ave

Sproat Ave

Greenwood Park

Dundas St E

48

Kerr Rd

Colgate Ave

Leslieville

57

59

Queen St E

56

Memory Lane

58

Sears St

Eastern Ave

SEE MAP 11

To Tommy Thompson Park

0   200   400 m
0   200   400 yards

PLACES TO STAY
1 Howard Johnson Selby Hotel & Suites
22 Allenby
30 Lavender Rose B&B
31 Aberdeen Guesthouse
48 Leslieville Home Hostel

PLACES TO EAT & DRINK
2 Café Brussel
3 Dora Keogh; Allen's
5 Silk Road Cafe
10 Astoria; Last Minute Ticket Centre
13 Myth
13 Ouzeri
14 πTAN
16 Mr. Greek
17 Ella's
20 Acropol Bakery

21 Beer Street & Granite Brewery
23 The Keg Mansion
26 Provence
27 Rashnaa
29 Phoenix
32 Jet Fuel
33 Now Café
34 Pope Joan
36 The Winchester Café
38 Lahore Gate
39 Madras Durbar
43 Chaat Rendez-Vous
44 Punjab Foods & Sweets
45 Bar-Be-Que Hut
54 The Real Jerk
58 Hello Toast
62 Montreal Bistro & Jazz Club
63 Betty's
68 Waterside Sports Club

OTHER
4 The Music Hall
5 Organic Fruits & Vegetables; Ottaway Herbalist
6 Eastminster United Church
8 Carrot Common; The Big Carrot Natural Food Market & Wholistic Dispensary
9 Canada Post
12 Billiards Academy
15 Cutty's Hideaway
18 Royal Bank
19 IGA Supermarket
24 Chapel of St James-the-Less
25 Choice in Health Clinic
28 Shout Clinic
35 Winchester Street Theatre
37 Cabbagetown Women's Clinic
40 Islamic Books & Souvenirs
41 Maharani Emporium

42 Toronto Public Library Gerrard Ashdale Branch
46 Royal Bank
47 Absolute Color Slides
49 Indonesian Consulate
50 St Paul's Basilica
51 Librarie Champlain
52 Space
53 Toronto Climbing Academy
55 Opera House
56 Value Village
57 Machine Age Modern
59 Streetcity Bikes
60 Goodwill
61 Toronto's First Post Office
64 Enoch Turner Schoolhouse
65 Toronto Sun building
66 Canadian Opera Company
67 Canadian Stage Company
69 Hydrofoil Lake Jet Lines

MAP 11 THE BEACH

PLACES TO STAY
1 Beaches B&B
3 Days Inn Toronto East

PLACES TO EAT & DRINK
4 Lion on the Beach
5 Jamaica Sunrise
6 Meat on the Beach
10 McDonald's; Royal Bank
11 Nutty Chocolatier
13 Second Cup
14 Starbucks Coffee
17 Swiss Chalet
18 The Beacher Café
20 Akane-ya

22 Chip & Fish
23 The Remarkable Bean
25 Antoinette
26 Otabe

OTHER
2 Alliance Atlantis Cinemas
7 Toronto Public Library
   Beaches Branch
8 TD Bank & Trust
9 IGA Grocery Store
12 Quiet Storm
15 Recycle
16 Planet Skate
19 Beach Pharmacy

21 Fox Cinema
24 The Church of St Aidan
27 Public Parking Lot
28 DD Summerville Pool
29 Kew Gardens Tennis Club
30 Skating Rink
31 Baseball Diamond
32 New Beach Park Lawn
   Bowling Club; Kew Gardens
   Snack Bar; Public Restrooms
33 Leuty Ave Lifeguard Station
34 Silverbeach Boathouse
35 Historic Leuty Ave
   Life-Saving Station

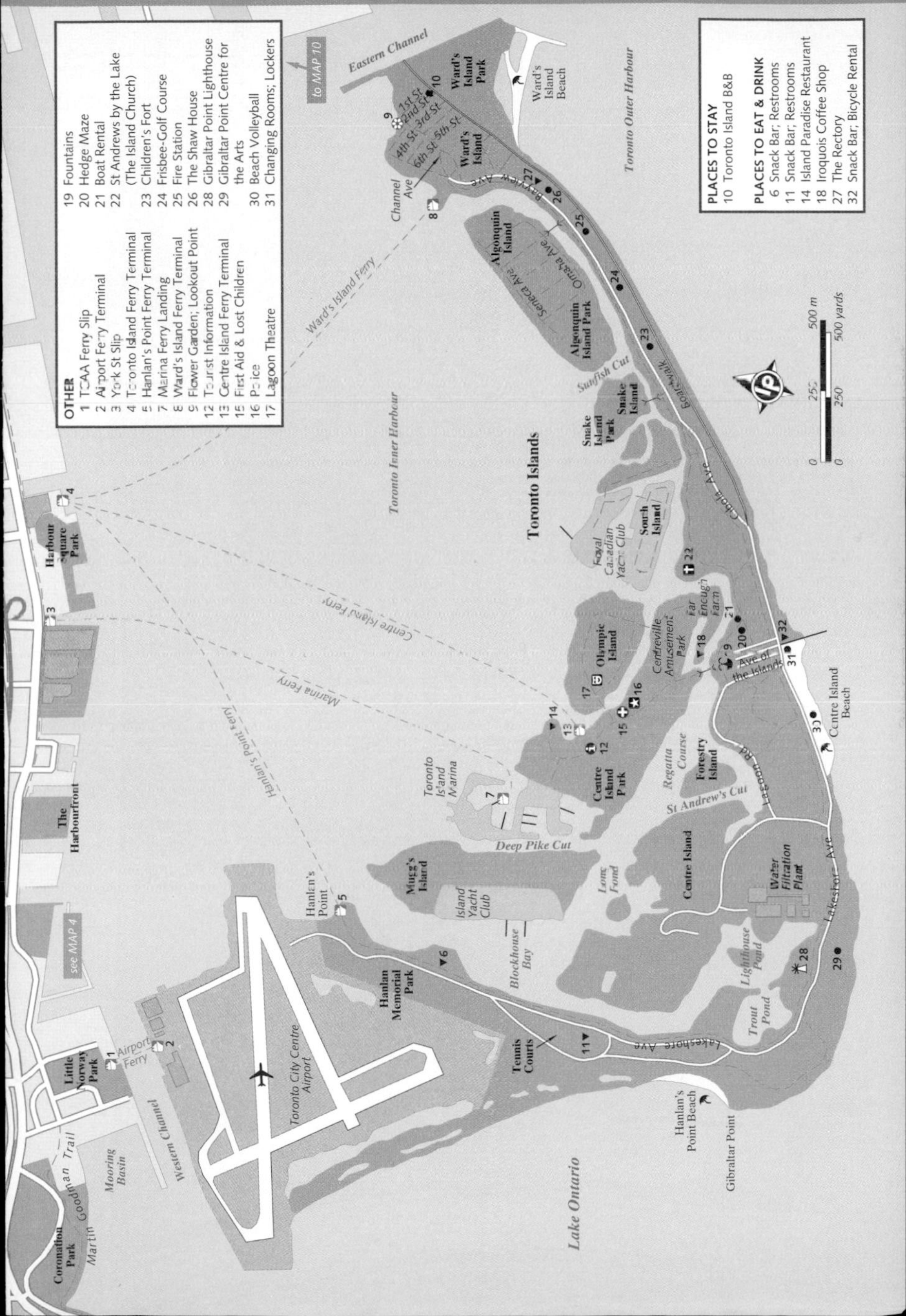

MAP 12 TORONTO ISLANDS

OTHER
1 TCAA Ferry Slip
2 Airport Ferry Terminal
3 York St Slip
4 Toronto Island Ferry Terminal
5 Hanlan's Point Ferry Terminal
7 Marina Ferry Landing
8 Ward's Island Ferry Terminal
9 Flower Garden; Lookout Point
12 Tourist Information
13 Centre Island Ferry Terminal
15 First Aid & Lost Children
16 P - ice
17 Lagoon Theatre

19 Fountains
20 Hedge Maze
21 Boat Rental
22 St Andrews by the Lake (The Island Church)
23 Children's Fort
24 Frisbee-Golf Course
25 Fire Station
26 The Shaw House
28 Gibraltar Point Lighthouse
29 Gibraltar Point Centre for the Arts
30 Beach Volleyball
31 Changing Rooms; Lockers

PLACES TO STAY
10 Toronto Island B&B

PLACES TO EAT & DRINK
6 Snack Bar; Restrooms
11 Snack Bar; Restrooms
14 Island Paradise Restaurant
18 Iroquois Coffee Shop
27 The Rectory
32 Snack Bar; Bicycle Rental

to MAP 10

Eastern Channel

Ward's Island Park

Ward's Island Beach

9 1st St
   2nd St
   4th St 3rd St
   6th St 5th St

Ward's Island

Avondale Ave

Toronto Outer Harbour

26

27

25

Algonquin Ave

Algonquin Island

Seneca Ave

Omaha Ave

Algonquin Island Park

24

Channel Ave

8

Ward's Island Ferry

33

Sunfish Cut

Snake Island

Snake Island Park

Boardwalk

Toronto Islands

Toronto Inner Harbour

South Island

Royal Canadian YacC Club

Cibola Ave

22

23

Centre Island Ferry

Olympic Island

17

Centreville Amusement Park

Far Enough Farm

18

21

20

19

Ave of the Islands

9

32

31

30

Centre Island Beach

Marina Ferry

14

13

12

16

15

Toronto Island Marina

7

Centre Island Park

Hanlan's Point Ferry

Deep Pike Cut

Muggs Island

Long Pond

St Andrew's Cut

Regatta Course

Forestry Island

Centre Island

Island Yacht Club

Blockhouse Bay

Hanlan's Point

5

see MAP 4

Harbour Square Park

4

3

The Harbourfront

Hanlan Memorial Park

Toronto City Centre Airport

Water Filtration Plant

Lakeshore Ave

Lighthouse Pond

28

29

Tennis Courts

11

Trout Pond

Hanlan's Point Beach

Gibraltar Point

Lake Ontario

Western Channel

Airport Ferry

1

2

Little Norway Park

Mooring Basin

Coronation Park

Martin Goodman Trail

0   250   500 m
0   250   500 yards

S

MAP 13 HIGH PARK

1 North Children's Playground & Wading Pool
2 Forest School
3 Allotment Gardens
4 Grenadier Restaurant
5 The Dream in High Park
6 Carlton Streetcar Stop
7 Hillside Gardens
8 Howard Tomb
9 Colborne Lodge

to MAP 8

High Park

M High Park

Bloor St W

Curtis Ave

High Park Ave

Pacific Ave

Oakmount Rd

Mountview Ave

Keele St

M Keele

Olympus Ave

Harcourt Ave

Wembley Rd

Wendigo Way

Wendigo Creek

West Rd

Deere Crescent

Hill Path

Spring Rd

Spring Creek Nature Trails

Parkside Drive

Spring Creek Ponds

Ridout St

Indian Valley Crescent

1

2

Sculpture Symposium Site

Colborne Lodge Drive

Sports Complex

West Ravine Nature Trails

Bowling Green & Tennis Courts

Spring Creek Nature Trails

3

High Park

Howard Park Ave

High Park Gardens

Constance St

6

4

5

Grenadier Rd

Geoffrey St

Howard Park Ave

Centre Rd

Creek House Rd

Spring Creek

Westminster Ave

Colborne Lodge Drive

7

Children's Zoo

High Park Blvd

South Children's Playground

Wright Ave

Grenadier Pond

Deer Pen Rd

Spring Rd

Algonquin Ave

Wanawanda Heights

Ellis Ave

West Pond

LP

0   100   200 m
0   100   200 yards

8

9 Trail

Garden Ave

Ellis Gardens

The Queensway

Duck Ponds

To Hwy 427 & QEW

Gardiner Expressway

to MAP 4

To Lake Shore Blvd

The CN Tower dominates Toronto's skyline.

The haunted Gibraltar Point lighthouse

Cathedral Bluffs

Ice skating, a local favorite

ROUTES

City | Regional

............Freeway	...........Pedestrian Mall
........Toll Freeway	.................Steps
.....Primary Road	⇒⟩= =⟨⇐ ....Tunnel
.....Secondary Road	---- - ---....Trail
.....Tertiary Road	•••••••• ..Walking Tour
........Dirt Road	=========Lane

ROUTE SHIELDS

(QEW)	Provincial Highway	(7)	Provincial Highway	[23]	County Road
(shield)	Trans-Canada Highway	(90)	US Interstate Highway	[62]	US Highway

AREAS

✕ ✛	Airport		Campus	❀ 🦁	Garden; Zoo		Park
🏊	Beach		Cemetery	⛳	Golf Course		Plaza
	Building		Fairgrounds		Military		Theme Park

POPULATION SYMBOLS

○ **CAPITAL** ....National Capital	● **Large City** ....Large City	● **Small City** ....Small City
◉ **CAPITAL** ....Provincial Capital	● **Medium City** ....Medium City	● **Town; Village** ....Town; Village

MAP SYMBOLS

▪ ....Place to Stay	▼ ....Place to Eat	● ....Point of Interest

........Airfield	........Church	........Museum	........Skiing - Downhill
........Airport	........Cinema	........Observatory	........Stately Home
........Archeological Site; Ruin	........Embassy; Consulate	........Park	........Surfing
........Bank	........Footbridge	........Parking Area	........Synagogue
........Baseball Diamond	........Fountain	........Pass	........Tao Temple
........Battlefield	........Gas Station	........Picnic Area	........Taxi
........Bike Trail	........Hospital	........Police Station	........Telephone
........Border Crossing	........Information	........Pool	........Theater
........Buddhist Temple	........Internet Access	........Post Office	........Toilet - Public
........Bus Station; Terminal	........Lighthouse	........Pub; Bar	........Tomb
........Cable Car; Chairlift	........Lookout	........RV Park	........Trailhead
........Campground	........Mine	........Shelter	........Tram Stop
........Castle	........Mission	........Shipwreck	........Transportation
........Cathedral	........Monument	........Shopping Center	........Volcano
........Cave	▲ ....Mountain	........Skiing - Cross Country	........Winery

Note: not all symbols displayed above appear in this book

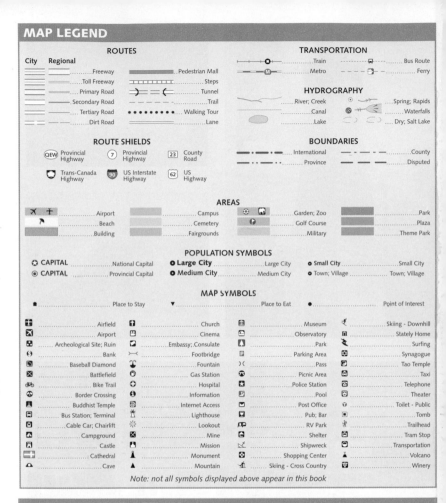

LONELY PLANET OFFICES

Australia
Locked Bag 1 Footscray, Victoria 3011
☎ 03 8379 8000 fax 03 8379 8111
email talk2us@lonelyplanet.com.au

USA
150 Linden Street, Oakland, California 94607
☎ 510 893 8555, TOLL FREE 800 275 8555
fax 510 893 8572
email info@lonelyplanet.com

UK
10a Spring Place, London NW5 3BH
☎ 020 7428 4800 fax 020 7428 4828
email go@lonelyplanet.co.uk

France
1 rue du Dahomey, 75011 Paris
☎ 01 55 25 33 00 fax 01 55 25 33 01
email bip@lonelyplanet.fr
www.lonelyplanet.fr

World Wide Web: www.lonelyplanet.com *or* AOL keyword: lp
Lonely Planet Images: lpi@lonelyplanet.com.au